MISTA

Acknowledgements

SPECIAL THANKS TO Jeffrey Dallas Moore and Benedict DiGiulio for keeping me on track when it was easy to quit. To Alice Elliott Dark, for reminding me to believe in myself.

Many thanks to Douglas "Niles" Eldredge, Chris Kipiniak, William Deubert and Mitch Wenger for taking the time to provide me with their real opinions. I also need to thank RJD and Douglas Weitz for giving me some very helpful advice along the way.

Thanks also to my email friends that took the time to read my stories over the last ten plus years.

And, of course, thank you to my students from RDHS and NHRHS who genuinely made it enjoyable to come to school (most of the time).

And I didn't forget . . .

Many thanks to Mike Dreeland for
the many cover layout ideas
and
to Angela Rocha for the cover concept.

MISTA

John J. Kaminski

authorHOUSE®

AuthorHouse™
1663 Liberty Drive
Bloomington, IN 47403
www.authorhouse.com
Phone: 1-800-839-8640

First published by AuthorHouse 6/11/2010

ISBN: 978-1-4520-3132-3 (sc)

Library of Congress Control Number: 2010907591

Printed in the United States of America
Bloomington, Indiana

This book is printed on acid-free paper.

For Danielle,
my lovely wife
and
My dear Mother,
who has worked for over 38 years
in public education

I.

Back to School

-1-

IT WAS A LITTLE AFTER 3:00 P.M., and I was looking out from the second-story window of a room that would be our new office. It was crammed mostly with boxes and books. People passed through it to get to the Day School math department office. Our program was called Twilight. The crack was that it was *The Twilight Zone*. Since it was summer, the school was only open to serve the needs of the Twilight students, so it was relatively empty.

According to other members of the Twilight staff, the Day School teachers disliked the Twilight teachers. Supposedly, these Day School teachers didn't think our students deserved a second chance at getting high school diplomas. So, I guessed the best way to express their animosity was to be rude to the people trying to help these students succeed.

The Spanish teacher, the math teacher, the history teacher, the social worker, the guidance counselor, the librarian and the clerk were in the Day School math office, which was the temporary Twilight office. There was little seating or table space available for our staff to do anything. The room was stuffy and cramped, and the dull colors weren't conducive to positive thinking.

Yesterday, my first day, I was sitting in a chair in the math office when I learned that it was the personal chair of one of the math teachers. One male staff member from the Day School said, "That's OK for now, but if he saw you sittin in it, he'll tell you all about it." I hoped a chair would never become that important to me.

I decided to work at the circular table in our future office. As I sat looking out at the smog, and after counting six smokestacks, I heard the students arriving and walking and talking in the hallway. One of the students popped her head in and said, "Hey, Mista K."

I said, "Hi." I wasn't sure what her name was, but I wouldn't know every name for the next few weeks anyway.

My main rule was that I wouldn't be called "Mista." I thought the students would show me more respect if they identified me as a person and not just any white guy they had to listen to in school. I introduced myself as Mr. Kaminski and wrote my name on the chalkboard. I asked the students to repeat it if they got it wrong, and I repeated their names if I mispronounced them.

When I was repeating my name, one girl said, "Ka-what? I ain't sayin that." So "Mista K" was the compromise. At least it wasn't "Mista."

Our urban district paid a lot of money to an educational institution to help the Twilight staff develop seminars for its students. The man who presented these models to us during the first three days of teacher training apparently made $49,000 for his efforts. I heard that number repeated numerous times in the temporary Twilight office.

Today, another lady from that institution came to present a seminar for the staff and the students so we could all familiarize ourselves with a new, modern teaching method. She was blonde, attractive, and from

Texas, but I was quickly turned off by her overlapping two front teeth and her wedding band. The history teacher, the Spanish teacher, the math teacher and I were all asked to participate in her presentation. We sat in a circle, said our names and drew up nametags to make the atmosphere more comfortable.

Whenever the math teacher spoke, most of the students laughed at him because he was Indian and had a very deep accent. To get to his job at the school, Dinesh drove his car to a train station about forty miles away before taking a thirty-five minute train ride to a PATH station. After one stop on the PATH, he transferred to a bus to get to our school. It took him about two and a half hours in each direction. I wanted to scold the kids and remind them about what respect was, but he needed to take his own stance to get respect.

Our Spanish teacher Mariella was from Venezuela. She was attractive and had the most gorgeous hair I had ever seen; it nearly reached her waist, and the girls always asked to touch it and she let them. Her daughter was still in Venezuela, so Mariella promised not to cut her hair until they reunited. Mariella had a science background but could not speak English well enough to teach it in the United States, so she settled for teaching Spanish. Her boyfriend was at another Twilight school and they were appalled at how little respect they got, because in Venezuela the situation was much different. The students asked her why she was so quiet. She didn't smile as much as she did during teacher training.

The seminar started with fifteen students and ended with almost thirty, as students arrived late to school. It lasted almost an hour and a half, while the temperature of the room got hotter. The students were incessantly restless.

It all began with a conversation about how people should speak to one another, before moving on to a discussion about a Quaker painting. To me, it was too banal and boring to be a conversational springboard. As the seminar progressed, I brought desk-chairs from other classrooms to accommodate students arriving late. I tried to prevent some students from just putting their heads on their desks and not participating. The history teacher was in the circle, but Dinesh and Mariella were squeezed out.

At one point, we were naming pictures of paintings being passed around the room and writing them on the board. Although I was sitting in the circle, my mind was in and out of what we were discussing. One student was really annoying me because he was playing a game on his cell phone. He thought he was being slick about how he was hiding it from us. No one told him to stop what he was doing.

I wrote a note on a sheet of paper that said, "Can you please stop playing that game and contribute to class?"

I walked through the circle, placed it on his desk across the room, and made it back to my seat without creating a distraction. I watched him stop his game, read the note, and ask his neighbor for a pen. I watched his hand make three jagged connecting lines followed by a circle, which was exactly how the word "No" was written. He then placed the note on the corner of his desk and used his cardboard nametag as a paperweight. Earlier, a gust came through the window and sent papers flying off desks and onto the floor. The student resumed his game.

Some were reading the titles from the board, and it was my turn to share my suggestion.

"Animal Habitat," I said. I read what I had written

on the paper on my desk. There was silence and a few gasps.

"What choo mean we animals?" one girl yelled.

I had no idea what she was talking about. Everyone was looking at me. It was so hot in the room, and I was still trying to cool down from carrying those desk-chairs.

"You're supposed to be picking a title for what the Twilight program is," one kid said.

"You don't know how to pay attention," another kid said. I realized how awful my flub was.

"I'm sorry, but I've been trying to get everyone involved in the seminar because the seminar works only if you contribute your own ideas and everyone can learn from each other, and when people are talking loud and playing games and playing on the computer..." I nodded toward the kids that were doing these things.

I continued, "These are fine examples of different kinds of distractions, and I'm sorry I was so affected." It wasn't said in anger and seemed like a worthy appeal. I looked away at no one to the left of me.

"Mista K mad," one girl said. The Texan consultant got the seminar back on track.

When it ended, she congratulated the students and said that each and every person did a great job and should be commended. I completely disagreed. This kind of compliment only reinforced the bad behavior we just experienced. I told her how I felt.

"I disagree. I thought it went well," she said. The history teacher agreed with her. I still disagreed.

After the seminar, the Twilight clerk divided the students into As and Bs, since she knew all the students and, more importantly, knew exactly who to divide. One group would go to one class, and one group would go to another. Because of the low attendance expected for the first few days back to school, the plan was for two teachers to teach double periods to each group.

"All the Bs should go to the other room," I said. All but one of the students got up and left, and I was sure that the one remaining student was a B. Since the guards weren't there, the mass exodus led to hallway chaos. Thankfully, someone shuffled the students back into the room.

Mariella and I worked together. We both prepared lessons we planned to teach consecutively. It cut down on students getting distracted while traveling to their next class. Since she didn't speak during the seminar, I asked her to teach first so the students could get to know her before she began teaching alone the Thursday after Labor Day. She presented them with a ditto, and once students were done, they lifted their papers in the air and told her they were done. She gave them more dittos. She was up to her fourth one.

During her teaching time, the fire alarm went off, and I presumed it was a student. It was the loudest and most irritating noise I ever heard. I covered my ears. All the students jumped from their seats and made their way to the hallway. Since I was unsure of the evacuation procedure, I tried desperately to maintain order. In the hallways were two guards giving teachers and students conflicting directions. Thankfully, Jack, the Head Teacher, took command of the situation. We were all directed back into the classrooms because it was apparently just a test. The alarm rang for more than a few minutes.

Jack was a flamboyant homosexual, whose partner was the Head Teacher of another Twilight school. He told me all about it during teacher training, as he told me how I was being reassigned here, which was the worst school in the city. He was very supportive and laidback. I was surprised the students didn't make fun of him.

After dismissing the students at 8:15 p.m., the teachers reconvened for ten minutes before going home. Yesterday, I clapped after Jack's encouraging and uplifting words at the end of the day, and everyone followed. We needed a good clap. Jack hugged everyone and kissed the women on their cheeks before we left. I made sure to shake Dinesh's hand and give Mariella's hand a squeeze, because she looked completely defeated. She smiled briefly when I did this.

"We made it through the day. It will only get easier now once everyone gets into the routine," I said. I hoped I wasn't lying.

-2-

This is a <u>story</u> about teacher training.

T'ODAY WAS THE FIRST DAY *at my new job as a high school English teacher in an inner city school, and since I had not had a full-time job with benefits for about three years, this was a major cobblestone in the cobblestone road of my life. More recently, I had a brief tenure as a freelance proofreader. I also worked a few times as a computer "consultant," who was responsible for turning off all the computers in a Manhattan skyscraper on a Saturday before returning on a Sunday to turn them all back on. To better assume my role as a teacher, I began growing a beard about a month ago, which meant that I had a beard I wasn't used to. I was still without the pipe and the tweed coat with elbow patches, but, let's face it, they're surely around the corner.*

I liked Twilight's alternative work hours. Students in Twilight came at 3:00 p.m., and their first class didn't begin before 4:00 p.m. These students used the school once Day School students left.

Waking up early to an irritating and grating alarm was a thing of the past for me. My regular workday was now from 1:25 p.m. until 8:25 p.m. The position paid more than the same one in the Day School, but Twilight had smaller classes and a later start time. Twilight was created to better accommodate students who were unable, for one reason or another, to attend Day School.

So on this very first day, I woke up at 11:00 a.m. Over the weekend, I was diagnosed with acute bronchitis and was the sickest I had been since I had the flu one Christmas in the mid-1990s. No matter how bad I felt, it would be impossible for me to miss my first day of work. But with encouraging words from my doctor and a prescription of strong antibiotics, I somehow felt great this morning. I was cruising down the Turnpike around 1:00 p.m. My destination was the Board of Education building, where three August days of teacher training were to begin. The first day of work for teachers was always before the first day for students.

Being sick had its obvious downsides: minor wheezing; thick, green phlegm in your respiratory system; and a wretched taste in your mouth that was surely just as disgusting for anyone unfortunate enough to converse closely with it. Although I brushed my teeth thrice before I left, the taste of infection lingered. I needed to get some gum to battle and defeat the odor.

I stopped at a gas station, and it only had the twenty-five cent gum. I bought a pack of green Doublemint, ripped the top of the pack off, pulled two pieces from it, unwrapped them, tossed them into my mouth, and began chewing like there was no tomorrow. I got back into my newly-detailed car and cruised to work. I was arriving early, and it was a great day to be alive.

So I was blowing bubbles and pop-pop-popping away, and I was scanning the radio for a song to sing and Heart came on. The band Heart recently made an appearance on my personal nostalgia road since I just found my old posters from childhood at my parents' house, my current place of residence.

I also found my Miami Vice poster. I remembered how cool I used to be.

Ann Wilson was singing "Never," and I was singing along:

> "Hey baby I'm talking to you
> Stop yourself and listen."

And then after that line there was a little riff, and I tried unsuccessfully to pop-pop-pop my gum to the beat. I started driving a little too fast in the traffic, but I kept on singing:

> "Walk those legs right over here
> Give me what I'm dying for."

I was really into it, so into it that I wanted to check out my soft and sexy singing lips in the rearview mirror. It was then that I saw all the green gum caught in my moustache and the hair below my lower lip.

I slammed on my brakes to avoid slamming into the car in front of me. I was lucky not to get into an accident, since I was just a few inches from its bumper. Slamming on the brakes, however, did not solve the problem of the gum on my face.

When I was younger, my mom had a book called Hints from Heloise. Heloise said that if you got gum in your hair, all you needed was peanut butter to remove it. It was about 1:10 p.m., and the Board of Education was around the corner. I couldn't be late for my first day of work.

I ran into a deli to see if it had any peanut butter I could rub all over my face. I covered my mouth with my hand.

I looked around, but there was no peanut butter and not a large variety of products either. The Indian guy behind the counter watched my every move.

"Do you have any peanut butter?" I asked.

"Huh?" he said. It is probably the kind of response to expect when you speak to another person while choosing to cover the hole in your face that emitted sounds called words that were needed to communicate with others. After two more similar exchanges, he said there wasn't any.

Here was where I used my ingenuity. See, I was graduating from graduate school in October, and that meant I would indeed be a Master. I had to start trusting my feelings. I thought about chocolate candy and about what varieties contained peanut butter. My eyes soon spied peanut butter cups on one of the shelves below the register counter. I grabbed them and placed them on the counter.

"Seventy-five cents," the Indian guy said.

My right hand was still covering my face, and my wallet filled with money was in my right pants pocket. Using the left hand to pull the wallet from the pocket while opening the wallet to get the money to give to the man...The task was too daunting.

"HAHAHA," laughed the Indian guy when I pulled my hand from my face. When I gave him the five dollar bill, there was a brief moment when his laugh began to wane, but once he got my change, he started laughing in my face again.

"Suck it!" I said, before running to my car.

I sat in the driver's seat, opened up the package of peanut butter cups, flaked off the chocolate, and rubbed the peanut butter on my face. Then I realized that the car detailers threw the napkins away. The chocolate was no longer confined solely to my hands but had fallen onto my shirt, my lap, my freshly shampooed rug and my new shoes. The gum was coming out though.

The second cup smear was moved outdoors, but the last of the peanut butter failed to remove all the gum. I had to go back into the deli. The Indian guy laughed at me again.

With the help of more peanut butter, bottled water and

napkins, my face was cleaned and ready for work. I was even able to clean the mess from the car. It was 1:18 p.m. when I entered the Board of Education building.

I took an elevator to the eighth floor and made it with a few minutes to spare. I found a chair on the outer perimeter of a rectangular conference table that was occupied by other teachers. The vice principal Miss Carter entered the room and asked everyone to sign in.

Our official lunch/dinner break was at 4:30 p.m. During the presentations and conferences, teachers made numerous comments about how they wouldn't remain in the meeting if it went to 4:31 p.m. The male consultant made numerous jokes about how official the time was, and many teachers laughed at the idea of leaving later than the official time.

After grabbing a quick lunch/dinner, I returned to my seat in the conference room. There were a few other teachers eating, reading and softly talking. I didn't know anyone. I tried reading a book since I was tired and worn down from being sick.

One overweight black teacher came in with a huge bag of McDonalds and sat in her chair at the table. I was struck by the pungent smell.

She was talking and pulling food from her bag. She was talking and eating. Her meal consisted of one Big Mac, one large fries, one large drink, and two apple pies. I couldn't avoid listening to her, and I wasn't even sure who she was addressing.

"This diet's flat," she said.

I chuckled to myself. I tried to read.

"When you fat, you don't get wrinkles," she said to the skinny Asian woman to her left. She laughed. I laughed too.

UNTIL DAY SCHOOL BEGAN the Thursday after Labor Day, the cafeteria was closed. For one hour a day, I had lunch duty, since Twilight kids began their day with lunch. The room was white and very bright, and I wasn't sure what was on the menu. Jack showed us the cafeteria on the first-day-of-school-for-teachers tour.

"Don't eat here," Jack said. "It's not good, and it's expensive." I couldn't imagine what it looked like with students because there was only a vast white openness without tables, chairs or any shred of hominess. In one area, there were more than ten large, clear bags filled with small, white cardboard boxes.

"If the students see those bags during lunch, they would be all over the cafeteria." I hoped they were gone by Thursday.

Today, our students started their day in the auditorium. Ten arrived by the time my duty began. Dinesh, Mariella, the history teacher, and I had a brief conversation while we waited for more students to arrive. We discussed how we would all begin working our actual class schedules, since the guidance counselor finally had the official student schedules.

Mariella was very nervous. She and I had the most students because every student, in order to graduate, needed to take four trimesters of English and three trimesters of a foreign language, a requirement that was just raised from two trimesters. Each of the four Twilight teaching blocks would have two separate classes, like Spanish 1 and 2, or English 1 and 3. Each block couldn't exceed fifteen students. Twilight also wanted us to teach separate lessons for each class.

Mariella had worksheets ready for her students. She wanted to get a Spanish book so she could design her classes, but the bookroom was locked, and the person with the key was still away on summer break. I told her to do her best to keep their attention until next Thursday because the absentee rate was so high— way over fifty percent. It was impossible to begin a focused curriculum if the students weren't in school. We were unregimented and disorganized. Absenteeism was a major problem before Day School began. I heard Mondays and Fridays were bad throughout the year.

At teacher training, the vice principal of all four Twilights, our boss Miss Carter, said that our lesson plans for the week would be due every Monday. Since there were so many absent students, it wasn't worthwhile to devote planning time toward classes with so many missing students. The standardized lesson plan sheet itself was complicated and wordy. The process was demonstrated to us quickly at teacher training, but I still hadn't seen one completed. On that day, all teachers received a two-inch pile of papers in an envelope. They were all punched with three holes, so I imagined we were expected to provide the binder. Since the history teacher was here last year, she promised to help me. Miss Carter had the right to view lesson plans at any time. She had been to school twice in the last four days.

Mariella knew that I thought it was a waste of time at the moment. Neither of us completed any of it. The history teacher began on time, and Dinesh's first lesson plan would be today. I doubted Miss Carter would be asking us for them until sometime after Labor Day, and if she did, I would tell her that I hadn't done them and I would tell her what I did do in my classes.

Yesterday, after the seminar with the Quaker painting, some students said that the teachers and the Texan instructor should talk about more relevant issues affecting their community. I decided to discuss some of these issues as my lesson. My students picked the topics. The first few were obvious, like AIDS, cop killing, terrorism, and racism. Then, they got even worse with issues like stripping, teen prostitution, giving head for Chinese food, and homeless teenage pregnancies.

"Look, education is important. With more education, you can make more money. If you don't take advantage of your teachers, who are paid to help you complete your high school education, you are just throwing money down the toilet," I said.

Some kids opened up.

"I was walking to singing practice yesterday, and I started crying because this would be the year I got my diploma," one kid said.

"This is my last chance," another said.

During our discussion, Miss Carter walked past my door a few times before popping her head in to listen. It distracted the students, but we were able to get back on track.

Later, she said: "Those were some of the worst students in the program. That was the best motivational speech I ever heard." At least she didn't bother me about the lesson plans.

Miss Carter hired me on the spot when I interviewed in June. She personally escorted me to Human Resources to make sure I filled out every sheet of paperwork correctly. Getting a job gave me a summer free of having to find one.

Jack and the history teacher said Miss Carter was a "bitch" and a "tyrant," and they mocked her for being unmarried and wondered how any man could ever deal with her. I tried not to let these comments influence my opinion of her, since she had never been a bitch to me.

While Mariella, Dinesh, the history teacher and I were talking, the Texan consultant arrived. She was supposed to help design lessons, and she assured us that she would arrive at 1:25 p.m. It was a little after 3:30 p.m. Earlier, Jack made a reference to the $49,000 her company was paid.

The Texan instructor wanted to conduct another seminar, and she created an ambitious one. When she looked to me for assurance, I said I looked forward to it and that it sounded great. Over these last few days, she told me that she was a graduate student in Texas. I hoped she wasn't writing a thesis supporting the value of her company's educational models. It was probably paying for her schooling. If she had to admit the failures of yesterday and today, her institution might not get its $49,000.

After her presentation, she asked if there were any questions.

In his garbled and accented English, Dinesh said, "I don't know how to write lesson plans, and I don't know how to incorporate this seminar teaching with math."

"If I get some time, I'll try to help you," she said.

We were beginning the school day with one huge

seminar of around eighteen students. We had yet to have an actual day broken up as it would be throughout the year.

During our meeting, I suggested we make new nametags, since the ones from yesterday were filled with small writing assignments and doodles. She began her seminar by passing out blank cards. Dinesh, who had been relatively quiet throughout this process, made a conscious effort to help.

I looked around the room and realized that some students wrote nicknames and symbols rather than real names. One student wrote "Miss D" on her nametag. The Texan noticed it too. We hadn't had this problem yesterday.

The Texan addressed Miss D by asking, "Can you please write your first name on the other side of the nametag?"

"If you tell me your first name, I'll call you that and write my name," Miss D said.

The entire class focused on the exchange. The Texan continued.

When I called Miss D by her real name when I first met her, she said, "Go fuck yaself." She was really nasty.

"That wouldn't be the first time someone said that to me," I replied, "and it definitely won't be the last."

The exchange riled up the class, but Miss D stopped talking and smiled. She told me to fuck myself every time I talked to her.

One male student drew a tic-tac-toe board or number symbol followed by an explanation point followed by a question mark on his nametag. Since he was sitting two desks over to my right, I asked him softly to please write his real first name on the nametag so everyone would know who he was.

"You know my name," he said.

"Sorry, but I don't." I wasn't good at memorizing everyone's names. "Should I just call you 'tic-tac-toe board, explanation point, question mark'?" I asked.

"Stop playin me," he said.

"I'm not."

"Well, your beard is playin you." I really hoped it wasn't.

As the seminar continued, he flipped over his nametag periodically. Sometimes it read "Ken," and other times, it was the symbols. I wouldn't forget his name for next time though.

Once the seminar was over, Benny the guidance counselor handed out schedules. My main reason for not doing lesson plans was because the kids weren't in their right classes to begin with. How could any teacher be expected to create a curriculum without a roster? When were we going to have a real day?

At some point, the librarian, who was black, came in and sat at the front of the room outside the circle to observe. I wasn't sure of her name because we only exchanged hellos in the Twilight office, and I hadn't had any time to work with her.

Once most of the students received their schedules, there was an uproar because they all had mistakes. Benny and the librarian couldn't possibly help every person in an orderly fashion.

Some of the students got up, and I tried to calm them down. Miss D was bopping around and I asked her by her name to please sit down.

"Why you callin me by my name, nigga?" she said.

Before I had a chance to speak, the librarian screamed, "Because that is your name.....NIGGA!"

They both stared at each other. Everyone was silent. It took me a moment to find the words to move on.

4

This is a second story about teacher training.

I AM ON MY THIRD AND FINAL DAY *of teacher training. It is getting quite boring since theories of teaching and learning techniques can easily become moot once the madness of the classroom begins. These presentations assume that all classrooms are problem-free and all students are well-behaved. Nevertheless, I have developed some camaraderie with my new colleagues, and I am excited about the new year.*

During the days, the teachers have been broken into groups, and after completing a short activity, the groups have opportunities to talk shop and exchange stories.

At our union-designated break at 2:50 p.m., most of the teachers exit the room to smoke or to go to the bathroom or to just walk around. These fifteen minutes are in our teaching contract, and we can do with them what we want.

So I found myself sitting next to one of the new history teachers named Anwar. Anwar is from Pakistan, and we have been shooting the shit the last few days. He tells me he is a Muslim.

I slap him on the back and say, "So Anwar, are you going to put the FUN back into Islamic FUNdamentalism this school year or what?" He looks at me funny, gets up and walks out of the room.

I look across the table at Pia. She is a staff member at another school, and she is precious. This has nothing to do with Webster's definition that describes someone as "excessively refined or highly cherished" though. It has to do with the huge PRECIOUS that hangs from her necklace and rests on her gigantic breasts. The letters are silver and adorned with diamonds, but hey, I'm no jeweler. It could easily be some bendable reflective metal and cubic zirconia.

Pia has a box of Chicken McNuggets and two, small containers in front of her. One is barbeque sauce and the other is sweet and sour sauce. She also has fingernails that are over six inches long; I watch her clamp two of her talons from her left hand around the McNugget, dip it into one of the containers and then the other before eating the entire thing in one bite. She continues the eating process with her right hand.

I consider some of the advantages of having eating utensils as actual extensions of my hands, but I can't think of any. I get gross and think about her #2 wipe-up. I then start thinking about Pia's sexual habits, and I hope she is a lesbian because a quick flick of her fingers could be damaging to the penis. I start thinking about the vagina. I hope she is not a lesbian either.

I return to the poem I have been working on for the last hour. It is called "Life of a Cup," and it goes:

> God makes trees
> Man makes paper
> Some companies make cups.
> I pulled a cup from the sleeve
> But I really pulled two
> And one fell to the ground.
> I used the other and threw them both away.

I am unsure whether the project is complete or not, but I am suddenly disturbed by the smoke breath of the history teacher at my school. I will call her Nicotina.

"I won't be at school next Thursday, since Jose and me are going to the U.S. Open," she says.

"That sounds like fun," I say.

Jose is sitting a few chairs away from Pia and has blue contact lenses. Nicotina and Jose are both overweight. I wonder if Nicotina is doing it with Jose. I can't get their naked bodies out of my head. I imagine two giant hands grabbing them in the middle of one of their naked trysts, squeezing them together, twisting them, and then pulling them apart. There would be a suction-like sound before they were both torn to pieces.

My thoughts are disturbed by another teacher, who has just returned to the conference room. Her name is KetchupBoots, and Nicotina gave me the scoop about her yesterday. The kids have been very mean to KetchupBoots. She got her name because she came to school once in a pair of gigantic, red boots. The kids started calling her that, in between saying they hated her and hoped she would die. So far in teacher training, she has been the person whose laugh ends last. It is also the loudest, which has made for an uncomfortable combination. She seems a bit sycophantic, but I'm not really sure. Nicotina told me that Jose worked with her last year, and this year she was transferred to another school.

Soon, the union-mandated break was over.

-5-

This is a <u>story</u> about the benefits meeting.

I RECEIVED A LETTER ABOUT A WEEK AGO *about a benefits meeting at the Board of Education. It would be my opportunity to sign up for a health plan. I walked into its front doors at exactly 1:00 p.m., according to the clock inside the security guard's office. He gave me a pass to stick on my shirt, and I headed for the elevator.*

I recognized the guy waiting from teacher training. He had a shaved head, a goatee, and large brown glasses and was wearing a long-sleeved button-down burgundy shirt and a beige tie. He had a bandaged knee. He was the most formally dressed teacher at training and wore a tie every day. No one else wore one. His head wasn't cleanly shaven though, since I could clearly see that if he did have hair, he would be bald on the top of his head.

His name was Carl, and he was a history teacher at another Twilight. It was his first year teaching.

"How are your students?" I asked.

"OK. How are yours?"

"OK," I said.

"They're not always OK," Carl told me. "I can't believe how bad they are."

"I expected worse. I taught at a high school in the Bronx for two years so I'm used to it."

"I have to yell at them all the time," he said. I understood his frustration.

"I've developed some patience, I guess. I know what to expect. This is your first year at an inner city school. You'll get used to it too," I said.

Carl was excited about the benefits meeting.

"This is one of the benefits of being a teacher," he said. I didn't laugh with him.

"I hurt my knee over the summer," he said. "I hurt it wrestling on the beach. I hope they pay for my physical therapy."

I looked at the watch of the security guard that was waiting with us. I was five minutes late. I wanted to walk to the sixth floor, but I didn't want to be rude to Carl and his bum knee.

The benefits meeting would probably overlap with my hours at school, but meetings at the Board of Education took precedence. That was what Shirley told me. She was the Twilight clerk who assisted the staff at our site.

On the first day, I told Shirley that I thought I needed a parking pass, and she told me she would take care of it. After a few days, I asked Shirley what the hell was taking so long and how come she was going to treat me like this. She got my sarcasm, laughed and told me I didn't need that pass after all. Shirley, who was black, told me how she had problems when she was younger. She liked helping students through Twilight since no one ever helped her. The students, teachers, and program were deeply indebted to people like Shirley.

At 1:10 p.m., the elevator doors finally opened. Carl and the guard rushed in and pressed buttons for their respective *floors. I let the five waiting women get on before I did. The doors closed. The smell of perfume was suffocating. Carl and I had to go to the sixth floor. The elevator stopped at the second floor, the third floor, the fifth floor and then the sixth floor. I was sure the elevator was an excuse for being late.*

According to the clock on the wall, I was fifteen minutes late. There were three tiered levels of long tables and chairs. I sat in one of the chairs that leaned against the back wall. People were talking quietly and occupying the majority of the chairs, but there were some empty ones. The front table was covered with stacks of catalogues, envelopes and piles of papers. There was also a cart next to a table covered in piles of papers. Two ladies manned the table.

I considered what to do for a moment, and Carl looked dumbfounded. I walked down the aisle to ask the lady at the table for help.

"Sorry I'm late." I said. "I don't know what forms I need."

"Was it that damn elevator? I been tellin them to fix that elevator for a long time. You know how long I've waited for that elevator?" she said, while gathering my forms.

"Get me one!" Carl yelled. About half the people in the room looked up. Most looked at Carl, and some looked at me.

I returned to my seat, and Carl snatched the package from my hand and perused its contents.

"Which one would be better for my physical therapy?" Carl asked me. I told him what I was signing up for. I told him I wasn't sure my plan addressed his needs.

"Yours covers major surgery. And dismemberment," he told me. It didn't bring me any relief.

The lady leaning against the table called for everyone's attention so we could go over our forms. The first was for life insurance. She went through the steps to fill out the card accurately. If you died, the Board of Education would give a total of $2,500 to whomever you listed on the card.

"I should just fill out the address for my credit card company," Carl said. He laughed for both of us.

As the lady was going over the next set of forms, there was a commotion in one of the rows.

"Can the audience be quiet please," someone yelled. There were numerous shushes. Some guy was on his telephone.

"Hold on a minute," he said, while holding up one of his fingers. "I'm on the phone with my medical insurance provider." He didn't look at her.

"Please take your conversation outside!" she said a little louder.

"Turn off the phone, you idiot!" Carl yelled. The man did, and the presentation continued.

After filling out my paperwork, I was about to bring it to the women to do a final check. Carl was still unsure what plan to get.

"You should walk down and have one of them help you," I said. We both got up. As soon as Carl took one step down, he tripped and fell down the three stepped levels to the front of the room.

"Oh my Gawd!" a lady yelled.

"Ow!" screamed Carl.

He was rolling around on the floor grabbing his knee, and everyone was looking at him. People stood up and moved to get better views of him writhing in pain. I didn't want to ask him if he was alright, because if he was, he wouldn't be screaming on the ground and holding his knee while being surrounded by onlookers.

Help arrived in the form of the old security guard that came up on the elevator with us. Carl was grimacing in pain on the floor. The old man radioed for an ambulance, and there was nothing I could do.

I handed my papers to the lady leaning against the table since she was not helping anyone now that Carl was the main focus. I got my papers approved and left the room.

As I walked down the stairs, I realized that our medical benefits didn't kick in until September 1. Carl was going to have to pay for the entire incident out of pocket because he currently had no benefits.

When I got to the street, I heard a nearby wail of an ambulance. It arrived when I reached my car.

-6-

I GOT TO SCHOOL AND REMEMBERED that Nicotina would be at the U.S. Open with Jose, and I felt bad for her since it was raining. I knew that her relationship with Jose was platonic, because she talked about her boyfriend. She was also going on a job interview in the morning.

A few days ago, she told me that when I signed my contract, it stated that I needed to notify the school system sixty days in advance before my departure. If I violated my contract, the Board of Education could have my state teaching credentials revoked. If she got a job, Nicotina told me she was going to give just thirty days notice. She didn't believe the state would pursue its case because our school was violent.

"You could always say you feared for your life when you went to work," she said.

Upon entering the Twilight office, Jack told me we were finally getting a science teacher.

"He is black and supposedly a big man," Jack said. "He used to be a chemist for a company that fell apart. This is his first teaching job."

Since Nicotina was absent, I had to cover her classes

and teach mine in my classroom. Substitutes were unavailable for absent Twilight teachers.

Fifteen students arrived for the first block of the four-block day. Officially, I needed to be teaching half of them Journalism and the other half World Literature. I told them all that we were working on current events, and I cut out articles from the *New York Times* and mounted them on black construction paper. Each student would read one and present it to the class. Hopefully, a discussion would ensue. My assignment was met with a series of teeth-sucking ticks and a symphony of sighs.

"I don't gotta do this I don't take Journalism," someone yelled.

War with Iraq, the anthrax investigation, the West Nile virus, and homicide bombings were uninteresting subjects. A discussion about a woman suing an airline for five million dollars, however, aroused the entire class.

"The airline should pay up," Miss D said.

"You wack," someone yelled out.

"Go fuck yaself," Miss D said.

"Remember that G-rated discussion code we talked about?" I asked. One student, Tanisha, was still screaming out her opinions.

"It's like a radio show. If too many people are talking at the same time, no one can hear anything," I said. Tanisha still screamed her opinions.

"No airline has to pay up because no cat is worth five million dollas," she said.

"If a lost cat on an airline can get you five million dollas, everyone would be tryin to lose cats on planes," someone added.

I noticed one student doodling and writing sayings all over the article I mounted. I took it back and asked him to not write on my papers. Everyone was focused on the exchange. I read what he wrote.

"What does this mean?" I asked. I was referring to MONEYOWABROADS.

"You got your shit wrong," Tanisha said. "Its money owa bitches. Owa means over."

"I got that," I said.

"I'm gonna get a tattoo that says N.O.M. for niggas owa money so all my niggas know that money is more important than they are." She laughed.

"You should rethink that philosophy for numerous reasons," I said. She insisted on getting the tattoo. Another girl folded up her article until it became one large and overstuffed triangle. I rolled my eyes at her; she sucked her teeth at me.

At the end of the day, Dinesh asked for a ride to the bus stop because it was still raining. I happily obliged and determined that Dinesh walked about three minutes to wait up to fifteen minutes for a bus. If I drove him one minute out of my way to another stop, buses came every three minutes. I told him I would drive him there every day because it wasn't a big deal.

When he left my car after less than a minute, I was glad that I had a four-day Labor Day weekend.

II.

In Session

1.

DAY SCHOOL OFFICIALLY BEGAN, and when I entered the school it was no longer the empty fortress it had been for the last two weeks. It was alive with the noises and the rustling and shuffling only the first official day of high school could adequately provide. As I walked to the Twilight office, I saw classrooms filled with students and teachers in action. A few students roamed the hallways. Security guards and disciplinarians immersed themselves in the start of their individual yearly tours of duty. I even experienced a bell followed by the proceeding class change.

Obtaining class rosters was the only thing on my mind. It was difficult to function without them. In four teaching blocks, there was no way to effectively keep track of anyone. I wanted to get my students regimented so I could begin an organized curriculum.

I entered the Twilight office to find we had officially moved out of the math office. To get to the round table I previously used, one had to move past a long, rectangular table with two chairs on each side. The space between the backs of the chairs and immovable objects behind them was slim. Dinesh, Nicotina, Mariella, and Jack sat at the table with their work. Jack got up to shake my hand.

"We only have 180-something more days until summer break," I said. Everyone smiled or laughed.

"The new science teacher is out again. His paperwork is still being reviewed," Jack said.

Before I walked into our former office, I saw Shirley sitting at a desk talking on the phone. Jack came in behind me. Shirley hung up the phone, and we exchanged greetings.

"Benny's been transferred, and I can't find the schedules," she said to me. My issue wouldn't be addressed today.

I returned to our new office and excused myself around the table.

"I can't believe Benny got transferred. I can't believe we still don't have schedules," I said. Everyone looked at me dumbfounded and shocked. Shirley's phone call had just notified her of this. I was the bearer of bad news.

Nicotina uttered her disappointment and departed for a cigarette.

At the table, I began cutting stories from the *Daily News*, the *New York Times* and the *New York Post*. I continued discussing current events in all my classes.

Soon, it was 3:10 p.m., and I had lunch duty. I went to the auditorium, because I forgot that students would be beginning their day in the cafeteria once school was in session. Mariella and Dinesh were a few steps behind me.

There were a bunch of familiar faces and a few new ones sitting in the auditorium.

Miss D walked by. "Hi Mr. Man," she said to me. "Hi Miss Woman," she said to Mariella.

Mariella quickly and defiantly reminded Miss D of

what her name was and what mine was. I was happy to see Mariella getting tougher, but it was equally sad to see a nice woman like her have to stick up for herself to disrespectful students like Miss D.

"Her name's Miss Barbie," Tanisha said. "Call her Miss Barbie. Just look at her hair."

"Get the names right please," I said. Even though she was rude, Tanisha was a decent student, whose loudness gave her the ability to be assertive about her viewpoints, thereby making her an asset to class discussion. I knew that she got easily bored and that was surely why she was in Twilight.

She was gripping her stomach, and I asked her what was wrong. She said she felt sick, and I wondered whether she had morning sickness. I hoped that it was just a terrible idea in my head because I would hate to see her pregnant and unable to get her diploma. I got over the Miss Barbie thing because Mariella was sitting next to Tanisha, and they were talking quietly.

Marvin came up to me and said, "What choo teach?"

"You know what I teach. Why are you tryin to play me?"

"I've never seen you in my entire life," he said.

Suddenly he yelled, "Oh shit. I can't believe it's you without all that hair on ya face." No one ever saw me without my beard before. Everyone laughed at my new look, and I laughed too.

"John, can you go to the cafeteria downstairs and bring up any students who are there?" Jack asked. Dinesh joined me on the task.

It was clear that Dinesh had become more confident in his job and was adapting. He had less than fifteen students taking math all day and felt he was successfully conveying his points. We got to the cafeteria, found some students, and sent them to the auditorium. I was glad to see that the cafeteria looked much better with tables and chairs. It was still not open for business though.

At 3:50 p.m., I returned to my classroom before Jack officially dismissed the students from the auditorium. I opened my door, and my room was filled with stiff and stale air. I regretted not taking a break from lunch duty to come and open the two doors to my room to activate the cross-ventilation breeze with five open classroom windows.

As the first block began, I got everyone settled, apologized that everyone wasn't in the correct class and said that these problems would be solved by next Monday, but I knew it wasn't necessarily true.

"I'm supposed to be in English 3 this period," Miss D said.

"English 3 isn't being offered right now," I said.

"Go fuck yaself," she told me.

"There is no way you're going to pass this term no matter what if you continue with this unjustified and unnecessary disrespect of me." She made me so angry.

"I'm gonna do all yer work and there is no way I'm not gonna pass." She also mentioned some Twilight guarantee. I considered many retorts.

"Start the class," Marvin said. I passed out the stories, and there were a few teethsucks.

As the second block was about to begin, a new male student entered my room and sat in the front row.

Tanisha popped her head in and said, "I'm goin to the hospital. This naval ring is giving me a pain."

The new kid said, "So Mista Pollock, what are we going to do today?" He pronounced Pollock like Polack.

As a Kaminski, I have been the brunt of many Polish jokes in my life.

I looked at him in utter disbelief. If I was a cartoon, my lower jaw would have fallen through the floor. I smiled and asked him what he just said.

"Mista Pollock, what are we doing today?" It once again sent the jaw of my cartoon self into motion. I got annoyed.

"His name's Mista K, stupid," someone behind him said.

The new student turned around and said, "Who you callin stupid, son? How come it says Mista Pollock on the board?"

I turned around. In the upper right-hand corner of the middle section of the blackboard, it read "Mr. Pollock" and under that "Social Studies" and under that today's date. He must be one of the teachers I was sharing the classroom with. I erased it and in the same place wrote my name and rewrote the date. I was relieved it wasn't blown out of proportion.

"Mista Kaminski huh? I'm G-Black, K-Dog." I almost started laughing.

G-Black was very funny. He made numerous contributions and asked relevant questions when we were discussing current events. I was happy to see that the students were becoming more familiar with the stories we were following.

We talked about the humanitarian aid provided by the United States to the countries of the world and how it exceeded hundreds of millions of dollars in some cases. Many students felt degraded.

"Why does America give so much money to people that hate us?" one said.

"Cuz America wants to be loved by everybody," someone else said.

Keesha chimed in, "Why can't they give any money to a poor black girl like me? I'm an American." I told her that was a valid point, and the conversation continued. I was deeply troubled by it.

When the fourth block rolled around, G-Black entered my classroom. I was glad that I had another student, because one day I had only one girl named Denise. She learned a lot during that class, and I told her that if she worked like this every day, she would do very well. When I mentioned it to Faith the librarian, she told me that male teachers could never be alone with female students and that I needed a chaperone whenever the situation presented itself. A class with two students would be ideal.

G-Black told me that he worked for an elevator company and had to be in Manhattan by 6:00 a.m. every day. He made $50–$150 a day in cash. Shenequa came to my door and asked if she could write a letter, since she had no teacher for her scheduled class. I obliged. She wanted to write a letter to her boyfriend, who was in jail on cocaine-related charges.

"It wasn't his fault," she said.

Then Denise wanted to write a letter to her cousin in jail. I obliged. I told them both they could ask for my help, although I understood their letters were private. We continued talking.

"I want to get an apartment after I graduate. I want to find a man that can pay for it," Shenequa said.

"Nothing's free," I said.

"Fuck rent," G-Black chimed in. "I'll pay the phone bill...maybe." We laughed, while Denise kept working diligently.

"Remember the G-rated classroom? Or at least the PG one," I said. He apologized.

He continued, "If I spend twelve dollars, you my girl, or give me back twenty dollars. If I buy you a bag, you better cook me dinner and your ass better be better than the last ass." Denise and Shenequa were laughing.

"Take it easy," I said. He apologized. They started questioning me about the girlfriend I didn't have.

"You better get your hos in line," he said, and I concurred wholeheartedly before saying, "Let's try not to refer to women like that." Denise and Shenequa laughed.

"You into jungle feverin?" he asked.

"It's never arisen," I said.

"We should go out and party at a club."

"Let's stick to the teacher/student relationship."

G-Black continued, "We could party in the jacoochi."

"What's that?" I asked.

"You know what I mean."

"You mean jacuzzi," Shenequa said.

"I mean jacoochi," G-Black said. "I ain't gettin anything less than coochi if I'm in the jacuzzi."

I couldn't stop smiling. All three students were trying to graduate, and I reminded them that we were going to do a lot of work. They all said they would do any work that came their way. I really hoped they would.

-2-

I ENTERED THE TWILIGHT OFFICE AND every available space was occupied and everyone assigned to the office wasn't even here. The little room served Dinesh the math teacher, Mariella the Spanish teacher, Nicotina the history teacher, the new science teacher, the supposed gym teacher, Jack the Head Teacher, Faith the librarian, Rhonda the social worker, the nurse, the guidance counselor who would replace Benny, Shirley the clerk, and me. In another turn of events, Benny the guidance counselor was transferred back to Twilight. We exchanged greetings, and I asked him whether we had student schedules. He told me he would work on it later.

For Journalism, I was going to repeat the same exercise of cutting out articles, passing them out and discussing them. I even prepared a pop quiz that was absolutely simple: Who are the President, Vice President, and Secretary of State? What is Al Qaeda and who is its leader? What country may the United States be going to war against and who is its leader? What country is the Taliban from? What bioterrorist weapon was mailed in the United States right after 9/11?

I did my prep work in the Day School math office

because it was empty. There were two long tables pushed side by side. At least eight people could sit around them.

As I was cutting out articles, I saw a man enter the office from the corner of my eye. I remembered him as one of three people who interviewed and hired me. We exchanged hellos, and he asked me how everything was.

"I've had my ups and downs, but I really appreciate the support I've been getting from my team," I explained. He seemed happy for me and began doing some work at a desk in the back of the room.

As I continued my work, out of the corner of my eye, I saw someone enter the office and immediately start yelling. He was yelling at me.

"This is the math office! You specifically have a room for the Twilight program! I saw you sitting in my chair a few days ago and I didn't say anything to you, but now school is in session and you can't sit in a chair in this room! Who do you think you are?"

I learned his name was Decocksta. No one but my father ever yelled at me like that, and he had both justified and unjustified reasons for doing so. Time has given more credibility to the unjustified ones, however.

Decocksta put me in some mild shock. I gathered my things.

"It's crystal clear," I said, before returning to our overcrowded office. Only Dinesh and Mariella were there. They were laughing, but my look succeeded in stealing their happiness. Due to the different background sounds, general noise, various angles of sound, and open windows, they were unable to hear the confrontation.

"What is wrong?" Dinesh said.

"We'll talk in the cafeteria," I said.

I sat and looked out the window. I kept thinking about that piece of shit coward of a man who hired me and didn't even remind Decocksta to at least have a minimal amount of professional courtesy toward other teachers. That fat and mustached weakling just sat there. He was probably some administrator who made a lot of money for doing absolutely nothing.

I started thinking about Decocksta and his curly dyed-black hair. It could have been plugged or was maybe just a wig. I wasn't the expert in hair replacement, but he sure looked like shit, him and his dyed goatee, the mullet of the 90s. I thought about him dying in the desert of dehydration, and as he crawled, I would roll up in a truck filled with cold water. I would pour out individual bottles of water onto the sand around him and if he attempted to get a drop, I would kick him in the face with the appropriate boot and continue my wasteful routine. I thought about burning him alive with a flamethrower.

I heard Decocksta behind me, but I didn't turn around. I tried to look at something in my sight, but I saw nothing in my view. I heard his voice fade away. In order to get into his office, he would have to walk through ours, so I would be seeing more of him. The math teachers always locked their entrance door.

I put all my materials in my bag and went to the cafeteria before my official duty began. There were two security guards chasing a student around the tables, chairs, and columns in the room.

"You can't catch me, traffic cop," the kid said. After a series of fakes around various objects, the student escaped from the room with the guards right behind him.

Since it was now vacant, I hoped to get some work done, but Twilight students were already showing up. I prepared a few articles before Nicotina, Dinesh and Mariella came to my table to ask what was wrong. I explained the situation, and everyone was appalled.

"This treatment is inhuman," Dinesh said.

"You gotta confront him about this," Nicotina said.

Mariella did an imitation of Decocksta in her accent, and we all laughed. She had never even met the man.

"I would have wept if I were treated like this," Dinesh said.

Later in the day, one of the Day School teachers disparaged Dinesh for using a part of her chalkboard. Mariella had her own incident. She was given a cabinet for her materials, and her name was written on the cabinet. Later, she found her name smudged out and her materials stacked in the corner. There was no professionalism here.

At some point, Benny asked to have a meeting with me. He showed me the "executive" male bathroom and even gave me a key. It was nice, and I was glad to have a key. The only other bathroom was in the Day School teachers lounge, and that bathroom had a "Women Only" sign. On one of the first days I tried locating the official male teacher's bathroom on the second floor, but I couldn't find it. I asked a black man in the vice principal's office for its location.

"All shit and piss goes to the same place," he said. "Use the women's bathroom downstairs. I don't have the keys to the other bathrooms yet."

I ended up leaving the stall door open for my number one. I was nervous and had stage fright. Sure enough, Mariella entered the bathroom and quickly ran out. I was glad we were able to laugh about it later.

Since then, I used the boys bathroom, and it was always filled with students smoking cigarettes between classes. Once, as I was urinating at one of the urinals, the windows were open, and I realized that anyone from the classrooms facing the courtyard could see me.

Before I was done, one kid said, "I have a burna and I'm gonna shoot ya."

"You should try shooting someone else, and not someone who is helping you get your diploma." He remained silent but started loudly banging on the stall walls before I left.

It was now 3:50 p.m., and I was so mad about Decocksta. I felt completely humiliated. Maybe I should have said something totally disparaging. Maybe I should have responded with some profanity. Maybe I should have just smashed his fucking face.

All the shades in my classroom were pulled down, and it was absolutely sweltering. The first shade I tried fell to the ground. The next shade was knotted onto one of the radiators. The other three shades worked. Students started coming in.

I told the first block of Journalism and World Literature kids that we would be doing the same article activity.

"That's boring," someone yelled.

"That's cawny," someone else said.

"First we will be taking a quiz. During the quiz, I need everyone's eyes on their own work." As I passed them out, every student wanted to argue. I was still upset.

It soon became clear that half the class had nothing to write with. I was still unsure whether these students were even really in my class, since we still didn't have official rosters. G-Black walked in late.

"Quiet please," I said. Everyone was asking everyone else for something to write with. I only had five pens and one pencil in my leather knapsack, and they weren't enough. I let one student volunteer go to the office for pens and pencils. Somehow everyone got started, and we had a few brief moments of students working in silence.

The volunteer returned, saw everyone working and said, "What am I supposed to do with these now?" Everyone looked at us. I took the pens from him and got him started on the quiz.

A few seconds later, Alysha yelled, "Al Gore is the vice president."

"You're getting a zero. You can't yell out answers," I said. He wasn't even the vice president.

"Go to hell," she said.

"I did, but your mom said you weren't home," I said in frustration.

"Kiss my ass," she said. She walked out of the room.

Shirley arrived with a new student.

"Alysha lyin," Shenequa said to Shirley.

"Yeah," Tanisha said.

"I'm glad I heard both sides of the story," Shirley said. She left the doorway.

"I'm done," Miss D said. I collected her quiz and asked her to please return the pen she borrowed from me.

"I hate white people. You can go fuck yaself." She continued, "I'm gonna tell the superintendent that you the worst teacher."

"I can't see you passing with this kind of attitude," I said.

"Shut your mouth, nigga," G-Black said to her. "Don't fuck with the K-Dog."

Everyone was looking up and not working.

"Please finish your quizzes."

"Don't listen to her shit, K-Dog," he said. "All you gotta do is tell her mama and she won't be talkin shit cuz her mama'll smack her upside the head." He explained how she'll even hit her in front of me.

"But that was years ago," Miss D said and remained silent. I asked everyone for silence.

I quickly graded the completed quizzes. Three students got over a 70 to pass. Fifteen students failed.

Soon it was Block Three, and I learned the class consisted of students in English 2 and English 4. I asked everyone to copy the ten vocabulary words on the board, to read a 4-page story from our textbooks and to answer five questions in the critical-thinking section. It occupied them for almost fifteen minutes.

Soon, most of the students started complaining about not being able to understand the questions.

"I cannot answer some of your questions, since it'll reveal the answers I want from you."

"That's not fair," someone said.

"Shut the fuck up, this work easy," Shenequa said. "I can't do mines lisnin to this shit."

Two students got so mad that they walked out. In the doorway, one girl said, "I'm gonna write a letter to Miss Carter sayin how you're the worst teacher I ever had."

I couldn't believe it was only September 9. I could honestly say that I didn't think I would survive here much longer.

3

I WALKED INTO WORK WITH A little more pep in my step and I didn't want to speak too soon, but I was very grateful the first anniversary of September 11 passed us by. I was uneasy for the last few days, and it was evident to my co-workers, who asked me about my glumness.

When I told them about my feelings at the end of the day in the office on September 10, Jack said, "If there is a terrorist attack, it had better happen in the morning because then we probably wouldn't have school." A few people laughed.

On the way to my car, Jack said, "I hate the direction our country has taken. We're responsible for 9/11, and we should not begin a war with Iraq. When Clinton was in office, we all lived through peace and prosperity." He hated Bush.

I said, "One of the best things about America is that people are allowed to have their own opinions."

At the front desk sat the same black security guard I saw every single day. On most days, I gave her a greeting from "Hi," "How are you?" or "Hello." She was either reading a newspaper or sitting with her hands folded in front of her with eyes wandering the hallways. She had yet to respond to me.

She was looking down at her newspaper. As I passed, I said, "Hi," and smiled. She looked up and back down. I continued walking down the hall toward my office. Tomorrow I was going to say, "Good Afternoon." Maybe that was the greeting required to secure a verbal response.

Our school policy was for students to carry hall passes, but there was no one making sweeps or ridding the hallways of roaming students. On this walk, there were two female students staring in through the window of the back door of one of the classrooms; each classroom had a front and a back door. One of them began tapping on the window to get the attention of someone in the class. Most of the students inside subsequently looked back to see who it was, and everyone was disrupted. Another girl waved back from the classroom. The two girls then walked right past the guard.

Midway down the hall, I saw Decocksta open the door to our office and enter. I was able to grab the doorknob before it closed. Everyone saw me entering the room since their heads were already up in reaction to his entrance. I was smiling and looking at Dinesh, Nicotina and Mariella and then in Decocksta's direction and then back at them.

Benny handed me a roster, and I was happy to be another step toward being organized. There was simply no room for me to work, so I announced that I was going to the cafeteria. On my way out, I saw Decocksta cutting through our office for the door. Just as he was close enough to think he could casually stop the closing door, I slammed it in his face. Why did he have to cut through our office? Why was there a television and VCR cart barricading their front door? I was sure Twilight didn't have access to the equipment either.

Later Mariella said, "Almost, you broke his nose." Her English was continually charming, and she especially hated Decocksta.

I arrived at the cafeteria downstairs, and naturally the doors were locked. I found a long table nearby so I pulled up a seat, unpacked my bag, and began preparing for the day. A review of my roster revealed that Miss D was officially in both my first block and my fourth block. I had to figure out a way to deal with her daily antics. Suddenly, a group of about five students ran past the foyer and past my table. Moments later, two security guards arrived to ask me if I saw a group of students run by. I told them which way they went and tried to get to work. A guard finally opened the cafeteria, and I gathered up my stuff.

Twilight lunch was upon us, and the students began arriving along with the other teachers. Before lunch officially ended, I wanted to talk to Shirley about Miss D. I wanted Miss D to do her work in the office; I could give her assignments to Shirley. Miss D simply didn't deserve to be in my class. As I left the cafeteria, I could hear Miss D talking about me.

"Look at them cheap-ass shoes," she said.

"But those Timbs," one kid said.

"Yeah, the faggot ones," she replied.

I found Shirley and told her about my plan. She and Benny asked me to please give Miss D another chance, and I reluctantly complied. Benny told me to begin a log of her comments.

I got to my classroom, and it was absolutely filthy with candy wrappers, crumpled papers, and empty beverage containers strewn all over the floor. There was no order to the disheveled desk-chairs that filled the room. I kicked all the garbage into an enormous pile in the back of the room and lined up the desks to make a classroom. Everyone always wanted to sit in the back row and would move their desk-chairs to the back wall. If the class was already arranged in an orderly fashion, it was less apt to happen.

The students began entering class, and within the first five minutes Miss D told me to fuck off thrice, said my mom could fuck off once, and called me a faggot. I wrote it all down.

"You should write a fuckin book," Miss D said.

"I already got it started," I replied. I wasn't referring to her comment log.

I went to the office to get Shirley to remove Miss D. I told Benny and Shirley what she said, and apparently calling me a faggot was very offensive. Benny said that she might get suspended.

In Block Two, a student I referred to as the Queen was in attendance. It was the first time she made it two consecutive days. She was also pregnant. I first met her in the auditorium during one of the first few days, and she had white powder all over her black shirt. Upon closer investigation, I realized that the Queen was sucking white powder through a straw from a box she had in a black plastic bag.

Nicotina and I asked about it.

"My aunt said you should eat cornstarch if you pregnant," the Queen said. "I think I'm addicted to it."

"That might not be the best food to be eating," I said.

"You have no right to tell me what to eat," she said.

Yesterday, on September 11, the Queen said that a

premonition of the World Trade Center attacks could be found in the Bible.

"Are you sure about that?" I asked.

"Yeah."

"Can you please find that passage for me? I would love to read it."

"I will," she said. We continued talking.

"How come you haven't given me a pass to the office yet?" she asked.

"Why do you need to go there?"

"You want me to call my pastor, right? Don't you want to find out what passage it is?"

"I don't need that information immediately," I said.

Yesterday, some students helped me clean up the room, and we began covering the corkboards with colored paper. I was sick of looking at the graffiti and the dark green. It was an awful reminder of how disorderly the classroom could get and wasn't conducive to any type of learning or positive thinking.

As we shuffled around the room, a rolled up projector screen fell from behind a file cabinet.

"It fell on me. I'm gonna sue the Board of Education," one girl said.

"You should get Johnnie Cochran," someone chimed in.

"All these lawsuits would be less likely if everyone was sitting quietly writing a boring essay," I said. The students stopped talking about suing.

In Block Three, Joe came in and said, "I like how much nicer the room looks, Mista K." The students called him JoAnna because he was extremely effeminate, and Shirley told me how he was terrorized for being gay. Last year, she lost two teeth trying to protect him from being severely beaten outside the school.

Joe was wearing a white T-shirt and a tie. He also had a style of wearing long-sleeve button-down shirts, from which he cut off the cuffs to wear as bracelets. He rolled up the sleeves to make the shirt short-sleeved.

Right before Block Four, Foolio asked if I could get him a bottle of water from the Day School teachers lounge. I agreed because the classrooms were stuffy and the water coming from the fountains was absolutely disgusting. We were obviously never supposed to get any students drinks.

"Give me a dollar," I said.

He pulled a huge wad of cash from his pocket. I saw lots of twenties. He found a dollar and handed it to me.

"Please never let me see all that money again," I said, and he obliged. Unfortunately for him, the machines were out of water, so I returned to class and gave him back his dollar.

"Why they outta water?" Foolio asked.

"I'm not the one in charge of the drink inventory."

"Maybe you should be," he said smiling. I smiled too.

"You crazy, Hootie and the Blowfish," he said. His eyes were really red.

"Maybe you should get some eye drops." He got more serious.

The day ended and I walked out with Nicotina and Dinesh. Dinesh decided to get a car because his commute was wearing him down and if he drove, it would take him less than forty minutes to get here. Nicotina and I said it was a good idea. As we left the school, Dinesh shook my hand.

-4-

IT WAS LESS THAN TEN MINUTES into my first teaching block, and Tamieka asked me if she could go to the bathroom.

"You know my policy of no bathroom passes for the first and last fifteen minutes of the class," I reminded her. Although my policy was simply the reinforcement of Twilight rules, the class reacted with a series of verbal complaints from practically everyone.

I looked over at Tamieka and forgot that she was pregnant. I wasn't sure how pregnant she was, but she was definitely showing.

"Sorry, Tamieka," I said, before writing her a pass. I had no idea how to address the needs of pregnant students. It turned into another series of questions about my children.

"Like I said, I don't have any."

"You don't have kids cuz you don't nut right," someone yelled.

"Hallelujah to that," I said.

The majority of students were able to return to their assignments. As I passed Miss D, she said, "Go fuck yaself." Then she gave me the finger, which she usually did when I walked by.

I went over to one girl who wasn't working.

"You're going to get a zero for the day," I said.

"That's alright. It's one zero. I'll work tomorrow," she said. It was more important to worry about everyone else and move on rather than begin a confrontation that distracted the entire class. She just sat quietly. She tried going to sleep a few times, but I woke her up.

Moments later, Destiny entered class with a baby carriage.

"I couldn't get a baby sitter. Since I'm here now and it's raining, can I do some work?" I gave her the editing assignment. Her baby boy was very cute and slept the entire time.

Tanisha got up from her work to ogle the baby. School policy forbid students from bringing their children to school, so Destiny was going to have to leave soon. On the other hand, it was better to have Destiny in school getting her high school diploma than not. Maybe they should provide daycare.

"I would have had a kid years ago if schools provided daycare," Tanisha said. Maybe school day care wasn't such a good idea.

The students were working on their own essays or editing the essays of others. Because of the horrendous amount of absences, it was difficult to get the entire class on the same track, but I managed to have everyone working toward completing individual assignments.

No one ever brought paper or pens to class, so I brought these supplies from the Twilight office every day. Today, the class dilemma revolved around the characteristics of the paper I distributed. Since I ran out of my white supply, I had to use yellow.

"I can't write like this," someone said.

"I'm goin to the office to get more paper," someone else said.

The color coordination of their essays was very important. I let a few of them go to the office, but I refused to write any passes. No one was checking them anyway.

In Block Two, it took longer to get everyone motivated. As I walked around the room to get everyone started, someone yelled, "Cracker!"

"Stop!" I said. Everyone looked up.

"What's a cracker?" I asked.

"It's what black people call white people," a student said.

"When I taught in the Bronx, students called me a cracker, and I didn't know what they meant. The only explanation I got was that crackers, the white edible ones, were white." Everyone was paying attention.

"I just learned that a cracker refers to the crack of the whip of the person who whipped slaves. When slaves were unruly, the cracker disciplined them." The silence continued.

"Maybe you should learn the definitions of these words before you call your teacher, the person who is trying to help you, this word," I said.

Someone in a hokey voice said, "Yessir." Everyone laughed. When I taught in the Bronx, the black students mocked the white teachers by talking in their version of a hokey cowboy.

"I get the voice thing," I said. "It's not that original." They got back to work.

For the last few days, there was some construction on the exterior of the school. Since it was hot, we had to leave the windows open. We tried ignoring the noise of the compressor. I apologized to the students when it disturbed them.

In the middle of class, a section of scaffolding passed by our window, and scared a few students and me. We looked at each other and smiled. The students got back to work.

The scaffolding rose back up. When I looked out the window, a worker said, "You better close those windows. Some dust is gonna drift back in."

The windows were shut, and the classroom got even hotter. The students were complaining about the heat and the compressor and the construction. I kept apologizing.

Once they got quiet, I ran down the hall to the Twilight office to find Jack. We needed a new room, and he got us one. He gave me a warm and supportive pat on the back as we switched rooms.

In Block Three, I began what I refer to as worksheet learning. I wrote 4 period-long (one hour) assignments of reading and answering questions about a book. Since student attendance was so erratic, it was impossible to have any consistent curriculum in the classes. On the other hand, there were a few students who were always here to learn. If you wanted to improve your English, you needed to be reading and writing.

I selected *The Old Man and the Sea* for many reasons: I enjoyed Hemingway, the book was easy to read, it was short, and the students might get a sense of accomplishment by completing a short novel. Also, fishing in Cuba was just so completely different than anything these students could relate to that maybe they would like it.

It was far more productive to have them working on individual reading assignments, since a class discussion with a rotating class of students was impossible. If I wanted to sit in a circle and talk about a book, many students wouldn't be prepared and would disturb the class. I pictured kids calling everything "boring" and corny without having read a word. If students were here, they could complete their work. If they were not, there was at least some kind of consistent curriculum in place for them to make up. Everyone would be busy doing something academic, and I could oversee the progress. These students were in Twilight for a reason, so we needed to make whatever adjustments necessary.

The novella was going over well, but I had to stop some students from yelling out the answers once they found them. I wanted to give them zeroes, but I knew that I was going to have to fail many students on my roster because they weren't even present. I prodded them along and quelled many instances of disruptive behavior. Nevertheless, the majority of students were able to accomplish some work.

In Block Four, I had one female student in attendance, and I got her reading. I remembered the school policy concerning male teachers and female students being alone together, and imagined having to defend myself against erroneous student accusations and having my career completely ruined. I ran over to the office to inform them of the situation.

"Go get a security guard to sit outside," Faith the librarian said.

"I don't know where the guards are," I said. As I stood in the doorway, everyone in the office sat at the table.

I looked down the hall to the sound of noise coming from Mariella's room. A security guard walked out of her room and then back in, before returning to sit at a desk-chair in the hallway near the room. I returned to my classroom and stood in the doorway. There was still noise coming from her room.

Soon, Nicotina barged out of her classroom and walked toward me. She had a scowl and looked livid.

"I've had enough," she said. "I need to speak to Miss Carter about how come we have no science teacher, and how come there is no control." I agreed.

"And Dinesh just sits in his room with his handful of students and never helps out." She was very frustrated, and I couldn't blame her. "Now everyone's in Mariella's room and you could hear that from here."

She continued, "Jack let a bunch of kids leave because we don't have enough teachers and now the rest of them want to go."

I went to Mariella's room with my one student. As I entered, there were numerous teethsucks and comments about my presence.

"Why he here?" someone yelled.

"You guys don't know how to be quiet." I said.

"Someone came complainin'," someone yelled. Apparently, a guidance counselor from the Day School came from the opposite side of the school because of the noise.

"I hate you," someone said toward me.

Mariella had tears in her eyes. She needed more office and security guard support.

"Let's talk later because they're all listening," I said.

"I am stupid. I cannot teach with all these kids," she said. I tried to be consoling and supportive.

"Try checking the roster more and learning who everyone is," I said. "Tell the students who aren't supposed to be here to leave."

"But where will they go?" she asked.

Miss D was in there too. She looked at me and said, "You the ugliest muthafucka I ever seen."

I turned to Nicotina, "I'm going to find Jack." I hoped

he would send everyone home and end the madness. There was simply no way to reason with the students.

As I walked down the hall, two male students descended upon Mariella's room. Their eyes were red and glassy. They had been in the bathroom. I ushered them both into Dinesh's room, so he could watch them.

I found Jack on the other side of the building in the hallway near the office of the guidance counselor who yelled at Mariella's class. I could hear the noise he complained about.

"I think we would be better off if we dismissed everyone immediately," I said.

"I can't. Carter's on the warpath," he said. He followed me back to Mariella's room, where he managed to quiet everyone down for a moment.

I went back into the hallway and was soon motioned by a student from Dinesh's room.

"Come here," he said. "Can you do this?" He began telling me about a math problem he had to do on the board.

"If I have four pounds and sell some bags, how many bags per pound?" I worked with him and actually answered his questions mathematically. I wrote the answer on the board.

"Oh shit," one of the kids said.

"And this remainder can just be converted into a fraction," I said.

"But I'd just smoke the fraction," the kid said.

I returned to Mariella's room rather than get into every issue wrong with the conversation.

I looked up at the clock, and there were only three minutes before school was over.

"That clock's slow," someone yelled, and everyone poured into the hallway. Nicotina and the security guards tried escorting the students from the building as they were screaming and running.

I walked back to the office with a dejected Mariella and Dinesh, who high-fived me that the day was over. Conversation turned to how Miss Carter needed to do a better job. No one knew why we didn't have a substitute teacher helping us. Before I left, Jack shook my hand.

I walked toward the exit with Dinesh and Nicotina, and we talked about how Dinesh was going to start driving to school next week. As we were about to exit, the Day School principal stopped us.

"You better keep your students quiet when they leave," she said assertively. "They better not wear their hats and do-rags in the school."

"It's crystal clear," I said, before we left. I really hoped she would show us how to effectively perform that task.

As we were leaving the school, Nicotina yelled, "I promise to be here to see your students doing the same things tomorrow. I'll be here early." I laughed.

"I hope I can get another job," she said.

I hoped so too for her sake.

-5-

RIGHT BEFORE HEADING TO CAFETERIA DUTY, I checked the condition of my classroom. Once again, the desks were in disarray and garbage was everywhere. Sunflower seeds were scattered somewhat evenly across the entire floor. The three computers in the back of the classroom were turned on, but the monitors were off. The twisting knob that was pressed to turn on the monitor was missing on one. The keyboards and the mice for the computers were also missing.

The two-door beige metal cabinet in the back of the classroom was open. One of the doors was pulled off its hinges. Someone pulled out some of the contents of the cabinet, and papers were partially pulled from shelves and left hanging while others rested on the floor. In a bunch of frustrating seconds, I was able to put the door back on its hinges and close the cabinet.

On the back table rested a partially destroyed mountain of pencil shavings from the sharpener that was screwed into the wall above the table. Shavings were strewn across that area of the floor. The blue paper on one of the corners of the recently-covered corkboard near the front of the room was torn off and crumpled into a large ball that rested neatly atop the desk-chair below it.

I saw the janitor sweeping the hallways and borrowed his broom. A few pushes combined with the careful movements of piles of garbage and desk-chairs made the room more presentable. I was sweating. I gave the broom back to the janitor.

I got down to the cafeteria; I wanted to talk to my colleagues about some solutions I devised to bring order to our day. Only yesterday, Mariella left her room in tears because Miss D was fighting with Joe, and they were both screaming and cursing at each other at the tops of their lungs. Joe was crying. Jack had to come and physically remove Joe. Two security guards were able to watch the action up close.

I showed them the essay topic for my two Journalism classes; it revolved around what teachers and students could both do to create a better classroom environment for learning. Everyone liked the topic. I also told them that I was going to start writing students up for the bad behavior we had grown accustomed to. Bad behavior was breeding worse behavior. I was constantly losing credibility because students like Miss D consistently undermined my authority. I was hoping my written testimony would lead to disciplinary action like a suspension, and once one student got suspended or expelled from Twilight, then everyone would behave better. Benny told me he would begin a folder of write-ups.

Mariella told me how her husband, who taught at another Twilight school, was also dealing with abhorrent conditions. Mariella never wore a wedding ring, and many people thought she was single. If anyone asked, she explained that she escaped Venezuela with her boyfriend, and they had been together in America for six years.

"What else is a husband to me than my boyfriend?" she said. I agreed.

"The other day, a student said to my husband, 'How can I say "I don't like you" in Spanish?'"

"I feel bad for both of you," I said. "You need to think about our three months off. Just think, after we get certified, we'll be able to teach better and more appreciative students."

"I don't know if I can wait that long," she said.

It was 3:50 p.m., and the only students in the cafeteria were sitting playing cards around a circular table. It was against school rules to play cards.

Benny went to the table and said in a soft tone, "It's time to go to class." No one stopped playing. A card fell off the table. I picked it up.

"It's time to go to class," I said, in a much louder voice.

One of the card players grabbed my arm and demanded it back. It was Miss D's cousin, who only needed to take one science class to graduate. Since there was no science teacher, he would come to my first block and talk to Miss D. Nicotina was nice enough to accept him into her class.

"Give me the card," he yelled, as he failed to twist my wrist.

"Get off me," I said.

I turned to Benny and said, "Can you believe this?" I left and took the card with me.

I got to my classroom and awaited my students, who arrived sporadically over the next thirty minutes. On my desk were my notebook, my knapsack, a pile of novels, a dictionary, and four piles of dittos. The dittos were of an outline of a Journalism essay, the third worksheet for *The Old Man and the Sea,* and two similar but different vocabulary tests to more effectively combat cheating. Some students were working on their 9/11 essays, while others were getting work for the first time.

As usual, Marvin sat in the front seat, asked for work, and got busy. Once he finished, he was allowed to leave. I always made sure that I had a consistent curriculum for those who came every day.

Foolio arrived and sat behind Marvin. "Hootie and the Blowfish," he said to me. Once he got his work, he began working.

Keesha arrived, asked for her work, and sat in the back of the room. She was very fat and was constantly eating candy, even though students weren't permitted to eat in class. Keesha always sat by an open window so she could throw her candy wrappers out. I told her numerous times to stop polluting, but it was like she was in denial that I knew about her antics.

Moments later, she said, "Give me more paper." No students had any regard for manners.

"I'm not a slave, and I'm not a dog so please don't treat me like either one," I said. She sucked her teeth at me. "Please get up and get your own paper."

"If you was a dog, you'd be barkin," she said.

"You got a point," I replied. I got the paper for her because I didn't think she would ever get up for it.

When I returned to my desk, Miss D arrived for her assignment. She had been relegated to the Twilight office. As I got her folder from my bag, she took Foolio's hat, put it on and slapped him on his head.

"Let him work, please," I said to her. "Please give it back." She continued staring down at him.

"Maybe you need to get another hat," I said to him.

She tossed his hat back when I handed her her work. As she left the room, she picked up two piles of papers from my desk, threw them into the air and said, "Go fuck yaself." Some students laughed.

"I hope you can all see how this behavior affects our learning environment," I said. I picked up the papers and sat down to write up Miss D. It was terse and eloquent.

Benny walked by my door, so I handed him the paper. He looked it over and said, "I'll take care of it."

Iverson finally showed up. I called him Iverson because he was always wearing Sixers gear with Iverson on it. He was about five feet tall.

"Thanks for making it to class," I said.

"Why you tryin to play me?" he asked.

I handed him the assignment for the teacher/student relations essay and two sheets of white paper. He went to his usual seat in the back of the room.

Seconds later, he said, "What the fuck we doin today, yo?"

"Try taking a second to read the assignment please."

Seconds later, he said, "I need a pen, yo."

"Thanks for coming to class prepared," I said. I walked a pen over to him. He fiddled with the pen, dropped it on the floor, reached to pick it up and began reading his assignment.

Seconds later, he said, "Why do I have to do this shit, yo?"

I said, "This place you're in, it's called a school. In a school, you do work so you can earn a high school diploma. And please don't end every sentence you say with yo."

Iverson sucked his teeth and said, "What choo mean why's everythin endin in yo, yo?"

"Just get started on the work please. If you don't do it, you'll be taking this class again." Iverson mostly showed up, but he was always late. He did enough work to pass, but I always needed to nudge him.

He said, "If I don't pass, you're goin to be in trouble."

"Ooooh, I'm so scared."

"All I need is one finger," he said, but not in a threatening manner.

Keesha said, "He means he's gonna shoot you, Mista K."

"Shooting the English teacher would not be in anyone's interest, believe me."

Iverson got to work, and momentarily, everyone was silent and working.

Suddenly from the hallway, G-Black yelled, "Yo, K-Dog! Yo K-Dog!" Everyone in the class looked up as he entered.

"Yo K-Dog, gimme some tissues."

"Please go to the nurse," I said. He began checking out a girl sitting a few seats away from my desk. "Can you please go to the nurse and come back later? Everyone is busy here."

For the remainder of the successful class, which was successful because everyone was working quietly, Faith arrived at my door and began asking individual students to the Twilight office. When they returned, they told me that Faith was asking questions about Miss D. Some of them were genuinely upset with the distractions caused by Miss D.

Shenequa arrived, asked for her assignment and began working at her desk, even though the class was almost over. I collected plenty of student work and planned on doing a lot of grading over the weekend. I wanted to have my gradebook up-to-date for next week.

Iverson handed in his work and began hanging

around my desk, since Foolio and Marvin were nearby. I read over his paper, which was completely preposterous. I asked Iverson about it.

"Jus cause I wrote cha fuckin paper, it don't mean I mean it," he said. I put it in my bag. He continued to linger.

As I was talking to Foolio and Marvin, Iverson said, "I got some ass last night." When no one responded, he said it again.

"Who cares?" I said.

He said, "What choo mean who cares, yo?"

Foolio and Marvin started laughing. Foolio put his hand out for me to slap it. When I went to, he pulled it back.

Faith was still pulling students out of class one at a time. Although Miss D wasn't allowed in class, she came to hand in her work.

As she left, she began talking to Iverson. She grabbed him by his crotch and asked him to come to the bathroom.

"Can I get a pass?" Iverson asked.

"Negative!" I yelled. Miss D sucked her teeth at me before leaving.

"You a hate-uh," Marvin said to me. I remembered how last week Faith said that Iverson was known for "putting his utensil everywhere."

Faith reentered and asked the class why everyone was complaining about Mr. Kaminski.

Shenequa said, "All these niggas don't wanna do any motherfuckin work. Mista K too nice."

When Faith was about to call out the next student, I told her what Miss D did. Iverson was called out next.

When he returned, he said, "You a rat."

Thankfully, the block ended, and the classes changed.

As some students left, they said, "One." It was what they said when they left any situation or conversation. They said it a lot.

During the next class change, I caught Marvin, Foolio and a few other guys in the bathroom smoking and shooting dice. They invited me to play. I also wrote-up Miss D's cousin and gave it to Faith.

When the fourth block began, G-Black returned. I asked him about *The Old Man and the Sea* assignments he owed me, and he began working on the first one. There were a few other students working already.

After finishing quickly, he asked, "What drugs you do?" I looked at him and got back to what I was doing.

"You ever been in prison?" he asked.

"What are you talking about?" I asked.

"I'm not talkin bout beef and broccoli, I'm talkin bout coke and dope," he said.

"Please take it easy," I said. I gave him another assignment.

Once he was done, he asked, "You need to stop hangin out with white bitches and start hangin out with black bitches." He gave me numerous reasons why. I asked him to take it easy.

Some students were finishing their work, while others were talking quietly. I looked into the hallway and saw Jack dismissing students at 8:00 p.m. He dismissed most of them early. I dismissed my class and got to the Twilight office completely drained.

Faith was sitting at the round table reading. I sat down, looked up at the bright light in the ceiling, closed my eyes, and stretched out in my seat. I was momentarily refreshed.

I opened my eyes and looked at Faith. She turned away. I again stretched my back out.

She said, "Don't think I didn't read what you sent me."

"I don't think that," I said. I looked up in a daze.

"I think we should put on a mock court," she said. I was unsure of what she meant.

"You just need a lawyer. Any one of the teachers," Faith said. I was confused.

"I don't know," I said. "If the students are running the court, they'll probably just side with each other. I know how they work."

There was a silence.

I said, "I don't want (Miss D) being found not guilty. What would that do for my credibility?"

"What do you mean?" she asked. "You're the one that's goin on trial."

I couldn't believe my ears. It was ludicrous *AND* ridiculous.

"Didn't you get my write-up?" I said.

"Yeah," she said, and paused. "You know how many students complain about you?"

I wasn't sure what to say.

"I can't be your lawyer because I'm the bailiff," she said.

Thankfully, Jack came into the office and started making announcements. He began at 8:10 p.m. and dismissed us five minutes later when he finally stopped talking. My mind was drifting intermittently.

The main issue revolved around whether Twilight should participate in a charity walk in a few Fridays. Teachers paid ten dollars to enter, while students paid five.

"Sounds like a ploy to make students give money to get out of going to school," Faith said.

"It wouldn't be worth ten dollars to get aggravated," Nicotina said. I agreed.

I spoke to Nicotina as we walked to our cars.

"I don't know what's going on," she said. "I don't know why you're going on trial," she said.

"I don't know what's going on either," I said. "I'm tired."

"You need to think more about this. You also need to give your write-ups to Benny."

Maybe I should get a lawyer.

One.

-6-

IT WAS FRIDAY, AND AS soon as I signed into the Twilight book, Faith came up to me.

"I apologize for not reading your written complaints yesterday. I forwarded all the information to Rhonda," she said. Rhonda was the social worker. Upon learning about my issues with both Miss D and her cousin, she suspended both of them until each returned with a parent. I was pleased.

Since it was Friday, most students were absent. By the end of cafeteria duty, only eight of twelve students arrived. Nicotina and Jack were also absent.

In first block, Marvin said, "I like your Infinity."

"I don't really like its four-cylinder power," I said.

"You should get an Acura," he said.

"That might be a good idea."

For the third and fourth blocks, I took my students to the computer lab in the library. Mariella brought her class too.

G-Black showed up at the beginning of the fourth and refused to complete the assignment he owed me. His attendance was sporadic, but he understood the list of assignments he had to complete. While Mariella read a magazine, G-Black and I were speaking.

He asked, "You gettin on that shit," as he motioned with his head toward Mariella.

"Take it easy," I said. He sucked his teeth at me.

As he looked back at her and at me, he said, "She should get some better clothes."

"Quit being a dick," I said. A few students laughed. Mariella continued flipping through the magazine.

I don't think Mariella heard or understood my exchange with G-Black. The other day when we were sitting at a cafeteria table during duty, she said, "Sometimes, I cannot understand people. Sometimes, they speak so fast." She admitted that sometimes she couldn't understand me. "Sometimes, I ask you to repeat or else I am quiet and embarrassed."

"I can't understand you sometimes myself," Dinesh agreed, in his heavily-accented Indian voice. "You speak too fast for me."

"From now on, just tell me to slow down," I said, much slower than I usually would.

Back in fourth block, G-Black continued, "You right, K-Dog, but can you tell me one thing?" I nodded my head.

"Where'd you get those muthafuckin shoes?" I smiled. Everyone laughed.

"They Timbs," someone yelled.

G-Black said, "They Timbs? K-Dog, how many miles you plannin to walk with those muthafuckin soles?" Everyone laughed again. I laughed. Someone said Mariella was laughing.

"And those muthafuckin pants, K-Dog? Why you gotta iron all yo shit?"

He extended his arms and explained how, "It's about

big, fuckin shit." He pointed to his jeans as an example of big.

"Take it easy," I said.

The block was almost over, and the students were getting antsy. Mariella escorted two students upstairs because they insisted on going to the Twilight office. Shelley, one of the security guards, remained.

The rest of the students were arguing about where they wanted to wait for the day to be over. One group wanted to wait upstairs. Another group wanted to wait in the lab. A few students refused to get off their computers.

Shelley brought one group upstairs, while I got the rest of them to shut down their computers. We made it upstairs, and Shelley dismissed her group. Once my students found out, they left as well. One student stopped into the Day School's principal's office on the way out.

I looked at the clock and realized it was only 8:10 p.m. The students were dismissed five minutes early.

No sooner had I gotten to the Twilight office when the principal made an announcement over the loudspeaker: "All Twilight staff report to my office." Faith, Rhonda, Mariella, Shirley, the nurse and I began talking.

"This is all my fault," I said. I tried leaving to go down alone first, but Faith and Rhonda called me back.

"Calm down," Faith said.

"We're going down as a team," said Rhonda. The nurse said she would get Dinesh from his room.

As we walked down the hall, I was the first person to see the principal as we turned the corner. She was a blonde-bobbed, robust woman. Her hands were on her hips.

I was about to talk when she put up her finger and said, "Wait a minute."

"Shirley, get Miss Carter on the phone," the principal said.

"She's in transit between the sites," Shirley said.

The principal got angry and flustered. She went into her office. Shirley went to another office and began fiddling with a phone. The rest of us, including both security guards, Shelley and Patrice, stood silently in the hallway.

Jack complained about the principal before: "She stays here until eleven, and no one knows what she does other than meddle in Twilight affairs."

The principal returned from the depths of her office and said, "I can't find Miss Carter's beeper number."

She gave everyone a look with her roving eyes. "What parties are responsible for the early dismissal of students?"

"I dismissed them early," I said. "I lost track of time."

"Explain yourself," she said. I told her how Shelley and me took the students upstairs too early from the computer room.

"So you can't keep track of time?" she said to Shelley. "Do you know school policy?" I felt bad for Shelley.

"I told Shelley to dismiss the students," I said.

"You dismissed the students?" she asked.

"I dismissed the students."

"If anything happens to any of them, there will be a humungous liability lawsuit against the school," she said.

"I'm sorry," I said.

"I don't want your apology."

She stared me down. I remembered how although I was in a high school, I was no longer in high school.

"Are you blind?" the principal asked, as she pointed

toward the clock above the front door. "How can you make a mistake like this?"

"It just eluded me," I said.

She went back into her office to answer her ringing phone. Since it was Miss Carter, she motioned us to leave.

When I got back to the Twilight office, Benny was in the math office.

"Why didn't you go with us?" Rhonda asked.

"I didn't have to," he replied. He called me over, took off his glasses, and gave me a clearer view of his eyes, one of which was entirely bloodshot.

"Don't let them get you down," he said.

"I'm trying not to let them," I said.

"The school would be better without bastard students like (Miss D)," he said. I agreed.

"In all my years of teaching, I always passed students like her, so I didn't have to hear them and their bullshit."

"I guess we'll see how this year ends," I said.

As we were leaving, I apologized to Shelley: "Sorry if I got you in trouble."

"Don't worry about it," she said. "Have a drink and enjoy your weekend."

I hoped I could.

-7-

IT WAS SEPTEMBER 23ᴿᴰ AND the dismissal situation was on my mind all weekend. I wanted to speak with Jack. When I entered the Twilight office, I noticed Dinesh got a haircut. Mariella also got some color from the fishing trip she was talking about last week. Jack had not yet arrived.

Nicotina asked, "You have your lesson plans ready?"

"I'm still working on them," I said. I hadn't done them. All I had were outlines of what I had done. I needed to put them into a lesson plan format I didn't completely understand. There needed to be ones for Journalism, English 2 and English 4. I didn't even have enough copies of the lesson plan template. "Miss Carter may be giving you a surprise informal observation," Nicotina said. "She'll probably look over your entire planbook."

"I'm more concerned about the early dismissal," I said. "It was totally my fault." She agreed.

As I was about to leave the office, I nearly bumped into Decocksta. He smiled and let me pass.

I was on my way to the cafeteria to put together today's lessons and to begin working backwards on my lesson plans. I was arranging and filling out forms. There was plenty of repetitious dating. If Miss Carter wanted my lesson planbook, I would tell her I forgot it. I made sure to have today's lessons completed properly.

At 3:10 p.m., Nicotina, Dinesh and Mariella arrived.

"Have you heard the news?" Nicotina asked.

"Do you know anything about anyone getting written up for dismissing students early?" I asked.

"I'm not sure of that," she said. "I am sure that we will be getting twenty-two new students today."

"Twenty-two new students?" I yelled. "Who the hell is going to watch them?" As I looked around the cafeteria, I noticed a bunch of new faces.

"Faith and Rhonda are going to keep them in the auditorium and introduce them to the school," Nicotina said.

"We're definitely going to have to watch them in our classes by third block," I said. Nicotina shrugged her shoulders.

Apparently, Miss Carter elected not to pay money for substitutes, so all the teachers dealing with additional students from absent teachers were paid twenty-five extra dollars a day. Shirley said that she would fill out the paperwork for us. Each teacher already accrued almost a thousand dollars. The extra money was still not worth the extra aggravation.

A student came up to me and said, "I'm for Mista K. There are parents waiting for him upstairs." It took me a moment to realize that the conference was a result of the suspensions of Miss D and Miss D's cousin. I took my time gathering my things.

As I was leaving, Faith arrived to tell me people were waiting for me upstairs.

"Relax," she said.

I was thinking about how I was going to deal with Miss D and her cousin. I wanted to speak to the parents without their kids. If the kids were there, I feared the conversation would deteriorate to me being called a liar. I was going to be very nice. I was relaxed, I thought.

I entered the Twilight office, and Miss D and her cousin were sitting with two older women at their sides. Rhonda was sitting at the round table near the window. Shirley was on the phone in the math office. I appreciated the air-conditioned hallway I just left because the windows were shut in here. It was stuffy.

I introduced myself to both women before having a seat at the table.

"Why are we here?" Rhonda asked me.

"Who should I begin with?" I asked. "Shouldn't this be a more private meeting?"

"We're sisters," one of the ladies said. I was urged to proceed.

I told them about the incident with Miss D's cousin and how he grabbed my wrist, and I told them about Miss D's disrespectful and foul mouth. I mentioned how Miss D's cousin distracted her in Block One and how I was forced to have him permanently removed.

Miss D and her cousin interrupted nearly every comment I made, and they were told to remain silent by their respective mothers and by Rhonda. Their countenances were reduced to pusses.

Faith entered the office and said, "Other witnesses have corroborated this."

Miss D's mother said, "I know my daughter's attitude. I assume that it's probably true."

"He always disrespects me and disrespects everyone with his smart mouth," Miss D said. "He sits on his desk.

That's no way for a teacher to act." She also complained about my stringent bathroom policies.

"He lies. He disrespects everyone with his smart mouth," Miss D's cousin said. "When I'm disrespected, I can never respect that person who disrespected me. (Miss D) never said to go fuck hisself."

He continued: "He bent up my card in the middle of a game. And he never lets me go to the bathroom. He even told me to go to the bathroom to wash my balls."

"What are you talking about?" I asked. He didn't respond. No one else said anything.

"Regarding the bathroom policy, sometimes pregnant students get more privileges than other students. You can always go to the bathroom during certain times."

"You never let her (the pregnant student Tamieka) go," Miss D chimed in. I gathered my thoughts.

"This is not about the bathroom or about a card I didn't crumple," I said. "This is about you grabbing me. It is unfortunate that we will never ever be able to clear the air because you will never be able to respect me."

"Liar," he said.

"How many times do you have to go down this road before finishing school?" Faith asked.

"You should shut your mouth and finish school so you can go after one of your many dreams rather than be stuck with these same problems," his mother chimed in. Miss D's cousin rolled his eyes.

"She can be a great student in class," I said to Miss D's mother, "but her complete disrespect of me causes such a distraction that she has to do her work in the office. Her grades are going down now." I found myself conceding.

"I know that we had a huge miscommunication. If we all got back to work, we would all benefit," I said to

Miss D. "I apologize for any miscommunications. I hope now you can just complete your education."

"I won't apologize," Miss D said. "I didn't do anything wrong."

"Listen to the teacher. Finish high school, get a job and start paying some of the bills," Miss D's mother yelled. "You need to apologize to him."

After a moment, Miss D said, "I'm sorry."

"Thank you," I said.

"If all the students hate him and if he has a bad attitude, it'll come out eventually," Miss D's mother said. "It's not your responsibility to open your mouth for everyone and everything."

"That's true," Rhonda said.

"It must be hard to teach these students," Miss D's mother said.

It was warm in the office. I thought about the state of my classroom. Earlier, I walked by to see what it looked like with a Day School class. Many students lined the entire back wall with the backs of their desk-chairs. The rest of the desk-chairs were crushed together into two masses in the available open space.

The teacher was writing something in Spanish on the board, but I was distracted when I heard a scream from another room. Through the open door of the next room, I saw a male student looking at me as a female student stood over him braiding his hair. A teacher was trying to teach a lesson.

As I walked through the hallway, I passed a teacher on desk duty. We exchanged glances that could have said, "This is just unbelievable."

The meeting was dragging on. There was the clichéd parental lecture about being better in school. Neither student showed any remorse.

"I hope we can have a clean slate now," I said. "Thank you for coming in." I shook both of their hands before leaving.

As I was about to begin class, the construction noise outside my window reached maximum decibels. Dust began pouring in through the open windows before I could close them. The still air stagnated as students started trickling in. The roar continued unabated. I apologized to the students for these conditions. How could they be expected to learn in such a noisy and uncomfortable room? We couldn't bear the heat more than a few minutes.

"Grab your belongings," I said. Shirley directed us to another room. It took another ten minutes before the students began their work.

Foolio, Shenequa, Marvin, and Tanisha were working attentively on an in-class quiz on *The Old Man and the Sea*. They completed all four worksheets. Because of absences and refusals to do work, less than half my students completed these assignments, which were essential to passing class. I made up more assignments for students who completed their work, so others could catch up. Plus, we were getting new students. I wanted to begin a new novel so more students could be working together on the same assignment.

Iverson walked in.

"Thanks for showing up," I said. "Where've you been?"

"Gettin some," he said. It was his uniform answer to everything. Sometimes he just gyrated his hips and slapped his hand in the air at the same rhythm.

I handed him his work, when he said, "I ain't doin this shit, yo." He put on a scowl but got to work.

When Iverson and I spoke, he wasn't loud and disturbing. Many students had loud mouths, and they didn't understand or care about how they affected others. Iverson sometimes needed to be prodded with whispered comments from me like, "There ain't no muthafuckin way ya gettin outta here without doin this shit." Even though he was barely passing and usually tried leaving my room to stroll the hallways without a pass, I respected Iverson for at least making some effort to finish high school.

About midway through the second block, Jack brought seven new students to my room. He told me they were here to observe before leaving.

"We have to stay here until seven," one guy said. No one had any schedules. No one wanted to do any work. The new kids distracted everyone.

Once the third block officially began, most students failed to show up. The hallway was instead filled with students meeting up with the new students. As the block progressed, there were over twenty-five students in and out of my room.

I saw Jack in the hallway.

"Can you get some of these kids out of here?" I asked.

He looked in. "I'll bring some of them to Dinesh's room."

As he walked away, he turned around and said, "By the way, nothing is going to happen with the early dismissal from Friday." Before I could react, he was down the hallway.

I had no control for the rest of the block. I was so frustrated.

By the end of the day, I was drained. Patrice walked by and offered me some Advil. As I opened the packet of two with my teeth, one of the tablets fell to the ground. It was that kind of day. I dry swallowed the other one.

As Nicotina and I walked towards the front door at day's end, Nicotina asked how my day went.

"Besides being absolutely demoralized, everything is great," I said.

"It will only get easier."

"It was easier before we got the new students," I said. She laughed.

As we walked out, the principal smiled and said, "Goodbye."

Thankfully, the next school day went smoothly.

-8-

I LEFT CAFETERIA DUTY AT 3:45 P.M., so I could clean my classroom. Looking through the glass window, I saw the usual mess. The door was locked, and I didn't have a key.

I looked for Rosa, who was the janitor for our hallway, but I couldn't find her. I knew she had a key. Sometimes Rosa helped me clean my classroom, but she mostly cleaned it after students were dismissed. We both commented on how filthy the classroom got and wondered what went on during the day.

Not only was my room locked, all the Twilight classrooms were as well. A Day School staff meeting was being held in the auditorium. Surely that meeting would end with teachers coming down our hallways at the same time the Twilight students would be arriving for class to classrooms that were locked.

I went to the Twilight office and found Faith and Shirley.

"What should we do about the doors?" I asked. Shirley brought me into the hallway.

"I'm going to the main office to find the main janitor who has the keys for the classroom," she said. "Rosa may be absent today."

I waited outside my classroom. I looked through the glass window of the door and saw the clock. The students would be here any minute. A few teachers exited the auditorium and were walking the hallways. I stood impatiently.

More and more students came up. More and more teachers exited the auditorium. The doors were all locked, and no one knew of anyone who had the keys. Nicotina, Dinesh, and Mariella arrived with the rest of the students.

"This is ridiculous," said Nicotina. I agreed.

Iverson came up to me and said, "What the fuck is going on with this shit, yo?"

"Please be patient," I said. "We're waiting for the doors to be unlocked."

He walked over to G-Black, and they began talking.

"Mariella said Rosa's absent today," said Nicotina. Mariella learned this information on the way up from the cafeteria. She was friends with some of the other janitors. I always saw them speaking Spanish.

G-Black grabbed the doorknob to Nicotina's classroom and started twisting and turning the knob and banging on the door and screamed, "Let me in this mutherfucka."

"Take it easy, please," I pleaded. "Try to act like a human for a few moments."

A Day School teacher walking by recognized one of the Twilight students, and they exchanged greetings.

"I joined Twilight," the student said.

"That shouldn't be *too* hard," the teacher said. "Good luck." Before walking away, the teacher gave me a blank stare.

Nicotina yelled at G-Black. He was making dice out of wooden blocks by drawing numbers on them, while

Iverson, Marvin and Foolio crowded around. The same wooden blocks were stacked all over the math office.

"Look guys, this place is a school and not for these shenanigans," I said to the *high-stakes gamblers.* G-Black was holding a wad of bills while defacing school property.

"But I'm addicted to gambling," Marvin said. He thought the comment would convince me to condone their antics.

"Please stop," Nicotina pleaded. "We teachers simply cannot let you continue." G-Black stopped writing to look at us. He threw both blocks down the hallway. Problem solved!

About twenty minutes later, the main janitor arrived to unlock all the doors. The students and teachers were agitated.

There were numerous complainers that yelled, "Why did we have to wait so long in the hallway?" I hoped they would all just move forward.

My classroom was in its usual state of disgrace, but before I could make a dent in creating a better classroom, everyone sat down throughout the room. I tried to line the desk-chairs into some reasonable fashion, while sweeping the garbage into a pile and collecting all the Spanish textbooks that were on numerous desk-chairs throughout the classroom rather than in the pile that I usually made for them each day on the file cabinet. Students sucked their teeth when I asked them to get up from their seats while I tried arranging them. No one made any effort to help me.

I picked up someone's notebook without realizing it. When I stacked up the books, the notebook fell behind the file cabinet. It took me a moment to figure out what was going on.

"That's my notebook," a student said. There were numerous groans and teethsucks.

"Why you disrespectin him?" another student asked me.

"Can you please think about the situation for a moment? I accidentally picked up a notebook and it fell on the floor." I was clawing behind the cabinet, so I could get the notebook and return it to the student. "If this is what disrespect is, I beg you to better understand what the word means." I was irate.

Since we had not discussed current events in the last two weeks of Journalism, I passed out numerous articles. Each student was supposed to summarize an article and then read it aloud to the class so we could discuss it.

I noticed Miss D staring at me.

"What do you need?" I asked.

"Don't talk to me," she said. She flipped me off.

Everyone else, however, seemed to be working. Soon, I caught Foolio writing on the corkboard I re-covered with blue construction paper.

"Please stop vandalizing," I said. He stopped, but continued once I moved on.

"Please stop," I said again, in a sharper but not louder tone. I tore down all the paper he tagged with the logo of his so-called music production company. Foolio had aspirations of a life in the music industry.

Miss D said, "We gonna read these?" She was referring to the newspaper article I just placed on her desk.

"We've done this same exact assignment before," I said. I repeated the assignment again.

"If we gonna read them, why we gotta write them?" she asked.

"I need everyone to write a short summary of the article," I said. "I want to hear what you think the main idea is and what the important details are." She sucked her teeth and put a puss on her face.

Foolio put his headphones on, so I had to ask him to take them off. He groaned while taking them off.

Miss D was trying to grub a cigarette, which the students called a "bogey," from another student.

"Can I get a pass?" she asked. Many students smoked, but most never had them. Whoever did have cigarettes would give out an entire pack in one evening of school.

The other day, Tanisha came into class to grub a cigarette.

"Can you not disturb the class please?" I asked.

"Don't black out," she said. Blacking out was when you got mad.

"Gimme a bathroom pass," Miss D yelled. I hadn't reacted fast enough for her orders. I gave her a disgusted look. She stormed out of the classroom with a bogey in her hand.

I heard her talking to someone down the hallway. I looked and saw her speaking to Faith.

"I wanted a pass, and he wouldn't gimme one," Miss D said. "He stupid."

Marvin turned on his radio. He wasn't supposed to bring a radio to school, but he did sometimes. No one ever took it from him.

I grabbed it, brought it to my desk, and scanned through the stations. Students yelled out different radio stations. Others told me to press play on the cassette player. I found the classical music station and left it on for everyone's enjoyment. Some students groaned.

"I'll turn it off once everyone gets back to work," I said.

"I can't do my work," a student said. He never did his

work. "But can you put on…." I didn't hear his station request.

"Look, if you really don't want to hear it, get to work. I will turn it off when everyone gets busy." It worked somewhat, but I still found myself turning the radio back on now and then.

Shenequa said, "This class crazy."

I was finally settling into the day when I noticed one of my new male students staring at me and not doing any work. He tried making numerous comments about me during class but wasn't getting any laughs. There was already animosity between the original students and the new ones.

"What are you looking at?" I asked.

"You better watch out," he warned me.

"When should I do that?"

"When you're walking to your car."

"Look, if you want to surprise me with flowers, you could do it in front of the whole class," I said. Some students laughed. He couldn't even fathom the comment.

In the fourth block, Miss D returned and G-Black arrived late. We were having a class discussion, and to me Miss D said, "Suck my dick."

"So ya gonna suck it, K-Dog?" G-Black said.

I tried to ignore it and got students reading our next book: *The Catcher in the Rye*. Everyone had worksheets.

As the block was ending, G-Black had some strong words with Joe.

"You're a fuckin faggot," G-Black told him. Joe started whining.

"Stop it!" I said to G-Black. "Shut your mouth." I couldn't have G-Black mocking Joe's homosexuality.

"It's alright, K-Dog," G-Black reassured me. "We live in the same neighborhood."

G-Black stood up and started swinging his curled arms into little circles.

He sang, "I'm so naughty," over and over again while turning in a circle. All the students were laughing. Joe was laughing. I tried not to laugh.

As the teachers left for the day, five uniformed officers congregated around the security guard desk near the front door. Mariella was waiting in the doorway for her husband.

"What happened?" I asked.

"There was some kind of violation," she said. I had no idea what she meant.

Jack came outside and lit a cigarette.

"What happened?" I asked him.

"Two members of the football team sodomized another smaller member of the team with a broomstick," Jack said. It happened during one of our blocks.

Before I went to my car, I asked Jack for a cigarette.

-9-

A FEW WEEKS AGO, Faith the librarian and Rhonda the social worker cornered me in the hallway and told me I was going to chaperone a field trip. I agreed, although I suspected they asked me together to be persuasive in case I hadn't obliged. I preferred the adventure of a field trip to another day of school.

They wanted me to chaperone a trip to Douglass College, one of the schools in the Rutgers University family, of selected students from the four Twilight schools. The bus would be departing from the Board of Education building at 7:00 a.m. and returning in the afternoon. We wouldn't have to attend Twilight that evening. They already told all the students that the bus would be leaving at 7:00 a.m. sharp on Friday. If you were late, you would miss the bus.

I slept over at a friend's house nearby to save morning traffic time but got lost on the way. I still got breakfast and arrived at 6:55 a.m.

Nevertheless, there was no bus waiting, no other teachers waiting for a bus, and only three students sitting in the foyer of the Board of Education building. They happened to be from my school. I was sleepy.

John J. Kaminski

At 7:10 a.m., a few more students showed up.

"We need to go to the store," Tasha said.

"We hungry," Joe said. I walked them to a store. Who knew when the next chance for them to eat would be anyway?

On the way, Tasha said, "We broke day." I didn't know what she meant until I learned that the breaking of day was dawn.

"We smoked weed all night," Joe said. I didn't say anything. I was tired. It was early. We arrived at a bagel shop four blocks away.

"Can you buy me some cigarettes?" Tasha asked. "Here's some money."

"As a teacher, I just can't do that. Sorry."

"It's OK," she said.

I considered buying bagels for the students, but the idea of plastic knives and butter and cream cheese being passed around a bus filled with students had the infinite potential to be an incredible burden. I decided to buy twenty assorted bags of twenty-five cent chips because there were not many options beyond bagels at the bagel shop. On the one hand, I didn't like supporting the poor diets of my students who drank soda and ate chips and candy all day every day. On the other hand, the students would be happy with free chips.

As I waited outside for Joe, Tasha persuaded a white, disheveled, scraggly-bearded man to buy her cigarettes.

Joe came out, but we had to wait for the cigarettes.

"You shouldn't associate with people like this," I said.

"Don't worry about it," she said. She got her cigarettes, and we walked back to the Board of Education. There was a crowd and a yellow school bus with some students in the back.

"Good morning," I said to Faith. "Please tell me what to do. I've never been on the chaperone end of a field trip before."

"Don't worry, I will," she said. "Rhonda's not here yet."

At 7:30 a.m., we were waiting for her on the packed bus. I had a double seat at the front for myself.

"How come we haven't left yet?" a student asked.

"We're waiting for someone," I said.

The girl next to her asked, "How come we haven't left yet?" I told her the same thing.

Rhonda's minivan finally arrived.

"You should help her," Faith said. I helped carry about two-dozen muffins, three cases of multiple-fruit-flavored juice boxes and some other things onto the bus. We departed for New Brunswick, NJ.

There were six chaperones for twenty-nine students. Another Twilight English teacher named Phyllis was on the trip. We bonded during teacher training. She was a disciplinarian in the school system for over twenty years before moving to Twilight. She was one of its few black teachers.

Seeing Phyllis conjured up images of another Twilight English teacher named Rema. Rema was an old and overweight white woman with dyed orange hair. She always brought a sixty-ounce plastic Dunkin Donuts coffee mug with her. Her name was in large-lettered black permanent marker near the rim. And she always had an open can of diet soda. It never ceased to amuse me.

At the last Twilight meeting for all four sites, Rema, Phyllis, my high school friend Niles who helped me get the Twilight job, and I sat together and talked about English education. Rema complained about her disciplinary problems.

Phyllis said, "When they get out of line, I just slap em upside their heads." If a white teacher did or said this, it would garner a completely different reaction.

"You can, but I don't think we can," I said, while pointing to me and Niles. He laughed.

On the bus, Phyllis sat next to a woman who was wearing what I will ignorantly call traditional African garb. The outfit was embroidered with black patterns. It was also green and had a matching hat. Rhonda and Faith sat in the three-person seat across the aisle from me. Another black woman sat behind me in a two-seater. Our individual spaces were cluttered with food, so we began dispersing it.

As I passed out the chips, there were lots of gimmes and no thank yous. I tried to make sure that the students from my school got bags of chips. Some kids put them in their pockets before asking for more. They were gone in seconds.

"Sorry, but we're out already," I said. Teeth were sucked my way. Juice boxes were dispersed as quickly as I could get them out of their plastic-wrapped case. Rhonda passed out the muffins.

The staff was now able to sit comfortably. I began reading the *New York Post*.

Suddenly, the bus driver started complaining.

"It's not my job to pick up the trash," he said. "No one's supposed to be eatin or drinkin."

"We have a garbage bag," Rhonda said. She handed it to me. I passed it behind me and asked the students to put their garbage in it.

I started to wake up and was starting to feel hung over from the night before. When I went to buy breakfast this morning, everything repulsed me, but I settled for a turkey sandwich, a food I liked and hoped would make me feel better.

The talk of food made me hungry, so the turkey sandwich became appealing. Since the garbage bag was being passed around and would be returned to me, I wanted to get a few bites in before my hands were covered in the kinds of bacteria that lurked on this Petri dish of a school bus.

I sat in my seat, took a sip of Yoo-Hoo and devised a way to eat with the minimal amount of contact with my filthy hands. I took a bite.

"How come you didn't get sandwiches for everyone?" Faith asked. I was chewing. I felt awkward.

"I'm just kidding," she finally said.

"Yo, Mista K," Tasha yelled. I turned around.

"It's not fair you got a sandwich," she said. "You only gave us chips."

"You must have missed me yesterday taking orders in my waiter's uniform," I said. She sucked her teeth at me, sat back down, and went to sleep. I took a few more bites before I had to find a place for the garbage bag. A nearly-full box of muffins made their way back to Rhonda.

From the chaperone conversations I overheard, it was clear that we were not going to Douglass College. We were going to some kind of convention. I didn't have anyone clarify where.

Students began yelling at the bus driver to change the radio station. As they threw out suggestions, they argued about which stations were better.

"We're letting the bus driver decide what he wants," Rhonda said. It quelled them somewhat, but I got a serious headache. Maybe I shouldn't have been reading in a moving vehicle with a hangover. Maybe I shouldn't have gone out last night.

Our bus pulled up to the Hilton in New Brunswick. I counted everyone as they left the bus, so I could double check everyone coming back on later. We didn't want to leave anyone here for the weekend.

Inside the building, there were three huge groups of students who were predominantly black like our students. Two white female staff members greeted us with smiling faces; they were bookending the escalators and waving us up to the rooms on the third floor.

Rhonda checked us in on the second floor. There were people everywhere. I was the only white person I could see. There were lots of hugs, greetings, and smiles. There were Black Panthers passing out literature. I smiled at a few people who were clearly in charge, and my smiles weren't returned. Eyes looked away from me.

A few students needed to go to the bathroom, so I took them to one on the third floor. We returned to find a job fair afoot, and students were looking around at the opportunities. I saw Rhonda, and she led us to the rest of the students, who were in the banquet room. There was a big banner exclaiming the occasion: New Jersey Black Issues Convention. It was the twentieth anniversary.

We were the first group in the banquet room and were seated in the front on the right side from the angle of the stage. The room was gigantic. It was 8:30 a.m. The festivities would begin at 10:00 a.m. I decided to search for a headache remedy.

I went downstairs and found a small bottle of ten aspirins for nineteen bucks, but I just couldn't support the egregious hotel markup. When I returned, I learned Tasha had Tylenol. She gave me a few, and I thanked her.

At 10:03 a.m., the master of ceremonies welcomed everyone to the conference. He named the schools in attendance, and his words were met with groups cheering and standing. When our school was named, our students did a great job showing their school spirit. The Tylenol was working.

A band played and a gospel singer sang. People were up and clapping. I was too. It was uplifting. Truly.

The master of ceremonies introduced a reverend with an impressive resume of diplomatic experiences and credentials. He was greeted with applause when he stepped to the pulpit. He was black but light skinned enough to look Caucasian.

The reverend began by stressing the importance of black educators and students congregating like this.

"African-Americans need to make their voice heard because the country needs new thinkers to think creatively and help the nation with its problems, which include racism," he said. He was making an important point.

"Racism against blacks is terrorism," he continued. "Black people must stop enslaving themselves within the present culture dominated by whites." People were cheering. I was uncomfortable.

The reverend moved onto how the "Jews" oppressed the Palestinians.

"The white United States oppresses the black Americans in the same way," he said.

The reverend moved onto the recent academic controversy about the black New Jersey poet laureate and his poem about how the "Jews" were to blame for 9/11.

"The Jews love to support free speech until a black poet writes the truth," he said. "They're on the front line for advocacy and then an African-American writes a poem, and the Jews are in line yelling censorship," I began taking notes. I never heard a speech like this.

"When the glaciers melt," he said, "it's gonna be

the black people running from the flood." He spoke more about how he opposed global warming, as well as globalization.

"Bush's policy of invasion means whites have preemptive strikes against blacks." He continued, "Since the United States couldn't get Osama, we're now going after this brother in Iraq." He weaved through a variety of topics.

"In Iran, before the revolution that overthrew the Shah, American children drove motorcycles in mosques during prayers and no one could do anything about it," he said. I was feverishly taking notes.

"I will repeat certain lines from now on, so the reporters in the room could get it right." he said, which very briefly stopped his commentary.

"Our beloved president will send us to war, raise taxes, and give up everything in the name of 9/11." I thought about the sarcasm in Mark Antony's eulogy for Julius Caesar.

"We shouldn't be hoodwinked by fake symbols. 9/11 was tremendously tragic but we must all consider what drives nineteen men to go to such extremes."

He concluded by stating how "airlines are no safer now than before 9/11." Everyone rose and stood clapping and cheering. I sat in my seat looking around in amazement. Faith was up and clapping and smiling. Sweet.

The master of ceremonies returned and directed us to the conference rooms where black issues were going to be discussed. The students and teachers split up, and I went with a few students to a discussion about money sponsored by American Express. We got seats, and the room filled up quickly. It got hot and loud, so I caught a breather in the lobby for forty minutes.

I returned to the area with the job booths and waited

for the rooms to empty. I found Rhonda and Faith, who were shopping at some stands. Rhonda gave me a ticket for the lunch banquet that was valued at seventy-five dollars. It was sponsored by a few distinguished companies. New Jersey Senator Jon Corzine was a guest of honor. It was clearly a legitimate luncheon.

Every conference ended at the exact same moment, so the job fair space quickly flooded with students and teachers. I thought I saw another white person. We managed to gather all our students, so we got on line for the banquet room. Students were complaining about being hungry.

Once we were seated, the master of ceremonies welcomed us. I sat with the chaperones and a few students, while the other students had their own tables. On the table were a pitcher of water, two baskets of bread, and a small plate of butter molded into seashells.

The master of ceremonies again repeated the name of every high school in attendance and was met with loud cheers. A distinguished teacher was introduced, and she spoke about the importance of education; she was exactly who should have spoken earlier at the opening ceremony. She stopped her speech numerous times to silence the crowd. Next, a student was brought up to read a poem and received the same lack of courtesy. Silence was never restored after the initial cheers.

Finally, our NJ Senator Jon Corzine spoke from the pulpit. Our table was close, but I had a difficult time hearing. So many people were talking and ignoring him. He spoke about how it was important for all Americans to respect one another in our present climate, but so many people failed to give him the respect he deserved.

At one point, Phyllis said, "I don't think there should be any white people at the Black Issues Convention."

One student said, "I think we're being starved."

The Senator concluded his speech to scattered applause, and the first course was served. It was a salad.

"I hate salad," a bunch of students said.

"Don't eat it if you don't like it," I said.

"But we're hungry."

"Eat more bread then."

"We already ate bread."

"We'll get more," I said. We got more, and they ate more.

"You eatin those tomatoes?" Rhonda asked. I let her fork them away. Many full plates were whisked away.

The main course was chicken parmigiana, a side of ziti with a smidge of ricotta cheese, and some broccoli florets.

Faith and the woman in the African garb asked the students how they felt about the conference.

"The food's disgusting," one said.

"I wouldn't eat it if I didn't have to," another said. The conversation about food lasted until another speaker closed the luncheon.

I soon realized that many of our students snuck out of the banquet room, and I had to look for them. I could only imagine the ruckus they could cause.

Thankfully, I found most of them smoking cigarettes out front and sitting on the couches in the lobby. After a brief discussion, they decided to remain here for the remainder of the convention because they were bored.

"But there are three hours left!" I said. "You have to attend another conference in an hour."

Over the next hour, I tried keeping them together, but everyone was off in different directions. I even accompanied certain groups on tours of the premises, so I could keep an eye on them. At one point, I was sitting alone on a couch in the lobby, while mostly everyone was smoking outside or riding the elevators up and down, up and down.

Faith finally came to the lobby.

"You are all going to the convention," she demanded. "It is your obligation as black students." We decided to attend a conference on gang violence.

A few police officers introduced themselves, as did a former gang member.

"Snitch!" someone yelled.

We heard numerous details about gangs from sexual initiation for females to the use of the American Sign Language for members to silently communicate. A district attorney stated that gang members would always suffer from stiffer mandatory sentences.

"Gang members can be identified by how their hats are worn. The inner labels reveal true gang colors," one officer said.

"Long white T-shirts and jeans are a gang member's outfit," the other said.

Many students dressed like this, but they weren't all gang members. Maybe I was just being naïve. It must be nightmarish when innocent students face these kinds of charges.

I learned that famous brand names were acronyms that conveyed different meanings. Reebok stood for Respect Each and Every Blood OK. Mecca meant Murder Every Crip Child Alive. Nike stood for Niggas Insane Killing Everybody.

The bus was to pick us up at 4:00 p.m. It arrived forty minutes late.

On the way home, I sat next to the woman in the African garb. Her name was Dianetta.

"Since you're not a person of color, how did you like the conference?" she asked me.

"It was good to have a convention to get these students together, but I was offended by the reverend," I said. "I think he could have been more positive by emphasizing education to achieve personal betterment rather than spew hateful rhetoric."

"Oh," she said. We didn't speak anymore.

Dianetta did speak to the students about the conference, and there was one clear and common theme — the New Jersey Black Issues Convention needed to serve better food.

-10-

THE HIGH SCHOOL WAS BUILT into a hill, but as you drove up it, you saw the back of the building. You had to take a higher road to get to the front entrance. The grounds were surrounded by an iron gate.

To the right of the school was a small parking lot for six cars. Below was a tightly-packed, slanting parking area built into the hill with an entrance at the back of the school. Since there were no lined spaces for cars, the lot was always in disarray.

There was another parking lot at the back of the school that was reserved for VIPs like the principal and her prominent staff of education professionals. There was also a giant satellite dish for the high school's television studio. It was one of the best studios in the state.

To the left of the school was a grammar school, which was right next to a police station. The state university was a few blocks away.

Each school day began with me searching for a parking space. By the time I arrived at school, the lots were full, so I had to find a spot on the street. I preferred parking within the gated perimeter where the security guards could see my car on their security monitors.

Available parking on the streets was scarce and had certain street-cleaning rules. The street in front of the school was always busy with traffic, and when the students were dismissed at 3:05 p.m., it was deadlocked. There was also some metered parking several blocks away.

A parking violation wasn't just a ticket that could be paid through the mail. Instead, offenders had one of their front tires booted. You had to pay one hundred dollars for someone to come and remove the boot. Parking fines provided the city with a valuable revenue stream.

Lately, I was lucky finding spots in the smaller parking lot. Nicotina always parked on the street. When I told her I was parking in the smaller lot, she said, "That lot is reserved for daytime staff."

"I'm going to pretend I didn't know that," I said. I felt I had a right to park there.

Today was a different story. On my first pass around the school, there was a white flatbed truck blocking the entrance to the smaller parking lot. There were a few spots open. I drove around to the other lot, but it was packed.

By the time I made a second pass of the school, the truck was gone, but the spots in the lot were occupied. Thankfully, I was able to parallel park on my second try into a spot in front of the school.

I got to the Twilight office at 1:30 p.m., which was five minutes late. I said hello to Faith, Dinesh and Nicotina. I was introduced to Mr. Williams, our new science teacher.

In a dramatic voice, Faith said, "Where have you been?"

"I was looking for a spot," I said. I signed in like it was 1:25 p.m.

"I'm playin'," she said.

I hung my jacket on a hook and grabbed a copy of *All Quiet on the Western Front*. As I was leaving, Faith asked, "Where do you hide before the students get here?"

"I've been going to the library," I said. "There's more room for me to work, and it has two computer labs. Everyone should go there."

"Everyone is worried about your antisocial behavior," Faith said.

"Everyone should get a new set of worries," I said. I heard Faith laughing as I walked to the library in the basement.

I waved to the older, blonde librarian whose name always eluded me. She waved back from her office. The second lab was empty, so I got to my prep work. A computer made my life so much easier.

Five minutes later, Mario entered the lab. He was white, a few years younger than me, and in his second year at the school. Mario was the media specialist, who served as a librarian and managed the two computer labs. We always talked about how bad the students were and how badly they treated the library. Often, substitute teachers brought their classes here and Mario was forced to supervise them once the sub lost control. Lately, he was receiving flack because the computers weren't functioning properly. He had to constantly ask students not to download software or play music or video games. Many of his hours were spent enforcing these rules.

Last year, his brand-new leased car was keyed in the large teachers parking lot. It cost five hundred dollars to fix. He suspected it was a student but couldn't prove anything.

There was also a back door to the library that was always locked. Students were always banging on it. Most of them wanted to use the library as a cut-through. It happened all day every day.

"A class is coming in here soon," Mario said. I had to type up worksheets, print them out, and have them copied for class. One pertained to *All Quiet on the Western Front,* another was a list of vocabulary words, and another was a list of vocabulary sentence fill-ins. I also wanted to move my car.

The bell rang before I finished. A male voice began a twenty-second countdown over the loudspeaker.

"You must be in your assigned rooms, or you will be brought to the late room and immediately suspended," the voice said. "Parents will be called."

"Nineteen. Eighteen. Seventeen. Sixteen…"

Students were pounding on the locked back door of the library. Mario had to stop them. Once he walked away from the door, they started pounding again. They begged and pleaded with Mario rather than walk another route. No one would accept that it was always locked.

"Eight. Seven. Six. Five…"

Students filled the lab, so I gathered my things and went to a table in the main room of the library. The knocking on the door continued. I tried ignoring it. A voice begged to be let in.

At 2:30 p.m., I tried moving my car into one of the school lots. I drove past the smaller lot, and every spot was occupied. On my way to the other lot, I saw plenty of activity around the university. Buses were lining up outside the grammar school. There were no spots in the other lot either.

On my second pass of the school, I saw a spot in the smaller lot, but when I turned around to get it, a Jeep pulled in. As I drove past the school again, the grammar school was dismissed. Students, cars and buses crowded the street. Two officers tried directing standstill traffic. It was 2:50 p.m.

I made another pass of the smaller and bigger lots, but there were still no spots. I tried making another pass around the school, but I found myself behind a traffic accident that prevented the car in front of me from moving ahead. A garbage truck was trying to make a wide left turn, but a lady in a burgundy car prevented that from happening.

I opened my window to hear the people arguing. There were lots of fucks and assholes and talk of lawyers and lawsuits. People were looking out windows from the apartment at the top of the street, and a crowd of younger kids was standing on the corner laughing. The driver in front of me failed to get by the mess. The driver behind me kept honking his horn. Beep. Beeeeeeeep. Beeeeeeeep. Beep.

It was after 3:00 p.m. when I got my car past the garbage truck. I pulled around to the smaller lot, but there was a blue student services car blocking the entrance. A woman sat behind the wheel. I grimaced at her when I drove by.

There was still traffic in front of the grammar school when Day School ended. I watched a deluge of students swarm the streets in my rearview mirror. I got around to the entrance of the larger lot but had to wait five minutes for an exodus of cars. It was a little after 3:15 p.m. when I got back inside school.

I skipped cafeteria duty, so I could finish my prep work. With the guards, Nicotina, Mariella, Dinesh, and Mr. Williams there, there was more than enough support. Incidentally, Nicotina was working on a supervisory schedule because everyone wasn't needed every day.

I went down to the library, but it was locked since the

Day School day was over. I looked through the window and saw no one. I didn't bang on the door.

I found one of the janitors in a basement supply room and asked him to open the door.

"Don't forget to close and lock it behind you."

"I will," I said. "I mean, I won't."

I walked into the first computer lab and found two black teachers whom I recognized.

"You need special permission to be here," one of them said. "We have permission."

"I have to type up a few things for class," I said. "It's urgent."

"You need special permission to be here," she said again.

"Where can I get this special permission?"

She directed me to a woman who was also the liaison between the Day School teachers and the Twilight teachers. I was unfamiliar with what her *liaisoning* entailed. She was in the principal's office. She gave me the special permission and her extension in case anyone wanted to verify the permission.

I returned to the library, but it was locked. I had to find the janitor again.

"I got special permission to work in the library," I announced to the women in the lab and told them the extension. One of them left to verify it.

By 3:50 p.m., I was in my classroom and ready for the day. All my materials were copied and stacked. As the students entered, I distributed their work.

Since I saw most of them twice a day, they were able to compare the books they were reading. It was unanimous that *The Catcher in the Rye* was better than *All Quiet on the Western Front*. Students gave their reasons.

"I'm glad you can compare them. It means you're

reading them, and it shows that you're educated enough to take part in a discussion about literature," I said.

The students settled into their work. A few kept finding ways to talk, and I told them to quiet down. Kia wouldn't stop laughing.

"Please be quiet," I pleaded. "If you don't get your reading done this period, I'm going to black out." Kia kept trying not to laugh.

As I sat at my desk, everyone was silent, but I felt eyes on me. I looked up at Kia, who was sitting in front of me. She gulped her bottled cherry soda and started laughing. She spit red soda all over me and my desk of papers.

I looked at her with dripping arms. The class roared with laughter.

-11-

FOR THE LAST FEW WEEKS, an alarming serenity enveloped Twilight. We were functioning with a full-time staff of a clerk, a social worker, a librarian, a guidance counselor, a Spanish teacher, an English teacher, a history teacher, a math teacher, a science teacher and a Head Teacher, as well as a part-time nurse and a part-time gym teacher. The Twilight office was more crowded than ever.

The addition of the new science teacher, Mr. Williams, helped tremendously since he had a large number of students, second only to my own, and now those students were where they were supposed to be rather than where they chose to go to not be held accountable. Although there were still daily problems, more work was being completed, and situations were more manageable.

I also changed classrooms from the pigsty that I had to clean daily to one that was spotless by the time my students arrived. The floors were swept, the desks were lined up, the chalkboard was washed, and the garbage bag in the garbage can was empty. I was directly across from the Twilight office as opposed to down the hall. More than once, I had to jog from one end of the hall to the other to leave a note or make an announcement about the classroom change. More than once, someone said, "Run, Forest, run!" as I darted by. I was no longer disturbed by construction noise, since the new room was on the courtyard side of the school. The courtyard looked like a tarred roof.

The new classroom belonged to an English teacher during the day. I admired the ambitious assignments that covered his blackboards before the janitor unceremoniously washed them away for my class. There was a poster of a photograph of Charles Dickens on the wall and a cartoon of the Globe Theater. The teacher left his materials and student work on a shelf on his desk. I jokingly considered taking them just to teach him a lesson. He also had many supplies. I took some paper clips, since he had a whole box. Sometimes I left a full can of soda or a bottle of water in his desk, and I found it the next day.

My new classroom came with a new janitor named Hero, who was Hispanic. I have seen him talking to Mariella. Throughout the school day, Hero made sure my garbage can was empty and occasionally swept around the room if it started getting messy. With all the food and drinks my students consumed, they filled two to three garbage cans a day.

Before they arrived, we spoke about how out of control they were.

"I like how you teach," he said. "You're tough on the students and make them work. No one does that. They're better in your class."

Hero also told me how he heard my students complaining about me to other members of the Twilight staff. He imitated a baby crying by making crying noises and rubbing his eyes.

"They're fuckin crybabies," he said. I agreed.

I barricaded the area around my desk with four desk-chairs, since I needed more desk space. I had a box of books, papers to distribute, papers to grade, papers to return, actual paper, a planbook, and a gradebook spread out and easily accessible. It was the best way for me to stay organized. Obviously, the students did their best to tamper with the arrangement. I kept the more important papers closest to me.

"You do dat cuz you're afraid of niggas and need protection," one girl said.

"Do you really believe that?" I asked. She didn't reply.

Just a few days ago, G-Black blacked out on me, grabbed a pile of papers that needed grading, and ran out of the room. Sadly, our relationship deteriorated to mutual malice because of his poor work habits and disruptive behavior. Although he was very funny, he did little schoolwork nowadays because he worked more to entertain the class, which undermined me. He had called me a faggot, a motherfucker, a cracker, and a bitch.

"No one's gonna suspend me," he told me. "If you fail me, you're gonna pay for it."

I had to inform Benny, Rhonda, Faith, and Shirley of his actions and had to write a long report detailing his exploits. After Shirley read it, she told me that she was going to talk with him.

"These are terroristic threats you can be jailed for," she said. "You shouldn't have to deal with this." Nothing became of it. Just yesterday, Faith had to sit in my class to keep him under control by holding his hands on his desk. When he freed them, he would give me the finger and deny doing it.

In another realm of reality, Miss D had been rather silent. About two weeks ago, I was walking down to the cafeteria and was greeted by the yapping of Miss D. She checkered her conversation with lots of muthafuckas and was talking about niggas eating her pussy and how she "eats pussy." She was loud about it.

"Be quiet or try not to swear or act like a lady or act like a human being please," I said.

"Go fuck yaself," she said. "Mind ya fuckin business."

Thankfully, the principal was walking around the basement and caught her monologue. She threatened Miss D with expulsion. Miss D was directed to the principal's office, where she must have gotten a serious talking to, because her behavior was much improved. These days when I gave her assignments, she was the first one done. The quality of her work was poor since she was working quickly and lacked skills, but she started slowing down and was somewhat improving.

Since there was no official bell to switch classes, I left my compound and went to the hallway to coax students to their next classes. I continually recited a similar speech. The volume of my voice was relative to the amount of people or the kinds of disruptions in the hallway. It went like this:

Let's go. Let's go everybody. This place you're in? It's a school! In these classrooms? That's where some sort of education is being administered. Oh yeah, and you're supposed to go to these things called classrooms. See this hallway? It's used to go from one classroom to another. No, it's not for standing in so you can talk to your friends for ten minutes, you silly. By the way, get to steppin.

I said it quickly, slowly, in a monotone, or accentuated by limitless combinations of accents, inflections and sarcasm. All lines could be easily interspersed with the goading of individual students along by name. It merited colorful responses.

Earlier, I got a parking spot in the smaller lot and walked briskly through the school and into the Twilight office. Rhonda and Nicotina were talking in the math office.

"It's not in my contract to get a picture for the yearbook," Nicotina said.

I wanted to say how it wasn't in my contract to be called a "cracker" or a "faggotass," but I thought better of it.

"Have you taken your picture yet?" Rhonda asked. "It's the last day for pictures."

"I haven't," I said. I grabbed my box of books and high tailed it to the library before I got roped into their conversation.

On my walk, I thought about whether I wanted to be in the yearbook and decided that I was going to do my best to be excluded. I could only imagine my picture being defaced by every student who bought the ninety-five dollar yearbook and knew me. I imagined profanity written around me and the addition of body parts spewing different types of bodily fluid all over my face. Or maybe that was just what my friends did to the people in my eighth grade yearbook.

During cafeteria duty, two students who were supposed to be there came from the office to remind me about the yearbook picture. Basically, they were sent to escort me to the auditorium to ensure that my photograph was taken. Five students were dressed for their photographs when I got there.

I'm not waiting on this line, I thought to myself. I sought out the photographers and said, "I'm here to take my picture." Two of my students in the front row began laughing.

One of them repeated, "I'm here to take my picture,"

in the hokey white person voice. They said it three more times before I left without having my picture taken. They were still saying it later in the day when I was moving the students from class to class between blocks.

In first block, Faith came to my doorway and asked to make an announcement. She told my class how it was the last day for yearbook submissions, so they all had to vote for illustrious positions like Class Brain, Class Couple, Best Friends, Class Politician, Class Comedian, and Class Storm, which meant that this student was most likely to black out when provoked or, more realistically, asked to complete his or her daily assignment.

The announcement destroyed all my plans for the day, since all the students became consumed by it. It morphed into every student campaigning for every position.

"Look at my best smile."

"We're best friends."

"I know everything."

It was the Hydra, and I was no Heracles. Students brought their campaign efforts to me throughout the day.

"I don't think anyone but students should vote," I said. They told me how Rhonda, Faith and Shirley voted.

"I already voted for these things when I was in high school," I said. "Once was exciting enough." A few students sucked their teeth.

I imagined my ballot being evaluated, reviewed, and discussed by the administrative staff sewing circle in the office.

"Just do it for the spirit of it all," Faith said, but I refused. I would have voted for the pregnant student and her boyfriend as Class Couple. When they won, I didn't congratulate them.

I spoke to Nicotina when we left for the day.

"This yearbook business was such a bad idea," I said. "These are the same students that have been thrown out of Day School. They need to focus on their work habits. Some of them are doing so badly. They're still always late." Nicotina agreed.

"They did this last year and it was just as distracting," she said. She ended up taking her picture. We hoped for a better tomorrow.

-12-

I MOVED MY CAR OFF THE STREET and into the smaller lot, and on my way back into school, I bumped into Jack in the foyer.

"Can you please help empty Rhonda's van?" he asked. I happily obliged. Rhonda pulled right up front. She had trays of food and bags that needed to be brought inside.

There were a few Twilight students in front whom Jack recruited to help. I forgot that it was already Halloween. We had our staff and student luncheon in the cafeteria during the lunch block. The occasion was also a celebration for any staff member's birthday from the previous month. That person got a gift bag.

I knew nothing about a luncheon until the food was brought in on the last day of September. Throughout that day, it was made clear to me that Faith and Rhonda paid for the entire event. We also happened to be celebrating Faith's birthday.

"How much should I chip in?" I asked Rhonda.

"How much do you want to?" she asked. Thankfully, something broke up the conversation before it could get any more awkward.

For the last month, I have asked Nicotina, Mariella,

and Dinesh if we were supposed to put money toward this, and none of them knew what the deal was. Before Rhonda revealed any magic number to me, Benny and I talked about the luncheon.

"Why are we having something like this when these kids don't appreciate anything?" he asked.

"I wish whoever was running the luncheons would just tell me what they were doing rather than just ask for money," I said. "Why don't they tell me what I should give them?"

"They've taken enough from me," he said, and I agreed.

"I heard it costs three hundred dollars. There is no way I'm paying like forty-five dollars to feed the same students who fail to treat me with any shred of kindness day in and day out," I vented. We were both on the same wavelength.

We agreed on a ten dollar "donation" and if anyone wanted more, we would need to be brought into the loop.

"Teachers don't make enough to sponsor luncheons," he said. I agreed. I eventually told Dinesh, Mariella, and Nicotina what I did, and I guessed we all paid on our own.

The students and I got all the food from Rhonda's minivan to the cafeteria downstairs.

Jack came down and said, "Rhonda just got a call on her cell phone. One of the children from the shelter she works at got hit by a car. She had to go." I started preparing the luncheon.

A gigantic cake wished a "Happy Birthday" to Mariella and a "Good Luck" to Benny.

"What greener pastures have taken you away from us this time?" I asked Benny.

"Today's my last day. I'm getting transferred to another Day School."

"Good luck," I said. At the end of the day when we shook hands, he said, "Don't let them get you down."

Students trickled down to the cafeteria and were surprised by the luncheon. Some were wearing Halloween masks.

To the ones not wearing masks, I said, "I really like your costume."

To the ones wearing masks, I said, "You've never looked better." Some laughed. Some didn't.

Many students were absent because of the gang specter associated with Halloween.

"They're gonna kill a mother and her baby," one girl said.

"They're gonna kill fifty people tonight," another said.

"There's simply no way any gang is going to kill fifty people tonight," I said.

"They will," she reassured me.

Last month, the luncheon consisted of trays of fried chicken, sausage and peppers, macaroni and cheese, collard greens, and a small pan of corn bread. We also had three cases of soda. This time around, there was eggplant parmigiana, chicken parmigiana, baked ziti, tossed salad, and a bag of sliced Italian bread. There were also four cases of different flavored soda. And a huge cake for dessert!

A buffet line formed, and the students helped themselves to the spread. Different groups ate at different tables. Since we didn't have tongs, I helped serve the food. I didn't want everyone using their own forks.

Overall, I was in a happy mood. I made a plate for myself and ate with the other teachers.

One of the girls started mocking Nicotina because she finished her plate of food so quickly. It was innocuous and funny. Nicotina went over to their table to joke with them.

When everyone was finishing, I noticed there was still plenty of food left since so many students didn't come in. There was also a lot of garbage accumulating on the tables. I got up to encourage the students to eat more food, and some did. I made sure the guards ate more food and asked the janitors to help themselves. Twilight needed to clean up the cafeteria after a luncheon, and I thought it would be best for us to eat the food rather than pack it up and transport it elsewhere. I also thought that if the students ate, they would be better behaved during classes.

I brought a garbage can around to the tables and made sure the students threw their garbage away. It became a compulsive desire to clean the entire area and have all the food eaten. I didn't want to pack it up and carry it upstairs. Where were we going to put it anyway? I threw away a lot of their garbage, while I encouraged everyone to eat more.

"If you get me some ziti, I'll eat it," one student said.

"Getting it is the only side of the deal you have to complete," I said. "Besides eating it." She sat until the remaining food was packed up.

There were at least three and a half cases of soda remaining, so I went from table to table taking soda orders. I cringed at the thought of all the aluminum cans being tossed into the regular trash.

"You're being really nice to everyone," Nicotina said. "A couple students said the same thing."

I moved from table to table, taking soda orders and

retrieving them. I figured if I did this once more, we would only have less than a case to carry upstairs.

"You have root beer?" one student asked.

"We have birch beer," I said.

"What's birch beer?"

"It's like root beer."

I passed out a bunch of orange sodas, black cherry sodas, and ginger ale. One student said, "Thank you."

I took orders maniacally because I wanted to hear another "Thank you," so I could congratulate that person on his or her manners. I never congratulated anyone. At least there wasn't much to carry.

Once in class, discussion was dominated by the imminent dangers of the Halloween evening. Some students feared getting egged once they left school. I heard a story about how some girl got hit in the head with a frozen egg and how it broke her head open. Like an egg.

"If you are going to pelt people with eggs, the normal ones will suffice," I said. "You may as well throw rocks if you're going to take the time to freeze eggs like a lunatic."

I looked out the window, and it was raining. I hoped it would impede any potential problems.

Fifteen minutes into first block, Jack entered my class to announce that students could go home if a parent signed them out. He told some students that parents, relatives, and friends were in transit to get them. When they began leaving one by one, I urged them to be safe. By 7:00 p.m., only two students remained.

Earlier, Foolio's mother stopped by to pick him up, but he apparently signed out with another student and his mother. Shirley immediately got on the phone to the student's mother.

"My son betta be safe," Foolio's mother screamed. "How could you ever let him go?" Thankfully, Shirley reached his friend's mother and got Foolio on the phone. The situation calmed.

Nicotina and I were in my classroom while the two remaining students rotated between socializing with the people in the Twilight office and us. Nicotina and I talked about Miss Carter.

"I heard she's going to be making observations," Nicotina said. "I also heard that she has it out for you since you let those kids out early. A lot of students are complaining about you too. I told you to be prepared for your informal observation she was supposed to do."

"I'm not worried about her. She can come whenever she wants," I said. "I hope she doesn't listen to the students who cry about me."

"Just make sure to have your lesson plans for the following week completed every Monday," Nicotina said. "She gets finicky with them."

Niles, my great high school friend who taught at Twilight, already warned me about Miss Carter's lesson plan madness. I had since prepared my planbook and gradebook.

Nicotina told me a story about Miss Carter's own issue with lesson plans and her lack of them when she was a home economics teacher. It was before she rose to power as the vice principal of Twilight.

The story began on an April day some years ago when Miss Carter was preparing to get observed and evaluated. She was meeting her department head, who told her to have her lesson planbook ready.

"I fell behind with the lessons in my lesson planbook," she said aghast.

"How far behind are you?" the department head asked.

"I hadn't been keeping a lesson planbook all year," she said. It was April. Seven full months had gone by.

It was decided that Miss Carter write lesson plans for the last two weeks and that day forward. She was to tell her observer that she lost the planbook that contained the others. I laughed at her supposed hypocrisy.

Nicotina and I also spoke about how Miss Carter had numerous crying fits to Shirley about the fear of losing her job. We both laughed.

The rain continued, and Miss Carter was supposed to stop in before 8:25 p.m. At 8:25 p.m., we all left.

When I finally got home to my suburban neighborhood, I was glad to see the remnants of Halloween trickery. One huge tree two blocks from my house was covered in toilet paper that streamed down its sides and clung firmly to the branches despite the light rain. I thought about how terrible it must be to have to stay in on these nights out of fear of being killed if one ventured outside.

The next day, I called in sick, because I really deserved it. At 1:10 p.m. and after encountering a busy signal, I reached the math office phone, which was the Twilight phone later in the day.

"Can I speak with someone from Twilight?" I asked. Jack got on the phone.

"I'm sick today," I said.

"Twilight's been cancelled," he said.

"What happened?"

"It's cancelled because of the shootings," Three students were shot outside the school in the morning.

"I have to call parents," he said, before quickly hanging up.

I watched the local news for more information.

On the first channel, the reporter explained that three students were shot two blocks away from the school. A melee apparently began inside the school and pushed its way out to the street. Someone ran into a house two blocks away to get a gun and came out shooting. Like a cowboy.

Our superintendent appeared on the screen.

"There is no evidence to suggest that this incident is gang-related," he assured us.

The reporter then reminded the viewer that the incident came "on the heels" of another shooting inside another city school just a week ago.

I switched to another local news channel, and the urban high school shooting was the next story. It said that three students were shot two blocks away from school because of a conflict between two posses from different streets in the area. The reporter named the streets. It also showed a shot of the house the assailant got the gun from. The reporter mentioned how the assailant had not yet been apprehended.

A police officer appeared in the report.

"We believe this case is gang-related," he said. A student was interviewed and explained how she "worried payback and retribution" was coming Monday.

I turned the television off.

-13-

I WALKED INTO THE TWILIGHT OFFICE and noticed Miss Carter sitting with Mr. Williams at the round table. It was 1:30 p.m.

"Mr. Kaminski," Miss Carter said, "I'd like to speak with you after I am done speaking with Mr. Williams." She always sounded so formal.

"Sure," I said. Since every chair in the Twilight office was occupied, I waited in the math office. It was empty.

Jack entered with the new guidance counselor.

"This is Ms. Garcia," he said.

He continued, "Today our new school schedule goes into effect." I forgot all about it. I also learned that the shooting really did happen two blocks away from school and that all the victims were alright. Jack and Ms. Garcia returned to the Twilight office.

Our schedule change had to do with the state exam that all high schoolers needed to pass to get diplomas. If you failed, then the state gave you another test to take that was easier to pass. Most Twilight students had to take the second test. These students would now have supplemental classes with a Day School English teacher and a Day School math teacher making overtime.

These sessions would occur every day from 3:25 p.m. to 4:00 p.m. If you were in this group, your lunchtime was now from 4:00 p.m. to 4:20 p.m. First block now ran from 4:20 p.m. to 5:15 p.m., second block ran from 5:15 p.m. to 6:15 p.m., third block ran from 6:15 p.m. to 7:15 p.m., and fourth block ran from 7:15 p.m. to 8:15 p.m.

If you didn't have to take the test, you would have lunch from 3:25 p.m. to 4:00 p.m., and then you would come up to one of the classrooms for twenty minutes. Two teachers had to supervise the newly formed class with an "engaging" activity.

Last week, we teachers sat around and discussed who would be taking the various shifts each day.

"I don't care," I said. We kept talking about it.

"I'll take the new class," I said. We talked about it some more. After wasting more of my life on every unnecessary facet of the issue, it was decided that Nicotina and I would run a Current Events class. It required little preparation beyond a newspaper and would provide students with a much-needed perspective on the world beyond the city.

Miss Carter's calling of my name broke up my thoughts in the math office. I went to sit in the warm seat vacated by Mr. Williams.

To my right was a sizzling radiator. It was hot enough to cook an egg. The windows were shut. I was wearing long sleeves.

"I am going to observe you," Miss Carter said. She showed me some paperwork concerning the different aspects her critique would be noting and took the most verbose route. I had to sign off on the last page, but my arm kept hitting the sweltering radiator. Minor adjustments needed to be made before I got my signature down.

I turned to open the window a crack, and as Miss

Carter spoke, a blast of air knocked all the papers on the table onto the floor and the other table. I left it open a crack before retrieving all the fallen papers.

I returned to my boiling seat. I made another attempt at a bigger crack for the breeze.

"Do you have your gradebook and your lesson planbook?" she asked. I pulled them from my bag.

"Can I see the lessons for this week and last week?" she asked, while flipping through my gradebook.

"I like how you have so many grades," she said. "You're giving them multiple chances to succeed." I was glad about this. I wasn't glad about the fact that I forget all about this week's lesson plans. On an even better note, I realized that I also forgot to update my lesson book since last Wednesday. It was so hot.

"I have notes for my lessons though," I said. "I know what I'm doing for the week too."

"Teachers need to have lessons for the week completed every Monday. I can ask you for them every Monday. If they are not prepared in the future, I can give you an unsatisfactory evaluation." I imagined it would be put in my *permanent* file.

"I will make sure my lesson planbook is better maintained," I assured her. The small breeze from the window could not compete with the heat of the radiator.

Miss Carter silently flipped through my lesson planbook.

"You need to further expound upon what you have written thus far about these lessons," she said.

"I've been writing worksheets that help the students along with their reading," I said. "I have been helping each student along." I tried grasping for more words. "I don't know what else to write," I conceded.

I needed to be more specific about the purpose of each

lesson. If it helped students with comprehension, I had to note that I addressed students' questions pertaining to comprehension. If it helped students with vocabulary, I had to note that I addressed students' questions about vocabulary. Same idea with grammar, and so forth. If I was reading a book in my World Literature class and another in my English class, I had to fill out fifteen similar lesson plan sheets for that week. I was already on my second binder, and they weren't complete.

"Your classes have no continuity," she said. I nicely begged to differ.

"In three months, if students took both of my English blocks, they would have already read three novels," I said. I reminded her how many students never even read a book before. She reminded me that she was a reading specialist.

"What is your next book going to be?" she asked.

The Great Gatsby," I said.

"It's great that you are exposing the students to D.H. Lawrence," she said. I almost started laughing. Instead, I smiled and nodded my head.

I addressed my concerns regarding my teaching certification. Since I wasn't certified, I was a candidate in the state's alternate route certification program. One major part was taking education classes at a state university though, and these classes were given once a week for four hours and one Saturday a month for a school year. Unfortunately, I taught at night, and there were no morning classes anywhere. I also needed a mentor who was supposed to sit in on my first twenty days of classes. If I didn't make any strides, I wouldn't be allowed to teach anywhere in the state next year.

Urban districts were filled with alternate route candidates because these districts needed teachers and couldn't attract certified ones. In suburban districts, a copy of your state certification was requested along with your resume. Often, teachers got certified while teaching at urban schools before making the brainless jump to nicer districts with higher salaries.

"Those issues are being dealt with at the Board," she said. "It is working with the state on creating concentrated certification courses at a college in the mornings so teachers in Twilight have an opportunity to take them."

She reassured me by stating how I would "definitely have a slot here in Twilight next year."

"I also don't have a mentor," I said. Dinesh, Mariella, Mr. Williams and I were in the same boat. No one really knew what to do. Nicotina was able to apply for other jobs with her certification.

After a year of these classes, you had to get a final evaluation at the beginning of the second year. Once all your forms were properly filled out, filed and approved, you'd receive your certification in the mail.

Since I doubted Twilight was going to succeed for me, I put in for a transfer to the Day School so I could take these classes in the evening next year. Then I could be certified in three years. Three years felt like a long time.

"You will still be able to work here," she reassured me. Then she chastised me for moving my classroom.

"That room is an official Twilight classroom and your new classroom is not," she said.

"Is there any way we could make my new classroom an official classroom?" I suggested.

"We cannot since your old one is the official one," she said.

"But my old room is filthy. I had to clean it every day," I said.

"You just have to get the janitors to clean it." I wasn't going to tell the janitors to do anything.

"I will be observing you in the next twenty days," she said. "I will be looking over your gradebook, your attendance book and your lesson planbook at that time as well." I was glad to get my attendance book together, since I wasn't keeping any formal record so far.

At 4:00 p.m., Nicotina and I went to her classroom for Current Events. We had no roster and were unclear about who was supposed to attend. By the time students made their way here after being told numerous times, it was 4:10 p.m. I passed around a sheet for students to sign.

There were students in the hallway, but I didn't know where to tell them to go. Boys went to the boys bathroom and girls went to the girls bathroom. They were surely hanging out and smoking cigarettes.

We let the Current Events class talk amongst themselves for the rest of the time. In the meantime, I looked into my old classroom, and it was filthy. I decided to use the new classroom until another objection.

Miss Carter helped many students in Twilight, and they all absolutely despised her. One would think that when the vice principal was here the students would behave. They didn't. They were actually worse.

In second block, I finally got the class reading. I was sitting at my desk and grading papers with my double-edged red and black pen. I was mauling a student with the red ink side when the class started giggling.

I looked up and saw a maxi pad on my desk looking at me. I looked at the class laughing. Foolio quickly turned away. Picking out the culprit was easy. I tried not to laugh. At least Foolio threw it on the desk and not at me. At least it wasn't used. If this was Foolio's rebellious endeavor, so be it. Maybe I should consider a policy of permitting students who did their work to throw maxi pads at me when they finished.

Between second and third block, Marvin charged down the hall to discuss the maxi pad situation.

"That's some fucked up shit. That's disrespectful," he said. "I done some foul shit, but nothin like that. I woulda blacked out. I woulda amped out."

"Take it easy," I said.

A few minutes into third block, the Queen arrived with her box of cornstarch and straw in a black plastic bag. Powder was all over her bag and her clothes. The last time I saw the Queen, I gave her a copy of *The Catcher in the Rye* and the worksheets. If she couldn't come to class or had to take care of her child, she could complete her missed work on her own time.

"I'm only here for those classes," she said to me. She was referring to the state exam reviews. Naturally, she didn't have any of the work or the book I lent her.

"Gimme some work," she said. I got her started on where I thought she left off. She hadn't completed anything. She started reading nonetheless.

Moments later she was sleeping, and I never tolerated sleeping. I woke her up and got her reading.

"I'll get you fired. I know Miss Carter," she said. Rather than argue, I tended to another student. Someone else referred to Miss Carter as a "fuckin bitch."

I returned to the front of the Queen's desk, and she was sleeping again. I nudged the leg of her desk, to no response. I started tap-dancing in front of it, and everyone started laughing. The Queen lifted her head up. She was mumbling, and I was dancing.

"If it means I have to dance on each and every one of the desks in this room to get you to do work, I will be regularly performing new routines of getting my groove on," I declared. The Queen loudly mumbled something again.

"Stop talkin gibberish," Joe said.

I pointed at Joe and said, "You get extra credit for using one of our vocabulary words in class discussion." I later marked it in my gradebook.

"You won't be working here next year," the Queen said, before dozing off again.

"Stop being a dumb nigga," Shenequa yelled out. The Queen was up.

"You dumb," the Queen replied. Touché! It escalated into a shouting match I couldn't control.

Shenequa was my best student in grades and attitude. Someone needed to say something to the Queen. From the corner of my eye, I saw Destiny throwing things at me. When I looked at her, she stopped. Miss Carter came into the room to quell the commotion.

She tried reasoning with everyone in her formal way, but everyone was disrespectful before quieting down. Miss Carter blamed Shenequa for being the loudest, and Shenequa apologized. Miss Carter insisted they talk about it outside in the hallway, but Shenequa refused.

Destiny was still throwing things at me. When I asked her to stop, she told me that she wasn't throwing anything, rather she was just making the throwing gesture. Once my eyes left her, she kept gesticulating.

Miss Carter left when the drama ended. Destiny continued throwing nothing at me.

"Why do you keep doing that?" I asked. "Please control yourself. This is not special ed." She kept making the same throwing gesture. She started laughing like someone sinister.

"Why are you in Twilight?" I asked.

"I don't know," she replied. I was hoping she would say she had to finish her high school education so she could support her one-year-old son but she didn't.

Faith came in to pass out fliers to everyone and then me. It explained how all students and their lockers were subject to random searches. It was in response to the school shootings.

"That's not fair," everyone seemed to say. I wanted to have a class discussion about it, but the block was over.

Between 8:15 p.m. and 8:25 p.m., I was talking in the hallway with Nicotina about how some students were blacking out today and how they made me want to black out.

Faith chimed in, "You can't black out because you're white."

"But I can," I said. I went home.

14

IT WAS ALMOST 7:00 P.M., and the head administrators had not yet made any decisions about the "incident" that occurred yesterday. Food was the furthest thing from my mind when I entered the Board of Education at 1:30 p.m. to report to Miss Carter's office. Now I was hungry.

I spent the last five and a half hours reading *All Quiet on the Western Front*, using Miss Carter's internet, having more discussions about the "incident," and waiting. I was so bored. Whenever I asked to step out for a few moments to get anything to eat, Miss Carter told me it would be best to wait a little longer.

Yesterday began with the concern that Miss Carter would be coming to observe one of my classes. I was prepared but still needed to make copies once I arrived at school. The copier was naturally out of letter-sized paper, and there was none available to reload it. There were boxes of legal-sized paper though; it just meant that I had to use a paper cutter to cut it into letter-sized paper to fit the machine.

Recently, I learned the secret about the copier. After it completed a job, the screen indicated a malfunction after every round or every other round of copying. All you had to do to get it to work again was to turn it off, turn it on again, and let it warm up briefly. It was always a gamble when you were pressed for time and needed to make copies.

After, I went to the library until 3:25 p.m. I then went to the cafeteria and sat with Mariella. We teachers no longer all performed cafeteria duty daily. Instead, each teacher was a part of a rotating schedule of twice one week and three times the next.

At 4:00 p.m., I went upstairs for a Current Events class that was only that by name nowadays. There was no accountability, so students were everywhere — in the office, the bathrooms, or elsewhere in our part of the school. Some students showed up to sit, while others floated around the hallway. They were supposed to be in the cafeteria, but no one was directing anyone anywhere.

Nicotina didn't even show up. I found out later she was in a parent/teacher conference with a student who kept calling her a "fat bitch." It was one of her better students.

"You like the fat bitch?" he recently asked me.

"Take it easy," I said.

"I don't like that fat bitch."

At 4:10 p.m., a piercing fire alarm tore through the school. My eardrums were vibrating. I covered my ears.

"Fire?" one student exclaimed. "I'm gettin the fuck outta here." She walked briskly in the entirely wrong direction. I pointed toward the right exit. I checked the bathrooms and exited the building covering my ears. We all stood in the rain until we were let back in. Apparently, one of the Day School kids pulled the alarm.

Before I went to my room, I stopped in the Twilight office to see if Miss Carter was here. I was getting that observation one of these days. Rhonda said she would tell me when she arrived. Five minutes later, Rhonda told me Jack was escorting her from her car.

After a few minutes into first block, I learned that many students needed writing implements. I estimated that since the beginning of the year, Twilight gave out over 1,500 pencils and pens. Our major supply was sorely depleted, and we wouldn't be resupplied anytime soon.

I tried charging twenty-five cents a pencil so I could buy more pencils, but no one would buy any. I was adamant against purchasing more pencils and pens with my own money. The ones that I did have were already gone.

Most of the students were reading, so I crossed the hall to the Twilight office to get some pencils. Pens were not that expendable anymore. Miss Carter was sitting at the long table.

"Does anyone have any pencils?" I asked the room. I was looking around the room for some.

"Mr. Kaminski," Miss Carter sharply interjected. "It is not your job to make sure the students have writing utensils." I wasn't sure what to say. I needed the pencils. If the kids didn't have pencils, they couldn't do their work. If they couldn't do their work, they failed. I didn't have the patience to discuss these trivialities.

"Here's some in an effort to make your job easier," Ms. Garcia said, as she handed over five pencils. In her first few days, she was already helping me in all the myriad ways. She also rolled her eyes at me numerous times after being confronted with absolute nonsense. I grabbed the pencils, thanked her, and got back to class.

There was a moment in the second block when I looked at the class and everyone was reading. It was completely silent. Keeping every student working on an assignment was the only way they ever got anything accomplished. They were so easily distracted when they were not on-task. I hoped more students would rather work then deal with my badgering and crassness when they did nothing.

The serenity was shattered once Tanisha walked into class and started talking to Shenequa like there was no one else in the room. I couldn't imagine barging into a class and starting to talk to someone when I was in high school.

"Please be quiet," I said. "And get back to work, Shenequa." She did.

"Gimme the last test I missed," Tanisha said. She was a smart student but could have an attitude, be nasty and be loud on any day. She also spent too much time walking around. Students were supposed to be suspended for walking around without a pass, but no one was ever even reprimanded.

I met Tanisha's mother numerous times in the building but had no idea what she was ever doing. Sometimes she came to classrooms to speak to Tanisha. Sometimes Tanisha went to the hall to speak to her mother. Sometimes Tanisha's mother had a baby with her. It all just happened sometimes.

Once after Tanisha had an outburst, her mother said, "I didn't teach her to act like that." I wanted to tell her that she learned her disgusting behavior somewhere, but I didn't. The school tolerated her attitude because she had great grades, but real world society wouldn't tolerate such violent outbursts. I sometimes wondered whether she could actually control herself. She needed to learn how to act like a nineteen-year-old woman.

Suddenly, Tanisha's phone rang, and she answered it. For starters, phones weren't permitted in Twilight.

Students had them anyway, and they rang all the time. Sometimes students apologized before taking a call in the middle of class.

"You need to feel remorse when you apologize," I said. Students never did. We spoke about the remorse concept before in class.

"Get off the phone, Tanisha," I said. When she did, her nasty attitude was in full effect. She yelled for a passerby in the hall and then at someone else in class. She didn't care that her booming voice was disturbing everyone around her. I asked her to be quiet more than three times, but she wouldn't.

"Can you please just shut up?" I said. "I just don't know how else to get you to not talk."

"This a free country," she said. "I could talk how I want. I could say what I want. You got children? You shouldn't tell anyone to shut up. Just gimme my test," she said.

"You'll get it when you begin acting like a human being by sitting quietly for a moment."

"Gimme my fuckin test!" she yelled.

When I ignored her, she screamed, "This is unfair you won't give me my test!" Jack had to pull her from the room. Somehow the class got back to normal.

Jack returned to ask for Tanisha's test.

"I don't want to. I don't have to put up with her mouth or her attitude. She needs to pass this class," I said. Jack said he understood and left.

Moments later, Miss Carter came into my room.

"I would like to commend the class for not getting that unsettled because of the disturbance. I would like to thank you for not making it any worse."

She continued, "Last year some of my students were

disruptive and they've matured. Mr. Kaminski, can I speak with you in the hall?"

She asked me for the test, and I told her my reasoning for not handing it over.

"Since you told her she could take it today, you can't let her bad behavior break that promise," she said. "I was going to observe you today, but I won't now because of this distracting event."

She continued, "She gets out of control, but she is better than last year. Her outbursts are getting shorter. We need to reward her for making strides." I handed over the test.

In Block Four, Miss D came in and started doing her work. She wrote a 300-word essay in like eight minutes, and it was one big block of barely comprehensible uppercased text.

"You need to break this into paragraphs," I said.

"I don't need to break it into any fuckin paragraphs cuz you didn't tell me to," she said. I showed her the paragraph symbol and showed her how to insert it into her essay. She quickly made some marks before insisting I take her work since she was done.

With no work, Miss D started strutting around and began bothering Foolio.

"Sit down." I said, but she continued walking around the room. She stopped to read a paper stapled to the closet door, which was, ironically, the class rules for the Day School classroom. Weeks ago, Miss D tagged this paper with her name.

As I walked to the back to coax her to her seat, I walked past the seat she should have been sitting in. Her glasses were on it, and they were facedown.

"You can't keep your glasses on the desk like this," I

said. "You're going to scratch your lenses." I moved them over.

"You touchin my stuff?" she asked. "I'll touch yours then."

She sat in one of the desk-chairs surrounding my desk and grabbed a pile of papers.

"Give me back my work please," I said. She refused. I went to grab them, but I missed her waving arm.

Miss D was wearing a headband. Students weren't permitted to wear headbands, hats, wraps, or do-rags, but, of course, these policies were never enforced outside of my classroom. Once they left my room, everything was back on. No one with authority was ever consistent.

Sometimes Shirley or Rhonda or Faith took hats, but they were always returned. Lessons were never learned. Rules were always violated. It was a relentless cycle.

Miss D continued waving my papers around, and I was yelling at her to put them down.

"I'm going to take your headband if you don't drop my papers," I said. She didn't care.

I began removing it, and she pulled her head away.

Jack came into my room from his meeting with Miss Carter, and Miss D dropped the papers. He pulled her from the classroom.

Moments later, Miss D came barging back into my classroom. She grabbed a bunch of papers and my gradebook off my desk and threw them at me.

"Go fuck yaself!" she screamed.

"Get out of my classroom," I yelled. She screamed obscenities.

I moved my other papers to the floor so she couldn't grab them again. I would hate to redo tedious paperwork she destroyed.

"Jack!" I yelled. I tried to clear my desk.

Jack returned screaming. He physically removed her from the room, which led to her blacking out in the hallway.

"He preventin me from gettin an education," she yelled at the top of her lungs. "I'm gonna shoot him in the fuckin head. I'm gonna get um. I'm gonna fuck his car up. I'm gonna smack the shit out of um."

Rhonda, Faith, Jack, Miss Carter, and a security guard tried to control her. I tried maintaining order in my classroom while it continued. Everyone was obviously listening to her, and some students were laughing.

"Fuck you, (Jack)!" she said. "Fuck you, Miss Carter!" She gave every staff member in the hallway the same shout-out. I wondered if she could be automatically expelled.

"This is beat! This is beat!" she screamed.

"You beat? I ain't beat," Foolio said. His little crew in the back of the room laughed. I was trying hard not to laugh, as I watched what I hoped was Miss D's swan song.

"You enjoyin yaself," Foolio said to me.

"There's nothing funny about a disrespectful student ruining school for everyone," I said. Maybe I smiled a bit.

"Suspend me! Suspend me!" Miss D screamed. "How many more fuckin times you gonna suspend me?"

Rhonda was on the phone so Miss D's mother could hear the outburst. The Day School principal was also in the hallway. After ten minutes, Miss D was removed from the building.

As the block ended, I realized that since I touched her head to take her headband, I was probably going to get fired. Once the students left, Jack and Miss Carter brought me to see the principal.

I waited in an office, while Jack and Miss Carter sat in a conference room waiting for the principal to finish a phone call in her office. Hero was dusting around the area, and we made eye contact. I waited to get fired.

Then I thought that maybe I was in some sort of shock. Why would I get fired? It was difficult to get fired from Twilight. At another site, there was a science teacher who pulled his jacket over his head when the students got disruptive. Then they would pelt him with paper balls. A bunch of students smoked in his classroom as well, and he still had a job.

I was asked into the conference room to sit with Miss Carter, Jack, and the principal.

"Are you alright?" the principal asked. "Have a candy bar." There was a bowl of small candy bars in the middle of the table. I was feeling faint. I didn't want anything.

"You look distraught," the principal said. I saw my reflection in a mirror across the room and saw how red my face was. I looked like I had been slapped around.

Jack tried to engage me in some small talk about my weekend. I didn't tell him that I was working diligently to try and accurately report my daily trials at this hapless job so I could entertain some friends on my email list with work stories. Nevertheless, the vacuous discussion was relaxing me.

Jack offered me an O-Henry, and I ate it and felt even better. Then I ate a $100,000 bar. Minutes later, a security guard came in and took all but two of the remaining candy bars from the bowl.

We discussed the incident, and Miss Carter was taking detailed notes.

"I thought I was getting fired," I said.

"Relax."

"That's not going to happen."

It was unanimous that I should never have touched her head.

"I made a mistake," I said. I thought I had a right to protect my work.

"I didn't want to redo a torn-up gradebook," I said. "I don't know what she's capable of."

Miss Carter read back her summary but missed the part where Miss D said she was going to smack the shit out of me. I told her exactly where to insert that in her report.

It was 9:20 p.m. when I left school. Miss Carter walked out with me. I later learned that there was a procedure in place where the police were patrolling the perimeter of the school so I wouldn't be harmed by any students.

On the front steps, Miss Carter told me to report to her office tomorrow.

"I would have been in tears over this entire incident," she said. "You have no reason to be embarrassed." I was wondering whether I should feel humiliated.

"My job is hard, but I like it," she said.

At 7:30 p.m. the next day, Miss Carter was finally able to meet with one of the heads at the Board of Education. I was led to a long table in a conference room, where I was introduced to a woman who I thought was a head honcho but was just a secretary.

"He hasn't eaten all day," Miss Carter said. The secretary offered me a tray of cookies, and I took one of the butter ones. It was chewy and delicious. I asked for another one.

"These are seriously some of the best cookies I've ever eaten," I said.

"They cost sixty-five dollars a tray," the real head

honcho said. "They didn't get finished today at the meeting."

"Someone complained they were too expensive, but I still ordered them because they are so delicious," the secretary said.

I repeated the Miss D story again. I regretted touching her headband.

"What do you want to do?" the head honcho asked.

"In the one sense, I want her expelled because she ruins the education of everyone around her. At the same time, another person without a high school diploma isn't helping society in any way."

It was decided that Miss D wouldn't attend my classes anymore this trimester but would do her work under someone else's supervision. Miss D still had another year's worth of classes and many other English classes to take. Her classes would be rescheduled for the third trimester.

Numerous times, Miss Carter sunk into another long-winded monologue. Once, the head honcho even rolled her eyes at me. I thought about a line that Niles and I heard Miss Carter say: "A lot of shit is going to hit your ass in the head." We laughed about that.

I raised the issue about Miss D's threats. I didn't actually think Miss D would go through with any of them. Once students were dismissed, they would never take their time to wait for me outside to do me any harm because even that took a certain initiative. I still felt that Miss D needed to be punished for her threats in some way though.

"I don't always feel safe around her. What is being done to ensure my safety?" I asked. "If Miss D decides to be violent one day, it wouldn't be surprising after the fact. I don't want to be the fact."

"You could always raise your concerns with the police. The administration fully supports you." And then the meeting was over.

I was told to report to Twilight tomorrow for a conference with Miss D and her mother. They all told me to enjoy dinner. As I left, I grabbed another cookie. It tasted so good on the elevator down.

-15-

THE NEXT DAY, I WALKED into school and saw Faith turning the corner ahead of me. I caught up with her before she reached the Twilight office.

"Are you going to the conference with Miss D and her mother today?" I asked.

"I'm refusing to attend that," she said, "unless I'm told to do so." She went into the Twilight office.

Nicotina, Ms. Garcia, and Rhonda all looked at me as I walked in.

"Don't worry, I'm fine," I said. I didn't really want to talk about Miss D anymore, but I knew they were generally concerned. I went down to the library to begin my prep work.

There was a crowd of kids in the stairwell to the library. As I walked by, one of them said "Boo!" into my left ear and his crew laughed. Thankfully, I didn't flinch. The attempt at intimidation was infuriating.

"The only thing scary is your disgusting breath in my face," I said. There was a chorus of laughter and oh shits as I opened the door into the basement hallway.

I entered the library and went to the computer lab. I talked to Mario about the Miss D situation and about how

I had to spend yesterday at the Board building and how she wasn't getting suspended or expelled for her antics and how there was a parent conference today at 3:00 p.m. and how Miss D was supposed to sign a contract and how all Twilight students already signed a contract but this was another contract and how the students in our program were completely out of control and how I was undermined on a daily basis.

"I need to get a new job," said Mario. "It's unbelievable how disrespectful they are to us."

I prepared for my classes, and at 2:50 p.m., I left for the conference.

"Good luck," Mario said.

At 2:52 p.m., I walked through the Twilight office and into the math office. Jack was there. He shook my hand.

"How ya doin?" he asked.

"I want to join the union," I said. I was advised by my mother, a grammar school teacher in the city for over thirty years, to join the union once I had a chance to, but I kept forgetting. Considering all the incidents I was dealing with, I needed them in my corner.

"I'll get the paperwork together," he said.

At 2:56 p.m., I saw Miss D's mother in the hallway but not Miss D. I requested to have the conference without her. She was incapable of attending a civil meeting. I gave Miss D's mother a whispered hello.

At 3:00 p.m., Jack, Rhonda, Ms. Garcia, Faith, and I were waiting impatiently in the math office for Miss Carter to show up.

At 3:11 p.m., I got up and went into the hallway. I hated just sitting there. I saw Miss D sitting in the Twilight office. I watched the clock tick for a minute before sitting back down.

At 3:22 p.m., Miss Carter called our office to say she was "arriving momentarily." She had a problem parking her car.

Miss D's mother came into the math office, and I stood up to shake her hand. Jack introduced her to Ms. Garcia. Miss D's mother already knew Jack and Rhonda, and they exchanged pleasantries.

Miss Carter finally arrived and apologized for her tardiness. Before she took a seat, she reintroduced everyone.

On one side of the table, I sat in the middle with Jack to my left and Miss Carter to my right. At the head of the table sat Miss D's mother. There was a vacant chair for when Miss D would join us later in the meeting. To the right of where Miss D would sit sat Ms. Garcia, and Rhonda sat to the right of her. Faith sat behind where Miss D would be sitting, right where the office phone rang incessantly.

"Thanks for coming," Miss Carter said to Miss D's mother. "I used to have (Miss D) as a student." She mentioned a grammar school.

"She never went there," Miss D's mother said. There was a short silence.

"I'm sorry for the confusion," Miss Carter said.

Miss D's mother's cell phone rang, and she answered it.

"I'll call you back in ten minutes," Miss D's mother said. "I'm at my daughter's school for a meeting." She hung up, and the meeting continued.

"There are serious problems in my daughter's classroom with him," she said. She meant me.

"He told my nephew to go to the bathroom to wash his balls," she reminded everyone.

"Clearly your nephew misheard whatever it was I said," I said. "I wouldn't say that. I'm a professional."

"But you admitted that in the last meeting," she said. I was flabbergasted. I never said such a thing.

"We should stick to the issue at hand," Ms. Garcia chimed in.

Miss D's mother's phone rang again. "I'm at my daughter's school. I'll call you back in ten minutes," she said. She hung up. The meeting continued.

Miss Carter discussed the incident and Miss D's subsequent outburst and how utterly out of control she was that evening.

"She got right in my face and would not speak with anyone calmly," Miss Carter continued. "She hurled profanity at anyone who tried to defuse the situation."

"She was really upset. She wouldn't even get on the phone with me," Miss D's mother said.

"You should not have been playing with her and her headband," Miss D's mother said to me. "You should have gotten some help."

"But he has a classroom of students. He can't just leave his post," Jack interjected. "I didn't even see him touch her headband, but I did see her waving his papers around." Other staff members could also verify being told to *fuck* themselves.

"I need to go outside," Miss D's mother said, and left the meeting. We sat waiting for her return.

"Before B, we really need to talk about A while not forgetting C," Ms. Garcia said. I couldn't agree more. Miss D's mother was trying to blame me rather than how her daughter caused it in the first place.

"It's ridiculous that we just can't have a meeting," I said.

"She's overwhelmed," Faith interjected. "This

is emotional. She needed to calm down. You don't understand, you don't have children." Miss D's mother returned.

"Her behavior was atrocious that night," Rhonda said. "I couldn't calm her down."

She continued, "911 was almost called to intervene. If we called 911, psychiatric services would get involved and I don't like how psych services treats people and especially children."

"I would have been displeased with that," Miss D's mother said. Her phone rang again. "I'm at my daughter's school. I'll call you back in ten minutes," she said. She hung up. The meeting continued.

"She should consider enrolling in anger management classes," Rhonda said.

"I thought about that, but I don't think it's necessary," Miss D's mother said.

Miss D was asked to join us. She sat down at the table with a puss on her face. She didn't look at me.

"Twilight has decided to retain (Miss D), but she is going to have to sign a contract to remain," Miss Carter said. I was unsure who else took part in making the decision.

"I want to read the contract," Miss D's mother said.

"The Board of Education has to approve it first," Miss Carter said. "This won't occur for another two weeks."

"Then I'm gonna come back to read it before she signs anything," Miss D's mother said. "What about the contents of *his* contract?"

"Mr. Kaminski does not have to sign any contract in regards to the incident," Miss Carter said. I had no idea what they were talking about.

"Since (Miss D) still needs to take two classes with Mr. Kaminski, we are going to schedule them both for the third trimester," Miss Carter said. For the rest of this trimester, Miss D would have to do my work in another classroom.

"Maybe they'll both grow up by then," Miss D's mother said.

Miss D's mother's phone rang, and she answered it. "I'm ready to go," she said. Miss D stood up. I shook Miss D's mother's hand on the way out. The meeting was over.

I felt punch-drunk when I sat down in the Twilight office.

"This is bullshit," Jack said to me. "I'm retiring next year."

Dinesh extended a hand to me, and Mariella gave me a sad smile. Nicotina lent me her support.

I still had all my classes to teach.

-16-

AS I DROVE UP THE HILL to the school, I saw blue Mylar tarps above and below every window of the four-story building. Some flapped in the breeze.

"What are these guys trying to accomplish?" I asked Patrice, the security guard, a few days ago.

"They're replacing bricks," she said. There was a construction crew of about twenty people. I wondered how important the project was for the school's structure and whether that money could have been used in a better fashion considering the high price of construction costs and overtime for workers who worked at night. These days I was more of a masochist than a logician.

I went to the Day School main office for my check. I looked over at the computer of one of the clerks, and it had a screensaver of an attacking great white shark with its jaws about to strike. I wondered why anyone would want to view this moment day in and day out. I opened my check to learn I was finally being paid for summer teacher training. That was almost three months ago.

Sometime a few weeks back, Nicotina was complaining about how the Twilight staff was getting paid.

"Our checks should be delivered here. They don't like

us as it is. Why do we have to get our checks from people who don't like us?" Nicotina said to Miss Carter.

"It's the policy of the school and will not be changed," Miss Carter said. I didn't mind walking a few seconds to the office to pick up my measly earnings.

I went down to the library and into the computer lab. Peter, the permanent substitute, was there with five students sitting at the tables. I talked to Peter before. His job was much harder than he let on. I began typing up some worksheets.

Peter wanted his students to find health-related articles in the magazines, so they could summarize and discuss them. No one was motivated. They all wore hats and do-rags, which weren't permitted in the Day School.

The first problem was having them select which magazines they wanted to peruse. There were complaints about the available titles and the cover pictures. There were constant spews of profanity. Peter was acknowledged in rude tones.

"We get extra credit for more than five sentences?" one student asked. Students always wanted extra credit when they decided to do any work. Some wanted it before they even began. One student moved away from the group to complete the assignment.

"Please be quiet," Peter said. He was flustered. The group got louder and louder.

"I'll give you zeroes!" Peter threatened. "I'll get you suspended!" The students weren't responding.

Being in the room was stressful. It was Peter's responsibility to control these five students. Some classes in the Day School had thirty-five students. I was nauseous. How could these students ever succeed in school or in life if this was how they treated their teachers? How exactly was the school preparing them for society?

"Can't you at least let *him* get his work done?" Peter said, and looked at me. Their behavior continued until the bell rang. At 3:25 p.m., I went to lunch duty totally stressed out.

Mariella, Dinesh and a substitute named Mr. R were there. Our new science teacher, Mr. Williams, had to go down South for a medical emergency involving his father, but thankfully we were able to get Mr. R. No one knew when Mr. Williams would be back, and the trimester was ending on the Wednesday before Thanksgiving. Only a teacher with the proper science credentials could give students grades for science. There was going to be an uproar if he was still out when grades were due. On the other hand, how could these kids expect to get grades for a class that had no teacher and for one they had done little work in? How can you get science credits with no science?

"(Nicotina) and Jack are absent today," Mariella said. Whenever Jack was gone, there was a power struggle amongst the administrative staff about who was in charge. There were also more student problems when he was out. And Shirley was absent lately because of a kidney condition.

Tutoring for the state exam was cancelled, so Twilight was going back to one of the old schedules. I made sure we all knew the time changes.

Out of the corner of my eye, I saw Miss D talking to another student. They were looking over and laughing at me. I couldn't believe I still had to deal with her.

I talked about the summer pay with Dinesh, and he started writing out numbers to determine the value of our work. It was hard to follow along because of his accent, the situation with Peter that lingered in my mind, and now Miss D. I went upstairs to make some copies in the Twilight office.

"Do you know where I could get a TV/VCR for next week? I want to show them *All Quiet on the Western Front*." I said to Faith, since she should know since she was the Twilight librarian. The last time I took students to the library, she didn't even come.

"I'm not a media specialist," Faith said. "You're gonna have to ask Jack. And you have to get your viewing material approved by Miss Carter." Faith was a specialist at passing the buck.

I really needed to have a conversation with Faith because we just didn't see eye to eye. Lots of students whined to her about me. I thought she was on their side.

At 4:00 p.m. I had few students. I learned from the office that over twenty were absent. Upon returning to class, I noticed Luther working at his desk with a pile of papers. Luther vacillated between doing absolutely nothing and sleeping. I never let him sleep, so we didn't get along at all. There was no reason for him to have so many items on his desk because he brought nothing to school but "hisself."

I realized that most of the papers were from my desk. He even had my pen! He was copying other students' completed assignments. I took everything.

"You're getting zeroes for all this," I said. I was so annoyed and mad, but it was a consequence for leaving students unsupervised.

"You're an asshole," Luther said. "And you have shitty pants!" The pants were fine.

"Do you have any remorse for violating my space?" I asked.

"Nope," he said. He just sat at his desk-chair.

"I'm going to get you suspended unless you tell me why I have to tolerate you taking my stuff." There was no punishment for calling a teacher an asshole.

I calmly sat back at my desk and wrote a suspension letter that detailed the incident. Iverson and Marvin came in reeking of marijuana.

"Where've you been?" I said.

"Gimme my work," Marvin said. Iverson asked for some too.

"Can you both please use breath mints to hide the smell?" I asked. They both laughed.

"So how was your suspension?" Marvin asked. He hadn't seen me since my day at the Board of Education.

"I wasn't suspended," I said.

"Yes, you was," he said.

"You shouldn't listen to rumors," I said.

"Someone in the office told me," he said. I believed him. The Twilight office was a sewing circle. It was turning into such a crappy day.

Once everyone was working, I brought the suspension letter to the office so I could have Luther removed. There were three students sitting and talking with Rhonda and Faith. Miss D was one of them. They were adding to the sewing circle, I guessed. Why were these students in here and not in class? How could the students take a suspension seriously if they were placed in a social environment they preferred to school? Why were policies not enforced? Why were all the kids wearing hats and do-rags if there were gang problems in the school? How was Twilight able to survive? I went to the math office to give the letter to Ms. Garcia.

"Why aren't those students in class?" I asked. "Why are they sitting there when there are kids roaming the hallways?"

"How come I have no place to do my job?" she asked. I smiled, shook my head and left, after giving her more work to do because of Luther. I heard her go to the Twilight office and ask, "How come they're not in class?"

I returned to class, and Iverson's eyes were barely open. He was very stoned. His book sat unopened on his desk.

"Books need to be opened so you can read the words," I said. Iverson started giggling. Moments later, the entire classroom stunk, and it was insinuated that Iverson did it.

"Can you be any more vile?" I asked.

"What's that mean?" he asked. When I told him, he laughed. I opened the window to let the fresh city air in. Faith came to remove Luther.

Everyone but Iverson completed work during the block.

"You have to get this work done," I said to him.

He mumbled something about how he was a "crazy nigga" and "under house arrest."

"You need to get a copy of this book and do this work, or you're gonna have to take this class next trimester," I said.

"You crazy if you think I ain't passin'," he said.

Students finally got to second block after my loud coaxing in the hallway.

One of the new female students said, "Stop bothering them."

When I looked at her, she said, "Go fuck yaself." I allowed her to get more riled up, so the office could hear her mouth. She told me to fuck myself a few more times. Faith finally came to remove her. Later in the block, I looked into the office, and it was Faith, Rhonda, Miss

D, Luther, the girl who just told me to fuck myself, and another girl. They were talking and laughing. I hated this job.

There were only three students in my third block, so I brought them to one of the small computer labs. They needed the time to catch up on their work anyway. This was why it was pointless to have plans for the week completed on Monday when day-to-day lessons were so erratic.

"Mr. Kaminski," Faith called to the lab, since it was not far from the office. I went to the doorway.

"Students can't be in the computer lab," she said. She was being bossy and assertive.

"I'll take care of it, don't worry," I said.

By fourth block, all my students were officially absent, so I stayed in the lab. My head was spinning from the clobbering nonsense coming from all directions.

A foul odor crept into the lab, so I went into the hallway to see a mist coming out of some classrooms. I went to the Twilight office, and Faith was on the phone. We had to shut the windows to stop the dust from the sandblasting outside. Rhonda called Miss Carter to request an early dismissal but was told that, "Dismissal was not until 8:15 p.m." Miss Carter ordered everyone to the auditorium for the rest of the day.

I told Rhonda I didn't feel well so I remained in the computer lab with the door closed. I didn't want to sit in the auditorium with the remaining students complaining about why they had to stay in school when it was like this. I just didn't have the patience to explain and reexplain how Miss Carter said there wouldn't be an early dismissal. I didn't want to incessantly repeat that I had no authority to let anyone leave early anyway. There would be talk of how unfair I was, and students would say how much they hated me. It was so inevitable and repetitive.

When school was finally over, I walked to my car to find it covered in a fine dust.

-17-

AFTER THINKING ALL WEEKEND, I decided to take a more proactive role in my own defense at school because I didn't really know whom to trust and I was not always sure who cared enough anyway.

"Stop caring so much about everything," Nicotina said. "Get certified and get a better job."

I couldn't bring myself to accept the madness and inefficiency. I didn't want to accept my role as just another cog in a gas-guzzling jalopy.

"I don't like how the students knew my business at the Board," I said. A bunch confronted me about it.

"Everyone was talking about it when you were out," Nicotina said. Some were still talking about it.

"It was definitely not someone on the staff," Nicotina reassured me. I hoped Nicotina, Mariella, Ms. Garcia and Dinesh didn't speak with the students about me behind my back. The students would probably name them if they did anyway.

Faith and Rhonda, however, were undermining me. They were enabling poor student behavior by not holding them accountable. I felt like an outsider as the white enforcer of rules.

My first step toward being more proactive in my own defense was going to the police station next to the school to speak with someone in the juvenile division about Miss D, her harassment, and, more importantly, her numerous threats. I was directed to the juvenile precinct, which was a five minute drive away.

I found myself in front of a non-descript two-story building behind a grammar school. I was buzzed inside and directed by a sign to the second floor. There was a giant corkboard with pictures of missing children. I went to the glass window.

"I'm a teacher, and I want to file a report," I said. A white-haired man came out from behind the glass. We both had the same last name.

"We're not related," he said, when I mentioned it. I told him all about Miss D.

"I can't help ya," he said. "You need to report this to one of the two officers stationed at the school. One is black, and one is white. Tell them what ya told me." I thanked him and went back to school.

I found the white officer, told him I worked in Twilight, and began yet another monologue about Miss D.

The principal appeared and asked him to bring a girl to the nurse's office. What did a student have to do and say to get a police escort? The principal said hello to me. I waited ten minutes before leaving.

By the time I arrived to the Twilight office after lunch, I learned the officer was looking for me, so I went to find him. I didn't want to elaborate to the staff about my decision to file a report against Miss D. I finally found him.

"What should I do?" I asked.

"It's your job to press charges, and mine to write

down the details," he said. "I'll use the school address rather than your home address. You don't need the aggravation," he said. I was glad I didn't have to give my home address. When I was younger, my house got inundated with obscene calls from one of my mother's students. I thanked the officer for his consideration.

"What room did this occur in?"

"I'm not sure."

"Don't worry about it," he said.

"Is this the kind of thing that gets picked apart in court and ends with a dismissal?" I asked.

"It's just a typo in the report," he said. "That stuff just looks real good in movies."

"I watch a lot of movies," I said.

He wrote down the details, shaking his head along the way. He told me to return to the juvenile office tomorrow to sign more paperwork and gave me a file number. I was sure he had done this many times before.

The next day, I got as far as the second floor of the juvenile office when I realized I left the file number in the car. I went back down to my car three blocks away to get it.

"Why don't you just use a bat to solve your problems?" the officer asked. I shrugged my shoulders. Maybe this was a more effective method than the meek ones that constantly failed me. The officer recounted the scene in *The Untouchables* when Robert De Niro as Al Capone smashed a man's skull at a dinner table.

"It got everyone's attention," he said. I agreed. He excused himself to get the file and to see if Miss D had been there before. He returned with her mug shot. There was one of her facing forward with a placard around her neck and another one from the side. Her bloated and disgusting face sickened me more than ever.

"Your school always had problems, and they're only getting worse," he confessed. He recounted his days as an undercover narcotics agent peering through holes in closets to witness drug deals.

"You ever teach before?" he asked.

"In the Bronx," I said. I told him a little about it.

"Why would you teach here?" I told him how I needed to get certified in New Jersey to get a better job. I also told him how my job here was more difficult than in the Bronx.

"I take classes sometimes, and for one, my instructor lived *there*," he said. "I used to wait with her at the stop until she got on the bus. She hated this city and told me it was much worse." I agreed with her.

"I was only in the Bronx during the day though," I said. He moved on.

"You gotta wonder about the school system and the criminal justice system. School violence has been on the rise since they took the power from the administrators," he said fervently. "When I was in school, the old Irish teachers would rap me on the knuckles if I misbehaved, and if I told my parents, they would only rap me harder."

He continued, "Teachers and administrators today cannot possibly have control because they live in constant fear of lawsuits." Students told me they would sue me and the school many times. I encouraged them to. The lawsuit concept was ingrained in their head.

Last month, I went to the dermatologist, and a chemical peel left my face very red in two areas.

"You should sue the doctor," many students advised me.

"It'll go away," I said, and it did. Many students called me "stupid."

"You lucky you got burned," one student told me. "I wished I got burned so I could have a lawsuit and get money."

The officer and I continued our discussion on school violence. The story was nothing new. My story was nothing new.

"There's a vicious cycle of angry students and single moms, and everyone is so damn confrontational over every single issue," he said. "It's rap music and movies constantly promoting violence that these students are devouring. What happened to the old days of boy meets girl and boy and girl had a nice family? Why can't we have it like the old movies?" Times were simpler.

"Now we have to deal with this specter of terrorism and how completely out of control our world has gotten," he said. "I'm looking forward to retirement."

After I signed the report, he explained that I had to appear in court when she faced the charges.

"What's gonna happen to her?" I asked, but he had no definite answers. She might be allowed in school, she might not be. They may address her charges and send her to court-mandated anger management, or maybe not. He told me his office would contact me, and I thanked him and wished him luck with his job.

Later in the day, I ended up telling Ms. Garcia, Mariella, Dinesh, and Nicotina about the charges.

"Miss Carter should've thrown out (Miss D) after her last outburst," Ms. Garcia said. "Twilight needs to be stricter and the students need to see this as their last shot at a high school education." I couldn't agree more.

Because of the Day School's parent/teacher conferences, Twilight students and staff were sent to the cafeteria to sit from 6:00 p.m. until 7:20 p.m. before being dismissed early. Since the students had nothing to do but sit, they were constantly complaining about why they had to be there. We told them about the conferences over and over again, but they still wanted to know why.

Despite our efforts, some students snuck out of the cafeteria, although I caught a few in the hallway. It was all a waste of time anyway for everyone; they had nothing to do but talk with their friends and look at the clock. I pictured one of them creating a problem upstairs and Twilight getting blamed for it.

When I sat at the table with the rest of the staff, Nicotina was discussing her theories on Nostradamus again. She talked about World War III and how it would occur soon when a retired Russian general united with a Middle Eastern prince, who was the third Anti-Christ, and how Napoleon and Hitler were the first two Anti-Christs and how the Wailing Wall would be destroyed and how five nuclear missiles would be launched at the continental United States as a result and how two would be intercepted and how one would hit St. Paul, Minnesota and the other would hit Washington, D.C. and how yet another other would hit New York and how since we were within the twenty-seven mile radius from New York, we would all be killed in a devastating hellfire, and this was all supposed to happen soon.

"I don't believe in that stuff," I said. Rhonda and Nicotina tried convincing me of the reliability of palm readers like Nicotina's mother. They thought I was a complete idiot. It was a long hour and twenty minutes.

-18-

I **WALKED INTO SCHOOL,** and all the guards I passed
reciprocated my greetings. They always did. It was a
direct result of me smashing the rude ones in the face
with my sledgehammer of kindness day in and day out,
leaving them little choice but to comply with my wishes.
After being with students that were so utterly rude and
unmannered, mutual kindness in the workplace really
did improve the environment for me.

Right before Block One, I entered the Twilight
office, and Faith asked me for Luther's work. He hadn't
returned to my classroom since he stole my papers, and I
tried unsuccessfully to have him suspended from school
rather than just from my class. He also needed a copy of
the book.

"He already has the book," I said.

"He was robbed," she said. "The thieves took the
book, his worksheets, and fifteen dollars."

"Why would thieves bother to steal his book and his
homework?" I inquired.

"He's lucky to be alive," she said. I walked out of the
office to get Luther's work. She didn't ask for Miss D's
work since she was absent.

In the middle of first block, Iverson wouldn't stop talking and wouldn't do any work, despite my ultimatum to him last week. He was going to fail if he didn't have all his work in by the last day of the trimester. I gave him new copies of all his assignments and a copy of the book.

"You're going to be enjoying this class again in the third trimester," I told him.

"You crazy as hell," Iverson said, before accepting my offer. He said he was already getting his work done at home and didn't have it with him to do anyway.

He focused his attention on a girl sitting at the front of the room working. I gave her the same deal with the work, and she provided me with the same excuse Iverson did. She turned around and wrote down her number for him. He looked over at me and began gyrating his hips when she wasn't looking. He was mouthing to me how he was going to get a "piece of that ass."

I always had to look away from Iverson because he made me laugh. He told me the other day how I was "a funny muthafucka" and how I was his "nigga."

"If I see you on the street, I ain't sayin hello," he told me. "My boys will think you a cop. And think I'm a snitch." I told him not to worry.

As I was going around the room, I passed Tanisha and looked at the screen of her cell phone. It said "Sex" down the right side edge and had a picture of a naked woman's breasts exposed as she was being bent over by a man. Their heads were cut off by the tight borders of the screen.

"Why would you want to look at that every time you use your phone?" I asked.

"It's just a picture," she said. "It's not a big deal."

Considering how advertising affects consumers, I wondered how that picture affected her sexual activity.

Suddenly, Iverson said loudly, "Time out, nigga. What choo think, you some kind of model uh somethin?" He had since moved his attention to another girl.

"I don't need no jailbird, nigga," she said.

Iverson sucked his teeth, and I was trying not to laugh at his funny facial expressions. I heard he had been to jail for drugs and gun problems a bunch of times.

Tanisha's phone rang, and I told her not to answer it.

"Sorry," she said, and proceeded to.

"Hang it up," I said. I said it again and again. She finally did.

"Who the fuck you think you is criticizin me and other people?" Tanisha said. "You're supposed to be a fuckin man!"

"I know I'm a man, and I criticize you and other people because I'm a teacher trying to prepare you for a merciless society. I'm trying to get you to act with some shred of professionalism."

"I said I was sorry."

"If you say sorry, you have to have remorse. You have no remorse, so don't say you're sorry," I said.

"You can't talk to people like that, yo. I'm a fuckin adult."

"It's this attitude that's going to prevent you from having any success in the world, whether it be at work or in college," I said. I was loud and irritated. "It's this kind of attitude that leads people to jail."

"A bunch of us already been to jail," Tanisha responded.

"Well, why don't you think for a minute why that is?"

The block and the confrontation came to an end when a commotion erupted in the hallway.

I went outside to see and hear Joe yelling and screaming at the top of his lungs. He was being separated from another guy, who was one of my students and looked furious. The other student kept trying to get to Joe.

Joe often flaunted his homosexuality. High school could be a cruel place, especially for homosexuals. I was an ardent supporter of students' right to express themselves, but this predominantly black inner-city school was making no effort to teach tolerance. Also, Joe made sexual comments to other male students. Even though it wasn't politically correct, I felt Joe needed to tone down his boisterous behavior. It compromised the safety of other students and staff members.

I tried to calm the student down as he tried to grab Joe, but he told me to, "Get out of my fuckin face." Rage was in his eyes. I wasn't going to take a punch.

The security guards arrived, and the staff tried dispersing the crowd in the hallway. Faith and I were screaming for everyone to get back to class. Thankfully, Faith and Rhonda were able to calm down both Joe and the other student in the office. To do this though, they asked Ms. Garcia and the Twilight nurse to leave the office. Ms. Garcia was furious and felt undermined.

I returned to class and let my students talk it out, because there was no way they were going to be silent and get any work done after the hubbub. From what I could gather, Joe said that Luther and the other guy were gay.

"They're faggots," someone said. A few others defended the other student and Luther. Someone hypothesized about an intimate encounter.

"You guys just have to leave each other alone. This

name-calling is so petty. It's not worth the problems it causes everyone," I said. A bunch of students agreed.

Throughout second block, students were called into the office to discuss the incident, and I could hear yelling.

Faith came to my class, and I said, "Maybe we should call the police for backup and send all the students home that were involved in this." There was "mad tension."

"They've already been called," Faith said. "And you don't want to send any kids home early, because they might get their friends." I didn't remind her that everyone had cell phones, and if anyone wanted his or her friends, they would already be waiting outside.

Before third block, I jogged down to Nicotina's room to hit her up for a cigarette. I was smoking more and more lately. Since the situation was obviously not going to end tonight, I decided to monitor the students smoking in the bathroom by smoking in the bathroom with them. Maybe I could gather information and possibly thwart another incident.

"Gimme a light," I said to Foolio. I took a drag. Everyone started cheering. Two girls even came in to see what the commotion was all about.

"You tryin to be a snitch," Foolio said.

"I just wanted a cigarette," I said.

Suddenly, Luther crashed through the door and started in on another student I didn't know. Luther was screaming accusations at him. The student swung his umbrella and threatened to stab Luther.

"Get out!" I said to Luther. Everyone rushed into the hallway and a commotion broke out. One kid tried to block my exit. I grabbed him by the shirt and tossed him into one of the stalls. By the time I got outside, Faith and Patrice, the security guard, were breaking it up.

By the time fourth block began, I thought it would escalate into something worse than fists. Some students thought homosexuals should be killed. Faith and Rhonda notified the parents of the students involved.

Before he left, the student fighting with Joe apologized for swearing at me. I accepted his apology before wishing him a safe weekend.

During fourth block, one of my students beckoned me to the hallway, and I went like the dog I had become. She told me about her science class. Since the trimester was about to end and Mr. Williams was on leave because of his father, and since only certified science teachers could submit student grades, the Day School science teacher was filling in.

And of all the lessons he could teach today, considering the incidents that occurred? What was the topic for class discussion? Bisexuality!

-19-

THE DAY BEGAN AT NOON because the teacher's union was sponsoring a luncheon for the Twilight teachers at their city headquarters. Last year the Twilight teachers weren't given an official reception, so this was the union's way of making amends. I tried to join for weeks, but it never came to fruition. The union reps were going to give a presentation and had all the paperwork to admit new members.

In the back of the meeting room was a table with food, so I made myself a turkey sandwich. I didn't have any salad because the bottle for the dressing was grimy. There was also an opened soda machine that was showering us with free soda. Diet soda wasn't popular.

I sat next to Nicotina, and we talked about our mutual excitement for the upcoming Thanksgiving weekend. Nicotina and her boyfriend were going to Atlantic City, and she was really looking forward to it. She deserved to have a wonderful time, and I hoped she had one.

Mariella was there with her husband. She said, "Benny told me the union was a waste of money for young teachers."

"You never know when you're going to need their

help," I said. She wasn't sure whether it was worth seventy-two dollars a month for her or her husband. I was never sure if they ended up joining.

Above Nicotina was a collage of photographs and headlines about the strike in the city a few years ago that ended with a better teacher contract. One newspaper cover of the picketing showed my own mother rallying in front of her school. That made me a legacy around here. Maybe I would be treated differently.

The union president began his presentation and spoke about the roots of the organization and the importance of the union and explained that the union got what it wanted in the last contract.

"I will go to jail for you and have been to jail for you," he said. As a union representative, Jack chimed in about the benefits of joining the union.

The union president returned to exclaim how the union saved a Twilight teacher's job last year. I knew it was our gym teacher, and Miss Carter was the one trying to push her out the door.

I imagined Miss Carter complaining about gym teacher lesson plans and insisting she write four long-winded ones detailing the activities of every Twilight gym period. It should be as simple as, "Passed out basketballs and organized games." Instead, they were tedious and wordy. They would be completely miserable like, "Took attendance in the classroom and chaperoned the students in a quiet manner to the gymnasium. There, basketballs would be distributed to the students. The rules of basketball would be restated to the students to make sure all students were properly immersed in the game. The students would perform drills to demonstrate their basketball ability and individual assessments would be made to properly record student progress. Games would be played and stopped to demonstrate how improved skills would further refine performance. Students would be quietly escorted back to the classroom where attendance would be retaken." There needed to be a more efficient way to do these.

The mere mention of Miss Carter brought a series of moans and sighs and hisses to the room. It seemed like everyone was talking about how she was the worst person to work for and what a witch she was.

"The union will protect you from people like her," the union president said.

The meeting moved on to the issue of back pay for the Twilight teachers who covered additional classes. Grievances were made. (Incidentally, after countless calls to various state and county union officials over the last eight years, I never received payment for my services, despite paying the worthless union a part of every one of my bi-weekly checks over that span.) Another was filed in the name of the Twilight teachers who wanted to write shorter lesson plans, like the ones written by Day School teachers. The union president announced that beginning next trimester they would be shorter. We were delighted.

"What about alternate certification?" I asked. The school was doing nothing to help us fulfill those requirements.

"We'll file a grievance," the union president said. "Maybe we'll organize classes in the mornings. We'll work on it *after* the Thanksgiving holiday."

I returned to school at 3:00 p.m. to find a furious Dinesh. No one told him about the meeting, and he was sitting around wondering where everyone was. I apologized for not reminding him.

I met Mariella in the cafeteria at 3:20 p.m. She told me that she and her husband were looking for a house, and she was excited. I was glad that she could find positivity somewhere. I hoped her relationship wasn't totally strained by their jobs and that they could find support in each other.

Iverson sat down and started talking; I had no idea what he was talking about, and I was sure Mariella didn't either.

"You owe me all of your assignments today," I reminded him, but he just kept talking.

"These diamond earrings are worth $25,000 each," Iverson said.

"They're at least twenty-five bucks total for that type of cubic zirconia," I said.

"You crazy as hell."

"If they were worth that much, someone would clip your ears off," I said. He referred to them as "frozen water."

"I took my cousin's car to school today," Iverson said. "It's got Sprewells." Sprewells were a type of car rims that spun on their own.

"Those muthafuckers are still spinnin even though we sitting doin nis shit," he said. He wanted me to go outside to see them, but I declined. I couldn't leave the school to see his spinning rims.

In first and second block, I planned to watch *All Quiet on the Western Front* since most of the class finished the book. Since Shirley was back, students switched classes quickly. She was yelling at everyone in the hallway to get to their classes and threatening some with suspensions. When a few students didn't listen, she suspended them. That day, she suspended six.

"Thanks for doing the best job," I said. "The school really missed you."

"Just tell me who needs to get suspended," she said. She was on the warpath.

Attendance was very high lately since the trimester was about to end, and everyone wanted to have their say before grades were submitted. The classroom got pretty warm for the movie, so I opened a window before we started.

Everyone was immediately disinterested by the black and white film. I couldn't sit here for hours quieting people down, so I let them talk as long as they whispered and didn't disturb anyone watching the film. No one was doing that anyway.

Alysha arrived late as usual and sat by the open window in a red sleeveless shirt.

"It's cold," she said. She closed the window. The room got hot and smelly.

"Can you just move to another seat?" I asked. "Or wear a coat?"

"I ain't changin seats, and I don't gotta wear no coat," she said.

"I have to open the window," I said, and I did.

"I'm gonna tell (Faith) about your attitude," she said.

"Then go." She left to do that. Some people were watching the movie when Alysha returned.

"(Faith) said you gotta close the window," Alysha said cheerfully. She closed the window.

"You need to compromise. The room is hot. You are choosing to sit next to the open window and complain. Why can't you just compromise and move to a seat away from the window?" I opened the window, and Alysha left.

Faith came over. "What happened?" she asked.

"Alysha needs to learn about compromise and not complain to you about every disagreement she has in the world," I said. "This doesn't require your intervention anyway." I was annoyed.

I returned to the movie, and Faith left. Alysha eventually came back and sat in the seat by the window.

"This old and in black and white," she said. "Why can't we watch *All about the Benjamins*? That's really good." First block came to an end.

As we watched the movie in second block, we were disturbed by a commotion in the Twilight office. I walked over to find Faith and two students, who were speaking loudly.

"Can you please quiet down?" I said. The students berated me, and Faith made no effort to stop them.

"They are talking about an important issue," Faith said.

"Can you close the door?" I asked.

"You can close *your* door," Faith said. I compromised and closed both of them.

With fourth block came G-Black's usual charade.

"If you don't pass this test, you are going to fail this class," I said.

"Gimme the fuckin test," he said.

"When you speak to me like a human being would speak to me," I said. I got the rest of the class working. He fell asleep.

Fifteen minutes later, he awoke to find his test on his desk. He took a pencil from my desk and began. In less than ten minutes, he finished *The Catcher in the Rye* exam and walked out of the room. I guessed he called it a day, since he never returned. I looked over his exam. He had no idea what was going on.

At 8:14 p.m., Jack told me to walk my students to the front door because the superintendent was in the building. One minute later, the students and the staff were all rushing down the hall. Hats were put on, and cell phones were pulled out. We tried keeping the noise level down. The superintendent was at the front door.

"How's school going?" he asked all of us. The staff gave the standard and blanket "good."

"You should all be thinking about how to make Twilight better," he said.

The superintendent continued, "Why weren't these students abiding by the dress code? Why weren't you enforcing it?"

"We support school uniforms," Jack interjected. The superintendent began pontificating about the prospect of school uniforms, so the rest of the staff snuck back to the Twilight office.

At 8:22, we left the office for the front door. Some of us left the building at 8:23 p.m.

The superintendent appeared and asked, "Why are you leaving early?" He gave me a crude look, like it was an educational travesty. Jack began talking to him, so I left.

-20-

IT WAS THE LAST DAY of the trimester, and the day was ending at 7:00 p.m., since it was the Wednesday before Thanksgiving. Many students were in jeopardy of failing. I made many deals and no matter what, the work was due today. Final grades were due on Monday.

The Day School students were having a pep rally, since they were playing their rival in football that afternoon. They built a float adorned with school colors and were walking it over to the other school. Supposedly, the cheerleaders would be riding in the float. In the last six weeks, four students from these two schools were shot both inside and outside their schools. Yesterday during Twilight, an announcement said, "Twilight students are not invited to this event."

Because of this, many students remained outside to watch the festivities rather than attend their so-called lunch in the cafeteria. Jack allowed most of them to leave for the game. By 4:00 p.m., there were only six students. None of them owed me work.

Mariella decided to show the movie *Selena*. I didn't want to watch it at all, so I sat in the hallway reading a book. Dinesh was doing his grades, as was the temporary science teacher. Nicotina was in Atlantic City, and Shirley was absent. Rhonda was working at another Twilight site. Ms. Garcia was working on schedules; Faith was on the telephone.

Jack was going to the boys bathroom periodically to smoke cigarettes, so I joined him twice.

For Thanksgiving, Jack and his partner Todd were going to their farmhouse.

"When I retire next year after thirty years, I want to open an antique shop and just relax," he told me.

Faith got off the phone and was apparently preparing a party for the students. There was pizza and soda, and cookies and cakes. Mariella baked a cake the night before.

"How can I help?" I asked. I carried some utensils and food to one of the rooms.

The students were psyched about the party. I was tossing Twinkies and cookies at students across the room, and everyone was in a jovial mood. Even Miss D's cousin was remotely tolerable. In the midst of this, Mariella took me out into the hallway.

"Who should I give money for this?" she asked me. I didn't know. No one ever presented us with figures for luncheons and parties, yet there were allusions to "contributions." We never got answers when we asked. It left us in an uncomfortable bind.

Suddenly, one girl opened a bottle of black cherry soda, and it blew up all over her, all over the table, all over the ice and all over the floor. Mariella and I started cleaning up the mess, but we found ourselves using too many napkins from the party. Someone got some paper towels, and some students helped out. The girl who opened the bottle kept watching *Selena*.

Mariella started wiping up the floor, and I told her I would do it.

"I'm used to it," she said.

"If that's the case, I'll do it." She smiled and returned to cleaning the table.

When it was finished, I went to the bathroom to wash my hands. Since there were no paper towels, I went to the Twilight office.

Faith was there. I found some paper towels buried in one of the crevices of the room.

"Who is paying for these lunches?" I asked. "Are we supposed to be paying? No one knows what to do."

"There's going to be another party for Christmas. You should just put some money in an envelope for that," she said. She reiterated how it was going to be "a lot of food." I surmised it would be a pricey event.

"How much do you want me to give you?" I asked. I was getting frustrated.

"That's up to you," she said. She wouldn't give me a number when I asked again.

I left the office; I didn't like being put in this position. I imagined the sewing circle counting the donations and making comments. Frankly, I didn't want to give a cent toward anything for some of the terrible people here. I couldn't rationalize paying money for food for people who were so utterly despicable toward me.

"What should we do with the rest of the food?" I asked Faith.

"Give it to the janitors," she said. That was actually a great idea.

I brought some pizza, soda and desserts into one of the rooms Rosa was working in. She said she liked the chocolate chip cookies the most. I got her another bag.

At one point, I was walking down the hall with a pizza box.

"What's in the box?" one student asked.

"Spare ribs," I said sarcastically.

"Don't play me, I'll slap the shit outta you," she said. She smiled. I kinda smiled back. She wasn't serious or being mean, but at what point must I not object to every sentence that comes out of a student's mouth?

We dismissed the students but were stuck hanging around for another ten minutes because Miss Carter might be stopping by.

I found a yellow book, and it said G-Black on the binding. Inside, it read: THIS BOOK BELONGS TO. In case he lost it, someone could return it to him.

In this space, he wrote MY NUTTS IN YOUR MOUTH. So in one sense, the book belonged to his nuts in my mouth. Sweet.

III.

The Next Session

-1-

THE SECOND TRIMESTER WAS UPON US, and my official schedule had me teaching English 1 and 3 during the first block and English 2 and 3 in the remaining three blocks. Some of the students taking English 1 were taking English 2 but weren't taking English 3. Most students needed to make up one English class or another. I began reading novels on the first day because I wanted to get my students into a routine right away.

I decided on *Great Expectations* in English 1 and 3, since the rosters of each didn't overlap, and *The Great Gatsby* in English 2. A bunch of students were going to be reading both. *Great Expectations* was almost 500 pages long and would take the entire trimester. Our novel options were limited by an older bookroom.

To my new students, I would say something like, "Reading (insert book title here) is the only way you're going to pass this class, but you will have an hour a day to work on it. And I'll be here to help you along the way." I thought that if they understood my expectations, we would begin on the right foot. Most of them immediately got to work.

There were some old faces, and some new ones. I

planned on giving everyone a clean slate. You couldn't hold grudges against students. Your job was to give them another shot.

I was somewhat overcome by optimism that the trimester was going to run smoothly. Students were more regimented to school. Everyone kind of knew what to expect from everyone; we had time to figure that out. In the first trimester, they were returning from their summers into a school with an entirely new staff. I hoped some of them came to the realization that they were going to have to work to pass my class. I figured in the third trimester, everyone would be so excited about graduating and about the summer that they would forget to do any work. And that would be rough on the staff. But who was I to try to predict the future?

Grades were due, and I was forced to make many decisions because so many students were going to fail. The total failure rate for my classes was twenty-five percent, and there was no way for me to be any kinder.

Since I taught World Literature, Journalism and English, there was potential to take and fail three classes. Some did. I warned them so many times about it. I pulled so many of them out of other classes and from the bathroom and the Twilight office when they were supposed to be doing work in my class. Maybe now they would better understand their responsibilities.

I feared student failures would result in an investigation into my grading policies and my assignments rather than on the students' usual cycle of doing absolutely nothing in school districts that continued to promote them again and again while giving them numerous second chances. I thought many students believed they wouldn't fail, so I hoped when some of them saw their actual grades, they would finally become better students.

There were some students who legitimately completed their assignments. I gave them extra credit points on their final grades because they deserved to be rewarded for doing fine work in a difficult environment. I was much nicer with my grades in the Journalism and World Literature electives than in English. Generally, the students with the decent grades were decent people as well and not consistently disrespectful to me.

Then there were the students who didn't show up at all. They're on the rosters and the bubble sheets, but they're never in school. They counted as failures.

Then there were the students who missed a lot of class but asked if they could make up their work so they could pass. I always let them, although there were policies that required them to be in school. I figured that if they were willing to make up the work, then I would make the concession. I spoke about it with Nicotina, and she was more stringent in her policies. She also had fewer students. It seemed like everyone had to take English.

Then there were the students who attended class and did all the work, but the quality of the work was poor. I could legitimately fail these students because they had really low grades, but they did try and generally behave. Failing them and making them take the class again wouldn't really benefit them in the long run. They were part of a system I couldn't change, and they needed to graduate. I hoped their attitudes would help them get jobs rather than lead to jail or death, which were prospects for many of them. Demanding more from this group would be too much.

Shenequa was my best student and had the best attitude the entire trimester. Her grades were in the mid-to-high 90s. She said she wanted to be a teacher, and I thought she could do a great job. She was interested in college, and I was trying to get her to attend right away rather than wait, because people who waited found it harder to go back once they became acclimated to the working world.

"But we need to make money now," said a number of students.

"You need to figure out a way to do both. People who get more schooling make more money," I would say. I even showed students some statistics.

Tanisha, whose mouth was one of the nastiest but whose work was decent, got low 90s in her electives and a low 80 in English. She was good friends with Shenequa, and they both wanted to go to college. I advised them to get applications for local schools and find out about the SAT so they could take it. Maybe they could even get some financial aid, but they needed to do that kind of research on their own. I offered to help them.

Miss D passed English with the minimum grade of 70 and also passed Journalism. I failed her in World Literature because her work was so poor. She probably thought she would pass all her classes since her mother complained. Miss Carter recommended that I pass her, but that was "off the record."

"Failing her is going to give you problems," said Ms. Garcia. I agreed, but I knew I could and should take a stand on her World Literature grade.

Destiny, since she made up her work, passed my classes with grades in the 70s. I failed the Queen.

G-Black, who told me he wouldn't fail and made threats about what would happen if he did, passed for the work he did in the first half of the trimester. He got a 70. At least he had a job already.

I gave the same grade to Iverson because he acted

civilly toward me and did some work, which was probably more than he ever did before

When I told him his grade, he said he deserved an 80. I told him I deserved a raise.

-2-

ON MY WAY FROM THE LIBRARY at 3:05 p.m., I went to the Twilight office to make copies before cafeteria duty with Mariella. Dinesh was using the machine.

Ms. Garcia had her work spread across the math office table. The past tensions involving these rooms and our staff and the math staff disappeared, since we needed the space for our growing staff. Most of the math teachers were gone when we were here anyway.

Ms. Garcia was inundated with the student schedule problems. Many insisted that they had already passed their scheduled classes, but naturally there was no written proof. Some questioned the reliability of their transcripts. Others failed to realize that failing a class years ago didn't mean they received credit for it. There were also ten new students.

Miss D's cousin came into the office to complain to Ms. Garcia about his schedule. He turned to me and asked, "You goin to court tomorrow?"

"I don't think so," I said, before I had a chance to stop myself. I wished I didn't reveal how out of the loop I was. All I could think of was missing Miss D's hearing and that resulting in my complaint, as well as the charges

I imagined she had against her, being dropped. I quickly grabbed my possessions and bee-lined to find the cop who took my deposition. He was just about to enter his office.

"Am I supposed to be in court tomorrow for (Miss D)? I heard about it from her cousin of all people," I said. "I didn't get anything in the mail." I was thinking that if I was sent anything, the school could have easily lost it, since I didn't have a personal mailbox.

The cop called around and tried to help, so I waited patiently, although I was going to be late for cafeteria duty. I heard Shirley's voice in the hallway. I didn't want anyone to see me in the cop's office, so I shut the door.

I learned that there was indeed a court date for Miss D tomorrow, and that she had another in three weeks. I wouldn't have to attend either. The cop also gave me the number for the juvenile district attorney.

"You should give the D.A. a call," he said. "He's probably going to want to reach you anyway."

I thanked him, left the office, and went downstairs to the cafeteria to apologize to Mariella for being late. She understood. We talked a bit, and then Dinesh arrived at 4:00 p.m.

I went to Nicotina's classroom for Current Events, and she was speaking with the gym teacher. No students had arrived.

"You and Mariella need to send them up after cafeteria duty," Nicotina said. We forgot.

Current Events was a colossal waste of time. Sometimes there was tutoring for the state exam, and sometimes there wasn't; there was never a consistent student regimen for anything. Today, there was a male English teacher doing the review. What happened to the other woman?

Students went where they wanted to: the Twilight office, the bathrooms, the hallways, and other classrooms before the first block began. If they showed up late for tutoring, they were not allowed in, so they ended up wandering the halls or hanging out with their friends. I was sure they preferred being late. I was unsure if any staff members knew where every student was supposed to be.

"(Miss D) has court tomorrow," Nicotina said.

"I know."

"You better be careful. She may accuse you of sexual harassment."

"That would be great," I said sarcastically. I couldn't imagine Miss D actually lying to the police after having these charges brought against her. Then again…

I tried not to worry about it.

"Without her here, classes would be much smoother," I said. Nicotina and the gym teacher agreed. The gym teacher had my back because she told me she did, and Nicotina knew how difficult our jobs were when no one was held accountable for his or her terrible behavior. I didn't blame Nicotina for not caring too much. There were so many problems, and we were just trying to keep our heads above water.

In Block One, one girl blacked out because I told her to get to work. She chose to berate me.

"You should take a moment to remember the miracle of the last trimester that let you just squeak by," I said. She failed to see the significance of the recollection. We had a distracting back and forth, but I stood my ground.

She left to talk to Faith. Faith returned and asked, "What happened?"

"The profanity. The racism. The refusal to do work.

The disturbance of the education of others. Pick one."
Faith left.

"You gonna get fired, everyone's complainin about you," Kia said. "You got one more chance." She reiterated the concept of this *chance*.

I brought order to the class, and everyone got to reading *Great Expectations*. It gave me time to reread parts of *The Great Gatsby*, answer a bunch of student questions, and take some notes about the day's events for my diary.

Most students were late for Block Two. Because of the scheduling problems, some students spent time in the hallways, which slowed down the other students who needed to go to class. I walked back and forth trying to get my students to class and getting the work to the students who showed up.

There were some students in the bathroom, and when I entered to retrieve them, they reeked of alcohol.

"Can't you at least chew a piece of gum?" I asked, before returning to my classroom. I shut the door.

Moments later, I heard a disturbance. I looked down the hall to see Shirley trying to put Iverson into a little garbage can. It was crazy, although I hoped he got stuffed in.

Soon Iverson walked into my second block class, but I had little patience. Since he didn't have a pass, I grabbed him by the jacket and tossed him into the hallway. He got one and returned.

"I need to wait here," he pleaded. "(Shirley)'s gonna suspend me for being in the hall." I looked down the hall and saw Jack and Shirley speaking to the male educational consultant from teacher training. That seemed like so long ago.

Iverson became distracting, since he had no

assignment to complete. Once they left the hallway, I told him to leave.

In the third block, the consultant entered my class and asked how I was doing.

"It's been a roller coaster," I said. He gesticulated up and down with his hands.

I told him what books we read, and he asked for my email address. His female colleague taught one of the same books for a special education class and wrote a paper about it. He wanted to email it to me.

"Can I stay and observe?" he asked.

"Take a seat," I said.

"I'll be back in a few minutes," he said. Third block was my worst, since both G-Black and Kia were in it and caused the most distractions.

I have reminded them: "You're going to read this book all trimester and the only way you're going to pass is if you work every day and not be disruptive."

"I'm gonna pass no matter what," G-Black told me. "I told you I was gonna pass last trimester and I did." G-Black already missed his first assignment.

Once the students began working, Iverson arrived. I referred to his passing grade as a "gift."

"You crazy as hell," he said.

Iverson was soon demanding five dollars from me, since I made him leave a deposit for the book he borrowed over the weekend. He didn't mention the assignments he failed to turn in. He was the only student that I made leave a deposit, and he was the only student who returned a book.

"Gimme my five dollas," he said. I checked my pockets and had only three. I always left my wallet in the car because I thought it would get stolen and then someone would have all my personal information.

"Take this," I said. "I'll give you the rest tomorrow."

"Get my money now," he said.

"Go bounce," I told him.

Suddenly to the class, he yelled, "He sellin me dirt." Dirt was low-grade marijuana. "He hasn't paid up for his bag." The comments themselves were hypocritical.

"That's *exactly* why I'm giving you money," I said, sarcastically, to the class. He left.

The southern consultant returned and took a seat in the back and in front of G-Black.

"So what are the police doing in the classroom?" Kia asked him.

"I'm not a member of the police force," he said.

"Yeah you are," she said.

"No, he's not," I said. She wanted to keep talking about it, but I went to her desk and whispered, "Please be quiet, and get to work. Stop ruining other people's education."

"Stop swearing at me," she yelled. I returned to my desk.

Everyone was working, and I began organizing the material on my desk. I realized my Gatsby worksheets were gone, as were my lesson plans. Some notes for a future diary entry were also missing. I had no idea where they went. It was impossible to watch my possessions at every moment. I tried backtracking to remember who could have done it. Was it Iverson? Maybe. But, maybe he didn't. I considered many diabolical scenarios.

For some reason, I remembered a few months back when Marvin and Foolio were telling me how they fought other guys. One of them would get in the face of the other guy, and the other person would smash him on the side of the head. I wondered who the decoy was in my case. What was the distraction?

Faith stormed into the classroom waving a paper.

"So who am I, Shirley or Faith?" she screamed. My face started to redden.

"Where'd you get that?" I asked.

"One of the students found it and brought it to the office because it had no name on it," she said. There was no way any student would ever do such a thing. Whenever I returned work, they mostly left it on their desks or threw it in the garbage. It didn't matter that the study guides were helpful for future exams. And then it was me at the end of the trimester making grade concessions because I couldn't fail everyone that deserved it.

"I really think we should speak about this in the hallway and not in my classroom," I said to Faith. All the kids were watching. She continued berating me.

"I may not have all of your fancy degrees, but I know what you're up to. I have never disrespected you before, but I will never respect you again!" she said.

The students cheered and hooted. It was very difficult remaining silent while being humiliated. I didn't want to stoop to her level.

"I will never support you in this school again," she said. "I'm going to show this to Miss Carter and the Board of Education." She left the room. At some point after, the consultant exited out the back door without saying a word. The students were still cheering. I looked at the clock. There was at least another hour and a half left.

Facing the students and getting them to do work now was virtually impossible in the wake of Faith's blatant display of unprofessionalism. She waved the paper as she spoke. Maybe I should have snatched it. Maybe she already made copies of it. I didn't care what she read; it was all true. All I was doing was recounting past events. I tried regaining my composure.

"See, you white fuckin bitch," G-Black said, "now you know niggas run this muthafuckin school." Everyone started cheering and hooting again. I couldn't look anyone in the face. I wished the day would end, but there was no escape.

"Can you please end your racism?" I asked G-Black. "It must feel great to yell at a teacher." I was upset.

"Why don't you call me a nigga?" he said.

"It's racists like you that are ruining the fabric of society," I said.

"Cracker," he said.

"Do you even know what a cracker is?" I asked.

"I'm lookin at one right now," he said. Everyone started laughing and cheering again. Kia's cackle reverberated through the room.

After letting one girl go to the bathroom, she returned to tell me how I was "tryin to get (Faith) fired." I wondered about the gossip brewing in the Twilight office. News of our confrontation was zipping from classroom to classroom, and who knew what it would morph into?

Between third and fourth block, I went to the office and asked Jack to speak with me in the hall.

"I was just writing a story," I said to him.

"(Faith) is upset over it," he said.

"This is just a huge miscommunication," I said.

"We'll speak about it later," he said.

I returned to class and couldn't stop thinking about who stole my papers, but my anger was subsiding. I was glad I didn't speak when emotions were running so high. Faith didn't have any authority to speak to me the way she did. I thought I couldn't get treated like that if I joined the union. I hoped there was something in my contract that forbid it.

Ms. Garcia appeared at my door and beckoned me to the hallway. She asked me some question, but my mind was so preoccupied that I didn't respond. I couldn't communicate. I wanted to know what everyone was talking about in the Twilight office.

"There is going to be a firestorm at 8:15," I said. I got angry. Students began calling me back to the room to answer their questions, so Ms. Garcia left.

I knew the outline made a reference to Ms. Garcia and how her job was sifting through transcripts and dealing with lies. She also had to contend with promises Benny supposedly made before he got transferred. I hadn't written about how a certain staff member was vehemently vouching for students who didn't have the paperwork showing certain class credits.

Jack dismissed the students around 8:00 p.m. Miss Carter was absent, and construction dust was seeping into the hallway and classrooms. Some areas were slightly foggy.

"Please return your work and your books to the front of the class," I said, but everyone walked out and left these items on their desks. I went around the room picking them up.

In the hallway, I asked Jack, "Can (Faith) please give me back the papers that belong to me? Can we have the conference now?"

"She has the papers, she's upset," Jack said. "We'll wait until tomorrow."

"Can I go home?"

"Yes," he said. I grabbed my jacket from the Twilight office without speaking to anyone and left.

I was so angry on my ride home. I didn't think I could

tolerate some of these so-called professionals anymore. There was just so much nonsense to deal with. I sent out three resumes before I went to bed. These new jobs were in suburban districts and paid much better. I had to see if I had options.

3

I TOOK WEDNESDAY OFF BECAUSE I wanted to think about my job with colleagues like Faith. On Thursday, school was cancelled because of a snowstorm that beat down on the entire country. I already had a personal day Friday.

I was sure everyone in school was talking and thinking about the incident the days I was gone, and it made me nervous. I hoped their imaginations were not as active as mine was. I didn't want to be ostracized for the remaining six and a half months of school. I wanted to deal with the Faith situation in a professional manner and imagined hypothetical scenarios. I felt I had a right to be angry, and that remaining meek and voiceless would only worsen the situation.

I returned to work Monday and parked in the smaller lot. Dinesh was walking up from the lower one.

"Where have you been for many days?" he asked.

"I needed an extended vacation," I said. He laughed.

We talked, but his accent made it difficult to completely understand him, and I hated asking him to repeat himself. I had no idea how the staff was going to react to me writing about them. Dinesh wasn't treating me any different though.

I saw Jack on my way to the Twilight office. He smiled and shook my hand.

"How are you, John?" he asked me.

"Not so good," I said. "I need to speak with you today."

"Let's do that later," he said, before walking off. I gathered all my strength and got ready for a confrontation once I entered the office.

Outside the office, there was a huge bulletin board that Faith prepared for the new trimester. "Characters Leading Students Forward" ran across the top of it. All over the board were cartoons named for different staff members. It wasn't original artwork; rather one student traced some characters. He just had a baby with another Twilight student. Maybe he should be doing something more constructive than artwork for the board.

Not every single staff member was represented, but naturally mine was there. My copied character had a burly head and eyes really close together. One of the eyes was looking up at poufy hair that was parted down the middle. Jack was a Doonesbury character that had a hat, was skinny, and wore a goatee and glasses. The only similarity between them was the glasses. I hoped people didn't really think my hair looked like my cartoon.

There was a hand drawn storefront, and students signed their names in its windows. Even the fictional setting was affected by the graffiti of the "A-Block," since someone tagged the wall in the drawing. "A-Block" tags covered desks and walls throughout the school. Some students even doodled it on work they submitted.

I entered the office after Dinesh and was ready for something, but there was no one there but a Day School math teacher in the math office. It was anticlimactic. It was 1:15 p.m., so I grabbed my books and darted to the library.

In the computer room, I found Mario, and we talked, while I settled down at a computer.

"My car got keyed again," he said. This time the culprit went along the side of the car and scribbled all over the hood.

"I can't afford this," he said. He just purchased a Christmas tree for the media center too. "I need to get another job."

"If I came out one day and my car was gone, I wouldn't be surprised," I said.

You didn't want to remind your students that your car was right outside the school. I told them about mine though because many had already seen me in it and mentioned it. I didn't want it to be a big deal.

"Did you check the cameras?" I asked. The lots were always recorded.

"Yeah. I just couldn't see anything," he said. We talked about getting new jobs. We talked about how students wielded a certain power around here.

At around 4:00 p.m., I went upstairs ready for a confrontation. I went into Nicotina's room for our faux twenty-minute Current Events class. She wasn't there, nor were any students, so I went toward my classroom.

I went through the Twilight office without really looking at anyone, although I knew Faith was there. Ms. Garcia was working in the math office.

"How've you been?" she said.

"Frustrated," I said. She talked about the continuing schedule problems and how she even had to speak with the principal. We both felt undermined.

I began making copies, and Faith came in.

"You gonna be long?" she asked.

"I hope not," I said. I didn't really want to talk to her, so I didn't initiate any conversation and looked away. There was silence for a few moments, and then she left.

As classes were about to begin, I looked through the contract agreement book I was given when I joined the union for seventy-two dollars a month. I was curious whether the incident with Faith was worthy of a grievance.

There were two articles that I thought could seriously be invoked. Article 6-1a stated: "No teacher shall be criticized in public." Article 20:2 stated: "Teachers shall immediately report cases of assault, physical or verbal, suffered by them in connection with their employment to their principal or other immediate superior." I thought she violated both. Why did I have to be in this entanglement with a librarian?

Foolio, Marvin and Iverson came in separately to find out where I'd been.

"I had personal business," I said. Marvin and Foolio looked at me skeptically.

"If you got any problems, you gotta speak to me, cuz I run this muthafucka," Iverson said. I told him I would next time.

At 4:20 p.m., the students shuffled into the hallway from the cafeteria. Mariella walked by and gave me a huge smile and a wave, and I reciprocated. I hadn't seen her smile like that in a long time.

As my class slowly trickled in, I learned three things: that Nicotina was absent, that Miss Carter was on indefinite sick leave, and that tonight was report card distribution and parent/teacher night.

Since the students were leaving early, the adjusted schedule confused everyone. Some parents came in to pick up report cards and then took their children. I worked in my classroom to avoid dealing with the disorder in the hallway.

In second block, a new student, who was a member of the A-Block, arrived fifteen minutes late.

"Where've ya been?" I asked. He mumbled something and went to the back of the room. He was one of those students that carried a hat and put it on the moment a teacher wasn't looking. I told him to take it off so many times already, and he apologized for it just as many times.

From the back of the class, he yelled, "Gimme my work."

"Try getting up and getting it yourself," I said. I noticed Faith in my doorway.

"Were you ignoring me when I was trying to speak to you?" she said to me, as I was across the room helping a student. I told her I couldn't hear her.

"Everyone at this school hates you," yelled the kid from A-Block.

"I don't care," I said to him. "Can you go get your assignment and pretend you're conscientious please?"

As the class was coming to an end, I heard that there was a man in the hallway from Atlantic City giving out jobs to students. I saw him earlier but had no idea who he was. He was a light-skinned black man with a security pass like the ones they distributed to visitors of the Board of Education.

Right before third block, a student came to tell me she no longer needed a college recommendation from me, and I was glad. I was having trouble with it, because I didn't really know what to write and didn't feel I knew her well enough. I couldn't imagine her dealing with a college schedule, and I knew she could have a really nasty mouth. As a student, she did some good work, but she could definitely have done better. I mean, it was Twilight.

I considered refusing but then envisioned the sewing circle talking about what kind of person didn't try to help an inner-city girl get into college. I wanted her to go to college; I just couldn't write a recommendation I didn't believe in. I didn't think the sewing circle would understand.

In Block Three, G-Black and Kia arrived late, and once I asked them where they'd been, I was berated as a "white bitch" and a "mutherfucka" and this and that. Since Faith blacked out on me in front of them, the class had been totally out of control. Today, I brought in a tape recorder and showed it to the class. It quieted them for a few moments.

Kia and G-Black started calling for Faith, who was in the Twilight office across the hall. "He has a tape recorder," they yelled. They were loud.

Faith walked in. "Don't be playing his game," she said to them. She left. Why wouldn't she say something about their behavior? Why wouldn't she want these students to actually learn something?

"She's gonna yell at you again," someone said. Kia and G-Black were yelling at me.

I had to go into the office and get Jack. He made Kia and G-Black sit in the office. The class was finally calm, and students were able to work on their assignments in peace. I could hear both students talking about me in the office. They were mocking me and laughing, and not getting any work done.

In Block Four, only two students showed up. While in the hallway looking for more of my class, Moses, the man from Atlantic City, introduced himself. After chitchatting a moment, I got the impression he wanted to sit in on my class, so I invited him in. He was supposed to interview with Miss Carter for a job coordinator position, but she was out, and no one called him to reschedule.

After explaining to one of the students looking for a job that he wasn't there giving out jobs, we began talking.

"Where'd you go to school?" Moses asked. I told him where I got my fancy degrees. He raised his eyebrows.

"What're you doing here?" he asked.

"I'm trying to work on patience," I said. "I'm a masochist." He laughed.

"Why are you a teacher?" he asked.

I thought for some legitimate answer. I said, "I started reading books in college and enjoyed it. I figured I could use literature to open up a new world for these students." It sounded good.

I told him what we read so far this year. "I don't know if any of them appreciated any of the books," I said. "Apparently I have *great expectations* for my students this year." I stole Jack's joke.

"The students appreciate you," Moses said. "If they don't, then they will realize that you are doing an admirable job." He was too optimistic. I got into more detail about my daily beatings and how disheartening it was.

"Maybe another job would be better," I said. I had no idea why I was opening up.

Moses started telling me about how he made mistakes when he was younger.

"And when I was thirty, I realized I had to take advantage of the only life I had," he said. That was when he decided to help the youth get on the right track.

"My brother should come speak to your students," he said. His brother spent eight years in prison for murder.

"He was innocent," Moses said, "but now he'll never get those years back because of the crowd he was involved with." His brother used to be a teacher but couldn't teach anymore.

Iverson came in and started rapping with me. When Moses asked him his name, he said, "It's Maurice Malone. Uh, Sean John."

'Maurice Malone, uh Sean John' got to talking about how he was going to be a lawyer and how he got accepted to Harvard, but how he "ain't goin there."

Moses explained how he applied to Harvard and was granted an interview.

"I didn't get in, but they told me that I could be more successful by getting better grades, since grades were used to evaluate you," he said. "You have potential to do more."

As he spoke, Iverson was making faces and looking at me, and I tried not to laugh. I could only imagine Iverson saying something like: "Who is this muthafucka?"

"You can be a lawyer if you want to. There are scholarships available so you can get an education," Moses told Iverson. It was positive, but no one was accepting Iverson into law school, and no one was giving him money for anything other than the illegal merchandise that he was involved with on the street. They continued speaking while I went to the bathroom. I saw Jack go in to smoke a cigarette. I reiterated my point about having a discussion.

"We will once the parents leave," he said.

After the Twilight day was over for the students, I found a mother waiting to speak with me. She was upset that her daughter failed my class and wanted to know why.

"She didn't do any work whatsoever," I said. "I gave

her assignments, and I told her what would happen if she didn't do them." I told her how I even gave her daughter a last minute deal to get her work in and how she didn't bother getting it done.

"Why couldn't you just give her a 70?" she asked.

"That wouldn't be fair," I said. "The other students did work."

The mother explained how it was around the anniversary of a bad accident suffered by her daughter. She mentioned a burn unit. I was sure this poor student had been through a terrible experience, but so have many Twilight students. There have been murdered and jailed parents, beatings, rapes, molestations, jail time for students, and numerous robberies. Every student can give me reasons to not do work. At some point, isn't learning a sense of accomplishment important in moving on from these horrors?

I eventually made a deal that allowed her daughter to make up her missed work. We decided on a date it would be completed. She also gave me her number to call in case her daughter fell behind again, since her daughter still had to take another English class with me.

With five minutes left before my contract said I could go home, Kia's mother showed up for a conference. I could tell by her eyes that she was angry. We sat at a table in the math office. Faith was on the phone. Earlier today, I heard her say, "You just gotta have a little faith," to someone on the other line.

Kia's mother was angry about her daughter's grades.

"You should be," I said. "Kia doesn't want to do any work. She is disrespectful, racist, and always late for class." Her mother was aghast.

"I've had to remove her from class many times. Then

she sits in the Twilight office and doesn't get any work done. Other times, she leaves class to go talk to (Faith)."

"Why do you have a tape recorder?" she asked.

"I'm trying to hold the students more accountable for the things they say," I said.

"Why wasn't I called earlier about this?" Kia's mother asked.

"Your daughter speaks with (Faith) a lot in the office. Maybe she can shed some light on the situation."

"He provokes them. And tape recording students is illegal," Faith wailed. Why was the librarian even at the conference?

"There is more that I want to say but won't in front of a parent," she continued.

I turned to Kia's mother, "We must use this conversation to focus on Kia's education and how we are going to improve it." There was a brief silence. Faith left the room.

"All the students say I'm unfair because I hold them accountable for their terrible behavior," I said. "When they don't like it, they go and complain. Their time is spent outside the classroom accomplishing nothing.

"Students are late and disrespectful all day and every day, and my job is to listen to it while trying to provide a worthwhile education to everyone else," I continued. "I go into classrooms to get students and into bathrooms to get them, and I make mistakes along the way, but I'm trying the best I can." Kia's mother listened.

"Getting parental support would make my job easier and Kia's education better. All these kids are adults or about to become adults. They all want to get treated like adults. Then they need to understand responsibility and accountability," I said. "And I am going to stand my ground every day." Kia's mother listened. She didn't look angry anymore.

"I'm here to help," I said. "I can only hope we can improve Kia's standing."

Kia's mother sighed. "It's difficult to raise a daughter," she said. "I'm a bus driver. I could barely get here tonight."

"Thanks for making it," I said.

"I never taught my daughter racism," she said. I told her the comments that came out of her daughter's mouth. "I'll speak with her about that tonight." She assured me that Kia's behavior and grades would improve.

Kia's mother gave me her phone number and her cell phone number in case her daughter continued behaving poorly. We shook hands, and the meeting ended amicably. I thanked her again for coming in.

It was 8:50 p.m., and the rest of the staff had left.

−4−

I GOT INTO WORK AND SAID "Hello" to Patrice, the security guard. Two days ago, she was selling Skittles for her daughter's fundraiser, and I bought five bags. I was glad to support her, because Patrice was a nice person and appreciative.

I signed in and headed downstairs to the library lab. Mario came over, and we recounted the individual insanities we were experiencing.

"Some of the other staff members are trying to undermine me," I said. "I don't think they should be coddling the students whenever they go to them and complain about how awfully I am supposedly treating them. Twilight was already supposed to be their last chance, but they're getting second and third chances every day."

Mario agreed that being a white staff member in an urban high school that was predominantly black was extremely difficult, because race was always an issue. He told me about an incident that occurred just yesterday.

Besides being a media specialist in the library, Mario also made ID cards for students. The school was enacting a new policy in which all students had to wear their IDs around their necks. It was to officially begin in January. Although the students were already given IDs at the beginning of the school year, the new policy led to a flood of students needing them.

"So this student came down to the library without a pass and with a hat that was not supposed to be on. When I asked him about these things, he called me a muthafucka and demanded I give him a pass so he could get his ID. You can't just treat me like this if you want me to do something for you," Mario said.

"I'm gettin my ID," the student said, before going to other staff members in the office. They also refused the request after hearing Mario's side of the story.

One black female staff member came over to investigate the commotion. She grabbed the student by the hand, caressed it and said, "What's a matter, baby?"

After the student explained his version, she said that he should take his hat off like a man because he was asked to. When the student did, it led to him getting his ID. The student was right when he said he would get it.

In first block, Joe came into class, and I gave him a bag of Skittles. He thanked me and went to work at a desk-chair in the back. Later in the block, I noticed him not really working, so I went to investigate. He made little effort to hide a sheet of answers to his assignment.

The problem with the worksheets was that sometimes students wrote down their answers and gave them to others. Since so many students complained that it was hard to write on one sheet of paper, I distributed additional paper to lean on to stop their whining. They then used this paper to make copies of the answers. Erratic attendance made it difficult to maintain a curriculum. It was all so frustrating.

The answers, by the way, were not always correct, and

some students copied misspelled words. I would be lying if I said I never copied someone else's homework when I was in high school, but at least I copied from someone who had the right answers. I put the right answers in the right spaces. These students were more concerned with just having anything on their worksheets. I wondered how often they got away with it when their teachers didn't actually grade their work.

Joe was upset that I caught him cheating, so he griped about how it wasn't a quiz or a test so it didn't matter. I discussed the word plagiarism, which was one of our vocabulary words.

"Copying the work of others is cheating," I said.

"I hate you," he told me.

"I hate plagiarism."

"I'm gonna pray tonight that a bus runs you over," he said. "Or a Mack truck."

"What kind of God is going to grant that request?" I asked. I hoped his prayers weren't answered. I hoped he enjoyed the Skittles. It irritated him enough to go to the Twilight office in a huff. I was sure he was complaining to the sewing circle about how oppressive the white teacher with the fancy degrees was. The next day he told me he didn't pray, so I was glad.

The Faith situation was taking a toll on me, and I responded by regularly smoking in the boys bathroom smoking lounge. A bunch of students were in there, and when I asked one of them for a light, they all started hooting.

"Take it easy," I said. Foolio was there. So was Iverson.

Since cigarettes were expensive commodities for those unemployed and poor like my students, students were constantly grubbing and even splitting one cigarette between two people. I didn't let Foolio grub one from me.

"What choo do, put bleach on yo shoes and walk on um?" Iverson asked. He was asking Foolio about his jeans.

"Yeah," Foolio said.

"Was you high?" Iverson asked. Marijuana was always a major conversation topic.

Back in the hallway, I saw Faith and decided to ask her for the papers that she continued to hold, despite the fact that they were not hers. She had absolutely no right to hold onto my property. She wasn't my boss. She was the librarian who was never in the library.

"Can you please return my papers?" I asked. She laughed.

"We'll talk later," she said and walked away.

Tanisha arrived, and I gave her a bag of Skittles. She was being much nicer this trimester, and her work was topnotch.

"I'm glad you are doing better so far," I said.

"I want to do well in your class," she said.

"Good," I said.

Once I got the class started on *Great Expectations* and *The Great Gatsby,* Shenequa arrived and went over to Tanisha. They never understood how rude it was to enter a classroom to speak with friends during class. It appalled me as usual.

I waited a minute and softly told Shenequa that she couldn't just come into the classroom. She softly told me to "shut up" and kept talking. It was disheartening to have your supposed best student treating you with no respect the moment she was no longer in your class.

When she was done, she said, "Nice shirt," before leaving.

In between second and third block, I went to the bathroom for a bogey. One student was eating a Styrofoam box of Chinese food. He had a few fried chicken wings and some roast pork fried rice.

G-Black entered, saw me, and said, "What the fuck you doin in here?"

"He's havin a bogey," Foolio said.

G-Black then shifted his attention to the Chinese food.

"I want some uh dat shit," G-Black yelled. He started tearing at the Styrofoam box so he could eat from a part of it. Food fell on the floor.

"I'm gonna put my whole hand in that muthafucka," he screamed. After getting some, he exited the bathroom.

In the hallway, Faith came up to me.

"We're having a twenty-five dollar Secret Santa," she said. "I need you to make a wish list of three things you want."

"Can I get back to you on this? I need to think about it," I told her.

My terrible third block class was soon upon me, although it had been much better lately. I could only dream that I was making some impact. Maybe Faith reminded them that it was me who was submitting their grades.

Students were reading two different books. G-Black was reading *Great Expectations*. He was acting better lately. He called me over.

"Miss Havisham's playin Pip," he said. "Estella's a bitch."

"I couldn't have said it better," I said. It was indeed a solid moment.

Sometime in the block, Shirley beckoned me to the hallway.

"You got your wish list?" she asked.

"It totally slipped my mind," I said.

"I need it soon because people need to leave, and everyone needs to pick from the hat."

I went back to my desk and considered what it was I wanted for twenty-five dollars or less, and I was unable to think of a single thing that I wouldn't just go to the store and buy, but I didn't want to fuel the potential of being viewed as a Scrooge. I couldn't think of anything, and thought a liter of Absolut would be a good gift. I wanted to add more varieties of alcohol, but I didn't want the sewing circle to review my list and paint some new picture. I thought about DVDs and wrote down *Pulp Fiction*.

Shirley returned for my wish list.

Between third and fourth block, I went to the bathroom and found Jack having a cigarette. We talked about the holidays, and I was unable to bring myself to discuss Faith and my papers or anything like that. I was just going to drop the entire issue because I knew I was right and didn't want to think about it anymore.

"There's an English teacher opening over at Todd's site," Jack said. Todd was his partner, who was a Head Teacher at another Twilight. "A union rep told me all about it. The teacher got transferred to an administration job. Are you interested?"

I told him that I would think about it.

I departed the bathroom to find Shirley in the hallway in front of my door with the hat containing the wish lists of others. I grabbed one. She went down the hallway to the other teachers. I opened the paper; obviously I had to buy a gift for Faith. I laughed out loud.

"What's so funny?" a few students asked.

"Nothing you'll find funny," I said.

"Who's your Secret Santa?" Destiny asked me.

"That's a secret," I told her.

I looked at the four items on the list; the first was salt and pepper shakers. I thought about restaurants that had this motif all over their walls, and I started thinking about some wacky options for her. I imagined a white penis for salt and a black penis for pepper. I thought about a holiday dinner at Faith's where these penises sat on the table for her guests.

The second item was a pocketbook. She wanted it to have a long strap. She also wrote "Bur" next to it, which I learned was her way of shortening burgundy.

Nine-inch round cake pans with spinners were her third option. I didn't bake cakes, so I knew nothing about them either.

Thankfully, at the bottom of the paper, she wrote, "If you can't find any of the above then a gift certificate for a book store." Now that would indeed suffice.

I went into the Twilight office at the end of the day.

"You're the vodka person," Jack said. I didn't write my name on the Secret Santa wish list, so everyone was trying to figure out who that was. He was correct.

-5-

YESTERDAY WHEN I AWOKE around 11:00 a.m., I called the prosecutor who was working on my case against Miss D. I wanted to "touch base" with him about my complaint, because the officer who took my report recommended I call a few weeks ago, but I forgot. After going through two underlings, I got connected to the prosecutor.

"She hasn't had to appear in court yet," he said. "There will be a few hearings before you are needed anyway. There was supposed to be an appearance yesterday, but someone called and said her mother was having brain surgery, so she couldn't make it." I hoped it wasn't really true; I wanted to laugh. When I got to school, I had no luck finding a parking spot, so I drove around and around. During one of these rounds, I saw Miss D's mother walking on the sidewalk as if she just exited the school. I stared and drove by in amazement because of how swiftly she had recovered from her brain surgery. I was delighted by her progress.

The construction on our school moved indoors the last week of December before Christmas break. Apparently, it was vital to remove all the fire doors to the stairwells. Without these doors, there wouldn't be adequate protection from the billowing smoke an erupting fire could cause. Those making decisions clearly frowned upon waiting a few more days for the students and the staff to depart for a nearly two-week break.

Since the school was violating fire codes, a twenty-four hour guard was posted at each stairwell. There were six on the first floor. I was unsure about the number of guards on the other floors, but I knew that these guards made twenty-four dollars an hour, not including the overtime a job like this provided each unionized worker. That meant to guard these doors it cost at least $3,456 per day and at least $24,192 per week.

The school was having problems recruiting guards for the Sunday shift. It needed a few people to sit in chairs and possibly warn an empty school about a fire. I wanted to sign up, but the idea of the bureaucratic channels I would have to cross to sign up was a frustrating deterrent. On a positive note, I noticed three brand-new metal detectors waiting to move into their new homes in some of the doorways.

Right before first block, I had a brief conversation with Jack in the bathroom while he had a cigarette.

"I used you as a reference for a job I interviewed for two days ago," I said. This high school was in a nice residential suburban district with groomed lawns and openness. There was no decadent crowd or seedy element pervading the grounds. I hadn't noticed a police presence.

Upon entering its doors for my interview, I found that it was the antithesis of my current school. There was no one in the hallways, because students were in classes where they belonged. There was no security force ridding the hallways of people that shouldn't be there. It felt like a serene and safe environment where learning could occur and an education could be had, which was unlike the atmosphere I worked in. I decided not to pursue the position, because despite all its positive aspects, the pay cut was unacceptable.

Teachers complaining about salaries was a cliché, but it was clear why the teaching profession failed to attract better candidates. The disparity of salaries paid versus the responsibility of educating future generations was alarming. In the next five years, a massive teacher shortage was predicted because of the number of anticipated retirees. Our state responded by lowering the minimum undergraduate GPA from 2.75 to 2.5 on its teacher certification requirements.

"I'll give you a wonderful recommendation," Jack said. He thought it was a wonderful opportunity and wished me the best of luck. He inquired whether I wanted the transfer.

"I'll think about it," I said.

Jack told me about how our staff Christmas party was cancelled since our reservations weren't made early enough. Maybe they didn't want me at the party. Jack and I still never discussed the Faith incident.

Since Rhonda, the social worker, worked at the other Twilight sites, I hadn't seen her much. My friend Niles knew about the situation with Faith and the sewing circle. Sometimes Rhonda was at his school. He spoke with her the other day, and when he asked about me, she gave a blanket, "No comment."

"He burned some bridges over there," she told him. "He needs to improve his relationship with the students." Obviously, she knew he would tell me that.

As Twilight English teachers, Niles and I confronted similar problems. There was one particularly troubling similarity regarding how black students responded to an

English education taught by white staff members. We both had students who asked whether we were going to teach Ebonics. Some openly rejected our classes as a white education they didn't desire. If this rationale was as widespread across the nation as it was in our districts, it was a major rift in American education.

On the Thursday before Christmas break, a few students were sent on a field trip to a Christmas concert in the downtown section of the city. Eleven students had permission to go, and chaperones weren't required. From what I heard, the ticket stubs ripped for admission to the concert would be verified later to make sure each student, represented by some number, was in attendance. The superintendent would be blowing his saxophone there as well.

Before Block One began, I went into the math office, and on the table were three partially eaten cakes and remnants of what I later learned was a Christmas luncheon that Rhonda attended. There was a plate of ziti and others with cold meats and cheese and a plate of warm pork.

I began talking with Ms. Garcia. Our conversation consisted of mutual complaining. She spoke very loudly when discussing various incidents, and I was sure that everyone considered her abrasive and didn't like her. She was pressured to give students passing credits for class. It must be overwhelming when most students cried about how past teachers and past schools didn't treat them fairly, while other staff members agreed with their pleas.

Just the other day when I entered the math office, Ms. Garcia was getting off the phone when she told me how Miss D's cousin just finished yelling at her about his transcript. I started surfing the internet on a new computer that recently appeared in our office.

Shortly thereafter, Miss D's cousin came in to apologize. Ms. Garcia wielded a certain amount of power because she had all of the transcripts and dealt with the credits.

"But I passed that class," he said. Ms. Garcia pulled out his transcript and showed him his failing grade.

"It's a conspiracy," Miss D's cousin said. "The teacher who failed me quit her job."

I couldn't listen to any more of his nonsense, so I returned to the Twilight office and its table of food. G-Black came in and explained that he had just spoken with Rhonda and she said he could help himself to the food. There were only a small number of plates and utensils.

"Please don't use everything up," I said, but I shouldn't have said anything. It wasn't my food and I hadn't even been invited to eat any. G-Black was about to tell me to fuck myself, but stopped when he realized that Ms. Garcia was staring at him from the math office.

"Bastard," he said on his way out. At least he didn't take more food with the fork he used.

I thought G-Black took my papers and gave them to Faith. I joked awhile back to Ms. Garcia that she shouldn't leave her papers unattended for long and definitely not overnight.

"I swear someone went through my bag when I left it," she said.

Fifteen minutes into first block, Nicotina moved to the classroom across the hall because the construction outside her window was unbearable. Late as usual, Alysha arrived and took a seat in the back.

"You gotta dolla?" she called out to a student across the room.

"You gotta dolla?" she asked someone else.

"Can you please stop asking people for money?" I asked.

"You gotta dolla?"

"You need to get a job," I said.

"You gotta dolla? You gotta dolla?"

"Can you please stop being so annoying?" I asked.

"You ugly," she said. "Fuck you and your class." This invited everyone else to respond with fuck yous to her. Once these replies subsided, Alysha individually asked everyone for a dollar again. Some people said, "Fuck you." One girl said, "Fuck you and ya dirty ass."

Alysha put her head on her desk. "I'm sick," she whined. "I need to sleep." Three other girls followed her lead.

"You all have to get your heads off your desks and get to work," I said. No one listened.

Faith looked in my door window, and I pointed toward the sleeping students, so she came in. She walked around and told them to get up and resume working.

"We're sick," they complained.

"I'll bring the nurse to you then," she said.

"The nurse just gives out pretzels and water," Alysha yelled. I thought that was funny.

Although there were only a few students in her class, I witnessed Nicotina blacking out from my classroom doorway.

When one female student was in the hallway, she called Nicotina a "fat ass."

"Be nice," I said, but not in the nicest way.

There was some conflict over someone stealing someone else's CDs and how someone stole someone's ten dollars and how that someone needed that money to get high and someone else chimed in about how no one should take other people's money if that's the money needed to get high. As the yelling continued, Foolio and G-Black arrived out of nowhere to watch.

Nicotina wanted two students suspended. I went to her room and brought them both over to my classroom. She was flustered.

Dispersing the students was difficult, and in my frustration, I shouted, "Come on everybody, let's just pretend we're putting tax dollars to work." Ms. Garcia was standing in the doorway of the Day School teachers lounge, while I was trying to usher students back to class.

Then another commotion erupted over the locked bathroom doors. Since the students spent so much time in them, the bathroom doors were locked sometimes, which was much to the chagrin of the students who needed to smoke and have a place to congregate. Sometimes Rosa locked them after cleaning them.

Miss D came down the hall and, after looking through me, set her sights on and confronted Ms. Garcia. Everyone needed to go to the bathroom.

"Who locked the doors?" Miss D asked Ms. Garcia sternly. "You can't do that. What does the principal think of that?" Ms. Garcia looked at me and rolled her eyes. Miss D's attitude was the worst.

Ms. Garcia was pushing for more discipline for the students, so this placed her at the top of the students' enemies list. She had a front seat to bad attitudes and constant disrespect. She was totally fed up with students violating her workspace with incessant problems, which generally related to their continued disagreements over class schedules and transcripts.

"I can't get anything done ever," she complained. "They go wherever they want." We both hated how the coat rack in the Twilight office was filled with student coats.

Ms. Garcia also despised how Jack let the students smoke in the bathrooms, which violated state codes. The hallway always reeked of smoke. I agreed with her complaints, although I didn't mention that I smoked there sometimes too.

The hallway disturbances continued unabated. Everyone needed to go to the bathroom. Everyone was looking for the keys to open these doors. Many students were saying it was illegal to lock the bathrooms. Finally, they were unlocked. All of the "boys" piled into the bathroom, and they had no intention of leaving.

I finally went in to get them out, since Jack was absent. I didn't want to ask the women in the office to get them out of the bathroom. The students were still smoking; my entrance barely affected them. I received the usual threats of how the students weren't going to let me out and how they were going to beat me down.

One past method I utilized to clear the bathroom was to simply turn out the lights and leave. It was somewhat successful. The students argued about who was going to turn the lights back on, so they ended up leaving since they were already at the door next to the light switch and finished with their cigarettes.

On this occasion, it was clear that Rosa just cleaned the bathroom, and now there were ashes all over the floor and in the sinks, and there were cigarette butts in the urinals.

"Can you guys be a little more considerate since this was just cleaned?" I asked. One student looked at me, smiled and ashed on the floor. He was the one who was always a problem for Nicotina.

I blacked out. "You don't have to be a complete

asshole all the time," I said. I walked out. I didn't care what I said. Someone needed to say it. I went back to my classroom.

I prepared packets of makeup work for a number of students. The other day at the library book sale, I purchased two three-dollar copies of *Great Expectations,* so I could provide a few students with books to complete their missed reading assignments. Lending books out and expecting them to be returned were mere elements of fantasy, and it became my burden to fill out the paperwork for them. On top on this, Twilight didn't even have access to the newer books in the book room.

I made Foolio buy one because he was really falling behind and not working hard. He didn't have the three dollars but said he would get it to me and that "word is bawn," which was how he and the other students pronounced what I believed to be 'word is bond.' That phrase won particular notoriety recently because it was written on one of the tarot cards left by the DC sniper that killed a bunch of innocent people.

Nicotina insisted that the students were saying "word is born," but I didn't think that made sense. Maybe she was right. Since many students failed to pronounce words correctly, I thought their bond was "bawn." When I asked them to verify what they were saying, "bawn" was repeated. I still thought it was bond though. "Aks" for ask was another common mispronunciation.

The day finally ended, and since Nicotina and a few other staff members would be absent tomorrow the day before break, we exchanged Secret Santa gifts. I gave Faith a gift card from a bookstore. I received a twenty-five dollar gift certificate from a DVD store from Patrice, the guard, who was absent today. Rhonda gave all the teachers a box of candy.

I gave Shirley a candy dish for Christmas with a card thanking her for her support. I placed it wrapped next to her bag so as to not make a deal about buying someone in the office something.

Before we left, Rhonda asked us all to stand in a circle and hold hands. She said a prayer and then wished us and our family and friends good tidings throughout the holidays. It was nice.

On the Friday before break, we had a small Christmas party for the students in the cafeteria, and most of the students were absent. Fried chicken, biscuits, tortellini in pesto, a cake, cans of soda, and bite-size candy bars were served. Some students were reprimanded for taking pocketfuls. All the teachers again wondered who should pay what. I gave Faith twenty bucks.

At one point, Rhonda visited each classroom to announce that the house of a Twilight student burned down a few nights ago and how his family lost everything so she wanted to start a collection. I felt bad considering I was confrontational to him the other day about why he was missing school and not completing his assignments. I gave her ten dollars. I wished I hadn't given the twenty dollars to Faith.

Near the end of the day, I was in a classroom with Shirley and a few students. She was making crude jokes about them and it was hilarious. At one point, they made fun of me because I was wearing my backpack. They wondered why I thought someone was going to steal my bag, but I shrugged it off.

"He's not stupid," Shirley interjected. "You bastards'll take anything."

The students were dismissed, I was tired, and our twelve-day break was upon us. Everyone exchanged Christmas hugs and Faith gave me a kiss. I hoped for a great New Year.

-6-

I T WAS 2003 AND we returned to school for a Thursday and Friday before our first full week back. Just like the last few days before our break began, attendance was poor. Some teachers and students openly wondered why we didn't just have these days off as well.

When I first got to the office, Shirley apologized to me for swearing at the students on the last day, saying that it was completely inappropriate.

"Nothing was more appropriate," I said as I laughed. She was really uneasy about it. Maybe she thought I was going to rat her out to someone for talking to them like that.

For my new look in the New Year, I brought back the beard for another run. When I first walked into cafeteria duty, one girl pointed at me from across the room, screamed, got up from her seat, ran out of the cafeteria, and then quickly returned.

She said, "Mista K, you gotta shave that muthafuckin shit off yo face." I guessed she didn't like my new look.

By the time the following Tuesday came around, students started calling me Santa. These were my retorts: "I'm not old like Santa," "I'm not fat like Santa," "I don't have white hair," "I don't have a flowing white beard," "I'm rarely jolly," "I live in New Jersey," "I don't have any reindeer," "I have no elves," "I wear not a red suit" and "I do not come bearing gifts."

On that first Thursday, Foolio came in during Block One, and after exchanging smiles, I asked him if he did his work over the break so he could be caught up. He didn't; he lost his worksheets. Destiny lost all her work as well. Most students completed theirs though. Others worked hard the first week back to catch up.

I was psyched that I had students working and reading, and I could now determine exactly where everyone stood. Threatening them with more classes with me was having a positive effect. I returned old work, and those who still made me wait weeks after due dates were held accountable and got zeroes. I didn't want any of them to ever think they could succeed by not doing their work. I was sure some succeeded by cheating or copying, but in another sense, at least they cared enough to do that. There were some students who didn't care whatsoever.

So it was Wednesday and I entered the Twilight office. Dinesh and Nicotina were sitting at the table, and we exchanged hellos. I removed my jacket, folded it in half, and placed it on top of the wooden shelf that ran along the right wall. I didn't want to keep my jacket on the teachers' coat rack with the student coats.

"Has anyone said anything to you lately?" Nicotina asked.

"I have no idea what that means," I said. I sat down.

"Have you heard anything about the other job opening?"

"Yeah."

"I've heard that you're getting transferred." Wow, I thought to myself. She talked about how that teacher had a tough time and just walked out. I would be taking over.

"They want to transfer you because of (Miss D) and your charges against her," Nicotina explained. "She still needs to take classes. Someone's gotta go. So what do you think of that?"

"I think I'm definitely going to get transferred," I said. "That makes absolute sense." Perfect sense.

The conversation ended when Mariella returned and I gave her back her chair. I walked down to the library thinking about leaving.

When I finally returned to begin classes, Jack approached me in the hallway.

"Are you interested in the other job, because it's available and if you want it, you can have it," he said. "The (Miss D) situation has taken its toll on you. The other English teacher finally got the administrative job she wanted. I'll miss you, but you'll be fine over there with Todd."

"When do I have to tell you?" I asked.

"By tomorrow," he said. "And the transfer will be expedited quickly, so you'll be there by next week. We'll look for a new teacher to take over your class."

The concept monopolized my thoughts for the reminder of the day. I knew that I was supposed to take the transfer. There was no reason to fight to remain here.

In Block One, the students were distracted by the Day School teacher subbing for our science teacher, who was expected back after he dealt with the affairs of his father's death. The sub was a black teacher from the Day School that many of them knew. I felt bad gathering my students from his classroom.

Joe, the flamboyantly gay student, was especially brazen lately. He never wanted to attend class on time, and I was obviously at fault when I yelled his name down the hall to urge him to class. Today, he entered with a scowl, and the second I brought up his responsibilities, he started whining.

"You have to work harder," I said. "You need to improve your writing if you want to pass the state exam." He failed it once before. In my class, he had terrible reading and writing skills. For the sake of his future, he needed to take school seriously and be more conscientious.

"I hope your house burns down and you end up in a shelter," he told me. Surely these ideas were in his head because of the student who suffered that fate.

"I'm glad you're thinking about me," I said. He continued to not do anything.

As Foolio was leaving, he said, "You enjoy givin brain?"

"I have no idea what you're talking about," I said. He sucked his teeth. There was a girl laughing behind me.

"That's givin head," Foolio clarified.

Before I could respond, he said, "You should write down 'givin brain' in the book you're writin."

"What book is that?" I asked, with a smile.

"The one you're always writin stuff down for," he said.

"Maybe I'll put that in it," I told him.

Between first and second block, Faith came in to tell me a parent was here to see me. I walked into the hallway and there stood Miss D's cousin's mother.

"My son is taking two classes with you next term," she said, and that was all she said. I agreed that he was, and that was all I said. Parents shouldn't be able to confront me in the hallway. There needed to be a better venue for parent/teacher discussions.

In second block, Rhonda's nephew came into class

with his usual smile and began "playin'" me. He came to Twilight a few weeks near the end of the first trimester. He showed me his 93 average in English in Day School.

"I expect a great job from you," I said. Passing was important to him. He completed all of his *The Catcher in the Rye* work.

His ambition had since plummeted, and he was often absent. A few times he signed himself out of school without permission and was never suspended. When he did show up, he just wanted to play around.

"You have anything for me?" I asked him.

"I don't have yer fuckin work," he said. He smiled; this was his idea of joking around. He was definitely going to fail this term, but he chose not to pay my warnings any mind. I showed him his terrible grades in my gradebook. His excuses and apathy infuriated me. Every day there was an assignment, and every day he got another zero. I told Rhonda about it.

"I'm gonna get it done," he assured me. "You better shave that beard."

After about eight minutes of this and after arriving ten minutes late, Rhonda's nephew said, "I'm out," and started to leave.

"I will get you suspended if you dare leave this classroom," I said. According to the rules that were never enforced, any student who left a class without permission got suspended.

As he walked out, he said, "There's no way I'm gettin suspended. There's no way I'm failin."

I went into the Twilight office, where thankfully Rhonda was parked in a seat. I relayed the present situation about her nephew. She said she would suspend him. I really hoped Rhonda's nephew regained his old form soon.

G-Black entered in third block and tried to captivate the classroom by sexually harassing the girls and mocking me. By calling me a "cracker," "white bitch," or "dumb bastard," G-Black worked diligently to get me to call him a "nigga." I just called him a racist.

After getting his assignment, he walked out and into the Twilight office, where he was going to try and captivate that audience. I went after him; he was already sitting down.

"He can't just leave my class," I said. "He has to return." Rhonda told him he had to go.

G-Black returned with a scowl and began berating me with "fuck you" and "fuck your mother." He told me he was going to "drop" me. Then he began his assignment.

Twenty minutes later, Kia began getting restless, so G-Black started up with more fuck yous. Students starting fighting back by saying "fuck you" to him, to which he cleverly responded, "fuck you."

Faith happened to walk by, and when I asked her to take G-Black out, he refused to leave the classroom until she babied and coddled him enough to soothe him into leaving. Minutes later, G-Black returned and sat in a desk-chair.

In the doorway, Faith said, "Rhonda said he has to stay, since when he tried to leave earlier, you didn't let him." So he sat. And did nothing but sulk.

During fourth block, Shirley came in and sat down at one of the desk-chairs surrounding my desk.

"I like this," she said, admiring my bunker. We laughed.

Shirley was somehow hidden behind a box, so some students couldn't see her when they walked in. Joe and another girl were talking.

"Please get to work," I said to them both.

"I'm gonna punch you in ya face," she said. "I hate you." She didn't see Shirley, who got up and removed her from the room.

When we briefly convened at the end of the day, Dinesh complained to me about Miss D and relayed her familiar attitude. I felt sorry for him.

Before I left, I told Jack I would accept the transfer.

-7-

I TOOK THE NEXT TWO DAYS off from school because I was hoping I would be transferred in the interim. I despised being the lame-duck teacher. Each day I waited for a phone call or a letter finalizing the transfer, but no official communications were made. It was difficult to continue onward when I knew that one day the students would be informed that I was no longer their English teacher, and I would begin working at a new school with new teachers and new students.

The trimester's grades no longer mattered, since I would only be giving midterm grades and not final ones. I felt as if I was duping everyone around me while I waited. I was unable to evade a gripping pointlessness.

The other day I thought I heard Rhonda singing "It's a whole new world" in the Twilight office, and I couldn't stop thinking that someone just told her the secret that I was being transferred.

Also, the other day, after I was annoyed by Joe, I asked, "Wouldn't it be great if I was gone?" He agreed it would be.

I could just imagine my students cheering and hooting at the news of my departure as they brandished gigantic smiles in the hallways or in the bathrooms during class time. Rumors would abound about how I had been fired and how I finally got what I deserved. Maybe Miss D would take credit for removing me from the school.

I was supposed to keep my transfer a secret, but I felt obligated to tell Mariella, Dinesh, and Nicotina. I told Mariella during cafeteria duty, and she wondered why the school would do that.

"Who is going to get the students out of the hallway?" she asked. "Who is going to teach English?" I didn't know.

"Your new school is supposed to be the best Twilight," she told me. "Working for Todd will be good also." She was happy for me.

I told Dinesh, and he was shocked.

"I always felt I could confide in you at times," he said. "I will miss you."

"I'll miss you, too." I said. He told me again how terrible and rude Miss D continued to be. He was having a tough time.

"You have to make sure to write everything down," I said. "Even if they don't do anything, they will at least have to respond if you keep reporting her." He told me that he would.

I caught Nicotina in the front of the school having a cigarette before classes began, and I asked her for a cigarette before I told her the news.

"The students won," she said.

"So they did," I replied.

"You're really lucky to get the spot at Todd's school," she said. Hopefully, she was right.

When I entered the Twilight office, Faith was there.

"Can you write me a letter?" she asked.

"For what?"

"It's a character letter." She didn't elaborate. I was able to get out of the office before giving any definite answers.

In the beginning of the first block, every student wanted to know where I had been, and although I explained that I was out on "personal business," it was unanimous among the class that I had been having sex. It also explained why I presently had a smile and a better attitude.

The talk continued, and one girl said, "Did she finally put it in her mouth?"

"We have to end this right now, please," I said. "If I actually did answer the kinds of questions you ask me, I'd be a pervert and not a teacher." The class quieted down and got busy.

Worksheets were boring. I wanted to be more interactive with my students, but I just couldn't deal more effectively with the absentee problems and the chronic lateness. The students had to be reading and writing to be better English students.

Since announcing how students needed to make up work to pass, some were making strides to catch up. I was glad that they were possibly beginning to understand my policies and were willing to complete their assignments. Any progress though was irrelevant, because I was going to be gone any day now.

Iverson appeared in the doorway. Foolio asked him if he wanted a bag.

"I can't smoke anymore," Iverson said.

"Who says?" asked Foolio.

"The judge."

A few students laughed, and I tried to hold back my own laughter as I escorted him to the class he belonged in. I got everyone back on task on *Great Expectations*. The class was about a third through the novel, but I doubted they would complete it after I was gone. My classes would be covered by a substitute until they found a replacement. The students wouldn't have any responsibilities. Maybe they would just give out English grades like they did with the health and science grades.

Block Two began, and the entire hallway reeked of marijuana. I went into the office to get Shirley.

When she got into the hallway, I said, "Take a whiff."

"It smells like weed in here," a few girls said.

I checked out the boys bathroom, but it only smelled like cigarettes and urine. Shirley said there was a "sweetness" in the music room that might have been used to cover the marijuana scent. Patrice said it was coming from the girls bathroom. As Shirley went to investigate, I had to get my students out of the doorway and back into class, where we discussed the current situation.

"In case you didn't know, drugs are illegal and cannot be brought into school," I said. Someone called me a "snitch." Someone else called me a "hate-uh."

"It's a crime in a school. It needs to be reported to the police. The teachers are responsible for you. You all talk too much about smoking and selling drugs as it is, but rubbing it in the school's face like this is pretty bad. Doing it in school shows a complete disregard for where you all are."

"At least the boys go outside in the courtyard," someone said.

"You shouldn't be surprised if the police come and search people," I said.

"They can't do that," someone yelled.

"I'm sure you have nothing to worry about if you

didn't bring drugs to school," I said. The room got tense; I was unsure of the validity of my statements.

Between Blocks Two and Three, Iverson came and wanted to complete Dinesh's work in my classroom. He tried to get into my room every period.

Although he had me for the first and fourth blocks, Foolio was in my room now as well. One girl was explaining how Foolio was her baby's father. She had no children but said this about two guys she liked.

Foolio playfully looked over at her and then at me. "If I was ya baby's father, then how come I don't get no kiss or no hug?" he asked.

Iverson chimed in, "Is that your baby's mother? Word? Is the pussy good?"

"Control your mouth please," I told him. He said he would.

Another girl walked in, and Iverson began telling me about how that was his "ass."

"Don't sexually harass the female students," I said.

"But that's my ass," he insisted. He told me the other day that he slept with six Twilight girls so far. I asked him to go back to Dinesh's class, but he ignored me.

One girl got offended by Iverson's treatment of women. She was loud about it.

"You're bein loud? You wanna be heard?" He was getting loud. A few people laughed, and the girl stopped bashing him. The girl sitting next to her made a comment that I missed. Iverson scowled at them. The girls both laughed and slapped hands.

In his own condescending manner, Iverson said, "You guys still high fivin? Shit."

A few students laughed, and I was smiling. Iverson focused his attention on me.

He said, "I don't mean to be racist, but do you get your hair cut with scissors?" I told him that I did.

"Literally?"

"Yes." I explained to him how asking me how I got my hair cut was not racist.

He pointed to my head and asked me if "they just put a bowl on that muthafucka" when they cut it. I kindly escorted him into the hallway and made him go to Dinesh's class. It was too difficult to refrain from smiling during the whole situation.

Then G-Black came in and said, "Give me my fuckin work." He was over three weeks behind. On some days, I would see him earlier in the day before he was absent from my class. When he did show up, he was always rude and disruptive.

"You can't speak to me like that," I said. I moved on to help another student.

A few days ago, Shirley took some students to the library so they could apply to colleges online. You would think it would be Faith the librarian's job. She was probably preoccupied with coddling students and putting me in precarious positions.

I didn't understand why G-Black was even allowed to attend the college event, because I thought it was much more important for him to attend my class, concentrate on his studies and attempt to graduate high school, rather than pursue an unreachable endeavor. His attitude would prevent him from remaining in college very long, if he happened to get in, which he wouldn't. I thought it sent a wrong message to some students.

As he sulked, I told him how poorly he was doing.

"You crazy as hell," he said.

"You've missed so many classes and so much work." He didn't deny this.

"Give me my fuckin work already and everything I missed."

"I'm not going to give you anything if you continue to disrespect me like this," I said. "I don't have to put up with being treated like this." He gave me a threatening stare.

"You're gonna get suspended if you keep talking like this," I advised him. I wouldn't relent. I wouldn't just give him what he wanted. I wanted to get Faith, but that would give him access to the papers and possessions on my desk. He wanted me to get Faith.

G-Black leaned on both extended arms and grasped the edge of my desk.

"Give me my fuckin work," he yelled. It was threatening. He wanted to intimidate me, as he probably intimidated other teachers before.

"There is no way you're going to get what you want by swearing and putting your hands on my desk," I said.

"I can grab all your shit and rip it up," he said.

"I dare you," I said. "Judges aren't very lenient to students threatening teachers." Our exchange was loud. Who knew how judges were anyway?

G-Black grabbed a pile of *The Great Gatsby*s and threw them across the room. One copy hit a girl. Another went through the doorway and hit Faith in the chest. Faith came in screaming at G-Black and pulled him from class.

"I'm gonna get you, word is bawn," he yelled as he was escorted down the hallway. Thankfully, he didn't return.

As the block progressed, numerous girls were removed from class and questioned by Shirley about the marijuana in the bathroom. Six students, including Miss D, were suspected. Such an offense was grounds for immediate expulsion. None of them admitted to it, but all explained how they smoked every day, just not in school. Rhonda explained that they would all be drug tested before they could return, and if they tested positive, they would be expelled. When the girls returned, the ones in my class were worried. I recognized the irony in Miss D getting expelled now that I was leaving.

Fourth block began, and as the students entered, they complained about how hot the room was. It was warm but not that intolerable.

"Take off your winter coats," I recommended. They wore them all day long.

I wanted to keep the windows closed because, for some reason, the air in the courtyard reeked like fish. Obviously no one believed me, so many students opened the window and let in the disgusting stench only to close the window again. I let one "hot" student work in the Twilight office rather than listen to the complaining.

Ken, who I once referred to as 'tic-tac-toe board, explanation point, question mark,' showed up. He was hardly ever in school. I wished Twilight would just expel him. He failed three of my classes last trimester and was presently failing two in this one. He did absolutely nothing, and his skills were deplorable.

Most male students ostracized him because he was effeminate and probably gay. When I told him that he needed to catch up on his coursework and how he needed to get here on time, he yelled at me. When some students blacked out on me like this, other students laughed, but no one laughed when Ken did it.

"Do ya work," someone said.

"Don't black out," someone else said.

To me, Ken said, "You're one of those bitches on *Oz* (a prison show on HBO) that likes takin it in the ass." I figured he was saying what other students said to him. Then he started really blacking out.

"Fuck you, muthafucka," he screamed.

Jack, thankfully, heard him in the hallway and removed him from class.

Like a bad routine, Faith soon came in to get Ken's work so he could do it in the Twilight office. I gave it to her knowing that it most likely wouldn't get done. Giving him a sheet of paper was a waste.

As we all walked out, Ms. Garcia said, "Thank God it's Thursday." I agreed. I couldn't wait for the weekend.

-**8**-

ON MY WAY TO WORK, I was driving in the left lane when a car drove by on my right, and it was Dinesh. I pulled by him and waved, but he didn't see me. In my rearview mirror, I saw him move into my lane. He signaled to make that move after he was already in the lane.

I later made a right and took a completely different route than Dinesh before finding myself a spot in the small teachers lot. I was a bit apprehensive because I noticed for the first time a sign stating that it was for "School Administrators Only." To think that I would get a ticket was too farfetched, since it was late in the school day and the day would be long over before anyone discovered the infraction. I wondered how long the sign had been there.

Since the exterior construction was complete, there was no longer wooden scaffolding hugging the facade of the school. To get through the front door, I used to have to walk below it. As I walked along the front of the school, I heard someone talking loudly above me. I looked to see three kids hanging out of the window of one of the upper floors. I looked at them while I walked toward the front door.

As I got up the three steps in the foyer to get to the front desk, I heard a woman complaining about how students were spitting out the windows. I hoped no one spit on me.

Two weeks passed since I thought I was getting transferred, so I chose to pretend I was never going to get the call. It would eventually happen. Jack apologized about it dragging on.

"I feel like an asshole," he said.

"Don't worry about it," I replied.

Jack explained how the woman who was supposed to finish the paperwork for my transfer had hurt her leg and had been absent. I also heard that the city was broken into grids, and since I was crossing grid lines to get to my new school, the process would take longer as opposed to switching schools within the same grid.

My classes were able to finish *The Great Gatsby,* and I decided to begin reading *Ethan Frome.* I doubted *Great Expectations* would be completed, since more than fifteen chapters remained.

One day, there would be no teacher to complete the novels or coursework I began. My transfer would be another disruption in the students' education. I wondered why the school would go to such lengths to help Miss D get her diploma, when everyone else wouldn't be getting any education whatsoever. She should be expelled. She could always get her GED.

The transfer delay meant that I had to submit mid-trimester grades. Grades were improving, since the students understood exactly what had to be completed to pass. I was holding them accountable, and they were becoming more responsible. The behavior of some vastly improved.

About two-thirds passed, and the ones who failed

mostly did so because of absences. Some failed two different English classes. The number of failures would have been much higher if I hadn't provided students with deals for missed assignments.

The marijuana incident involving Miss D yielded no punishment. I nonchalantly asked one of the culprits about it and was told nothing materialized. Threats of school drug testing were just that.

G-Black was never suspended for throwing my books and hitting Faith. When he later grabbed my papers and ran to the Twilight office to have Faith pry them from his fingers, he was never held accountable. He completed his assignments, but it was contingent upon me providing him with packets of missed work and not under supervised conditions.

"I've been playin too much," G-Black told me.

"I appreciate you doing what you have to," I said. Ms. Garcia may have had a word with him, since I saw them talking in the office a few times recently.

Every day we were supposed to sign in by 1:25 p.m., and I always came in a little late and signed in at 1:25 p.m. without anyone saying anything. I wasn't sure who came in at what time, but I was sure that everyone was not on time every day. At the other sites, there was a late book that teachers had to sign because the regular sign-in book was removed by the clerk after 1:25 p.m. We were not as formal with our sign-in policies.

Cafeteria duty turned into a complete waste of time, because no students showed up between 3:20 p.m. and 4:00 p.m. anymore. Some students were exempt for state exam tutoring, but others were not. Without a strict policy, students could just be late or at the store across the street or in the bathrooms or in the Twilight office or wherever.

Selfishly, I started skipping duty because it was basically Mariella, the security guard, and an empty cafeteria that could be cold enough to require a jacket. When I was unable to rationalize why I should be there, I *forgot* to go. Mariella kindly asked me to guarantee my attendance, and I told her I wouldn't let her down anymore.

"Mariella doesn't feel safe," Nicotina told me, since sometimes the guard didn't even show up. I felt like a total dick.

Supposedly, my transfer was a secret, but it was the kind of secret that everyone knew. The other day, the gym teacher wished me luck. It made me feel bad about not telling Ms. Garcia. When I did, she already knew. Jack told her to keep a secret.

I told Mario that I was getting transferred, and he was happy. To my surprise, he told me that he was also getting transferred, since the Board of Education made some mistake with the paperwork regarding his certification. He didn't have enough credits to even be teaching in a high school. He hoped to be relocated to a nicer elementary school.

"I'm gonna insist on it," he told me. His job frustrated him so much.

In the beginning of Block Two, Shenequa asked me if she could distribute some papers as she was about to.

"It's so quiet to read in here compared to last trimester," she said.

I was curious what she was distributing and upon further inspection realized that it was a cheat sheet for science class. I blacked out. I couldn't condone it. A few students pleaded with me about their innocence.

I would be a hypocrite to say that I never made a cheat sheet or looked over at someone else's test, but I never rubbed it in any teacher's face because I understood the consequences of cheating. These students failed to understand accountability. And the school didn't help matters by giving so many second chances. It was doing them little justice in the real world. Some of them would surely realize consequences when they heard their sentences from the judge.

In third block, a janitor opened my door and sprayed some chemicals on the floor in the doorway. Within seconds, a pungent odor filled the room. I opened the window for a rush of cold air, but not before a few students complained about having to stay in the room.

"Take it easy," I said. "Fresh air is coming through the window as we speak."

I couldn't blame them for complaining because the janitors shouldn't be spraying during school hours and disturbing the students in any way. Sometimes to communicate the janitors used the loudspeakers to call each other. It was another example of how Twilight students were treated poorly by the school.

During fourth block, Faith came to my door to ask whether she could disturb my class and pass out some papers. Since she already disturbed the class, I allowed her to come in. She began distributing prom information, an event that would not be occurring for four months.

Numerous students put down their books to look at the material. Everyone started talking about dates and limousines and parties. Faith left.

"Can you please read that later and get back to work?" I asked them to no avail.

I snatched one packet, and students got back to work.

Someone said that Iverson was going with the Queen, and I started laughing. They seemed like a funny couple for so many reasons. When I asked Iverson about it, he became irritated and started playing me by speaking in the white person's accent and ending every sentence with either "dude" or "man."

At 7:20 p.m., the students were dismissed because it was the third evening of Twilight Open House for parents and guardians. We came in at 1:00 p.m. Working extra time for Open House was rewarded with a half-day on Friday, which was Valentine's Day. Then we were off Monday for Presidents Day.

In preparation for Open House, teachers had to fill out individual forms for each student in each class detailing his or her progress. These were handed to Open House attendees or would be mailed home after. One girl's mother picked up her midterm evaluation but chose not to meet with me. Foolio's father came in, and I spoke with him briefly.

During a free moment, Ms. Garcia told me that she had to submit final grade forms for students who were supposedly graduating. Someone posted a list of our class of 2003, and it included a few of my students who really needed to shape up if they expected to graduate in June. It didn't help that some of them were confident that they would graduate without completing their academic obligations simply because their names were on a list.

Miss D couldn't graduate unless she passed the class she was taking with me. She already had a full course load in the third trimester. She was failing for not reading *All Quiet on the Western Front*. She spent her time talking in the Twilight office.

"Are you standing by your F for her?" Ms. Garcia asked me.

"I absolutely am."

"She won't be graduating then," she said. It was fair. Her grades supported it.

As we were leaving for the evening, we had to exit via another route because the janitors were cleaning the floors with very strong, bleachy chemicals that brought tears to my eyes. I wondered what would have happened if a parent had to walk through this decontamination to get to Open House.

When I said goodbye to Jack and Rhonda, who were in the Twilight office finishing a conversation, I heard Jack say that he would love for someone to write a book about Twilight.

Maybe someone would.

-9-

FOR THE LAST TWO DAYS, Twilight teachers had to report to the Board of Education for professional in-service days. The students had the days off.

On the first day, I arrived in the nick of time. Waiting for the elevator so I could get to the eighth floor took fifteen minutes. The slow elevator was such a blatant inefficiency in the system. Once on the elevator, everyone was going to different floors, and I was going to the highest one.

When we stopped on the third floor, a man asked, "Is this the fifth floor?"

I chose to remain silent rather than explain to him that there was an electronic screen above the elevator door indicating the floor number with a big, red digit. I wanted to ask him how he usually got to his correct floor when riding in an elevator since he was not attuned to the scheme of having the present floor displayed somewhere in the elevator for those occupying the elevator to see. He finally realized aloud what floor he was on.

I got to the conference room and found a seat at the back of the room. I liked sitting in the back rather than at the conference table.

The meeting began with a presentation by two women from the educational institution. I recognized one of the women from the summer. I was glad to hear the two women use the word "accountable" over the next two days.

They asked everyone "to consider the positive and negative aspects from the school year thus far." The women had an easel with a large pad of paper and a column for pros and one for cons. Jack was sitting at the head of the table with his back to the women. We were expected to contribute.

"The behavior at our site is getting better this year," Jack said. Replacing last year's teaching staff must have had a great effect. One of our staff members continued the positive sentiment.

The third speaker was a Spanish teacher from another site.

He said, "The kids are out of control. They have no respect for anyone. They have no desire to learn." He was bitter. After a pause, the presentation moved on.

My turn came. I chose not to mention the many problems with our site, since I didn't want Jack to look bad.

I said, "My students never read any books before, and I think I am succeeding in holding them accountable for completing their work. I made it crystal clear as to what is expected of them."

Soon it was Faith's turn.

"I don't like how poorly the school system is treating the students," she said. "There are no field trips, no lunches and no jobs that were promised. And we have no boss." She was referring to the absence of Miss Carter.

She had some points, but I couldn't agree with how sympathetic she was toward the students. It was easy to gripe; acting locally was all one could do. I didn't feel that she was making enough contributions to help. Rhonda spoke next and conveyed the same tone.

One sickening aspect of the entire affair was how rude the teachers were to one another in the meeting. Some teachers were having conversations, while others were trying to contribute to the discussion. Whispering was one thing, but speaking without even making an attempt to lower your voice or subdue a laugh was unacceptable. The teachers were the students here.

The conversation moved on to how we all needed to make more efforts because we were in an alternative program. Obtaining an education took time, effort, and work on the part of the students, and they weren't getting it. Making too many adjustments and lowering standards could never be constructive. To me, arriving to school after Day School was alternative enough.

As the round robin ended, I was disgusted by terms such as "success story," "superb," and "excellent." I didn't think the delusional optimism was benefiting anyone. People had to be honest about the situation and attack the problems rather than slap each other on the back for what I considered extremely small steps at best.

"We are an ingenious group of people capable of making real strides," someone said. Too often students were praised just for showing up. What kind of lesson was being conveyed when students got rewarded for showing up and not for their academic accomplishments? This attitude was truly depriving students of an education, which was the grossest injustice of all. I considered my own four years in high school, where I took four years of English. Twilight students needed to take English 1 through 4, and each class could be completed in three months and one week. How were they being prepared for the rigors of the real world? It was better than nothing, but it was too minimal an accomplishment. Twilight could never attain credibility if it continued like this.

Another issue raised had to do with how there were no special education aides at our sites. Our classes might have special education students whose needs weren't being properly addressed. Not only was it illegal, but it might also be the root of many Twilight problems and explain the horrendous attitude problems of some students. Subjecting teachers to such shortcomings was unfair.

The consensus of the discussion concluded that the Twilight staff was responsible for successes and the administration was to blame for not addressing our needs. These same cons were identified at our summer sessions.

Soon, we were introduced to the new head of Twilight, Mrs. Davis, who was an older white-haired woman with glasses. She was replacing Miss Carter. I heard many positive things about her. Her exact title was still a mystery, which took a certain zeal away from the moment. I hoped she was held more accountable for Twilight.

"I'm going to be taking a more active role," Mrs. Davis said. "Twilight is a wobbling boat that needs to have everyone working in unison. There are big changes in the works. We have the full support of the Board of Education."

She said the superintendent wanted our staff to be "thinking outside the box." The phrase "Let Twilight be Twilight" was repeated over and over.

"We have to let students do the work rather than have teachers emulating the same atmosphere of the Day School." She was vague. "Twilight in Newark was on the news yesterday. Why weren't we in the story?" Mrs.

Davis asked. I thought we were one assault or shooting away from the lead story.

"Our goals should be to get students more involved and interested in school," she said. She emphasized the need to have "student councils, guest speakers, special classes and projects."

She mentioned a quote from an education book that read, "How can you teach me when you don't know me?"

She warned that with "more flexibility to pursue these goals, we would surely garner lots of criticism. Some parents have said that they would never send their kids here. They think there is nothing educational ever accomplished here." When she was done, everyone applauded.

"What took you so long?" Jack asked, sounding relieved. Twilight needed someone positive like this.

The two women consultants explained that our lunch was going to be from 5:30 p.m. to 6:15 p.m.. This announcement was met with numerous groans and sighs.

"Lunch is always earlier," someone said.

"We're all hungry," someone else said.

It was decided that lunch would instead begin an hour earlier, much to everyone's delight. It was stressed that we all needed to come back on time so we could promptly continue.

One of the women began explaining how the sites would be holding a series of seminars for the students. A packet of ten was distributed; each site was to choose four and determine when they would be presented.

We had time to look over the packets before lunch. When we did break, it was easier to walk down the stairs than wait for the elevator, which would take at least two trips to bring everyone to the bottom floor. Only my friend Niles followed my route while everyone waited. We arrived back at 5:15 p.m., but it was 5:35 p.m. before we reassembled.

Our sites were divided into four rooms so we could write up lesson plans. The Head Teachers congregated in their own room. The two consultants walked around to the different rooms to give suggestions and check progress. I was stuck writing the lesson plans. Since I was the English teacher, I was apparently the only one who could perform the task. I didn't complain about the fact that if we divided the work, it would get done quicker.

"I am not entirely familiar with how to write these up," I said.

"Why didn't you read the manual that was given to you over the summer?" Faith asked.

I knew I would never be presenting these seminars at our site, since I was on my way out. I also hated these seminars. To have a worthwhile group discussion, there needed to be a respectful classroom, and most of our students had no idea how to act. It took the rest of the day to select four seminars and to read the rest of the packets.

We resumed writing seminar plans the next day. Our group discussed what role each staff member was going to take. I worked diligently, but it was pointless to discuss what role I would take because of the transfer.

"I'll just do whatever you guys want me to," I said. Over the next hour, I was asked numerous times about what role I wanted. I kept writing the plans, and no one offered to help.

When we reconvened with the rest of the Twilight sites in the conference room, Niles explained that I wrote my seminars incorrectly. He helped me fix them. In the end, it didn't matter, because no one looked at them anyway.

After we discussed our seminars, Mrs. Davis discussed the new Twilight direction for the third trimester.

"I want all the sites to develop a project that the students will work on each day of the trimester," she said.

In her plan, all one-hour classes would be trimmed to a half-hour, and the extra time would be incorporated into an Interblock that allowed students to work on an unspecified project. The Interblock would help develop a school community of teachers and students and provide time for speakers, assemblies, watching movies, watching the news, parties, and other activities.

Lunch would be converted to a homeroom where students could eat their lunches and teachers could tutor students who failed the state exam. It would be called Literacy Lab. Students who passed the exam would help others who did not.

"This is all a work in progress," Mrs. Davis said. "We need to all be flexible within this new structure." She continued by explaining how she had ordered display boards for student work.

"The Day School kids wreck our displays," someone said.

"We should strive for beautiful projects," she said, without making reference to the teacher's concern.

"I want the students to engage in solving real-world problems," Mrs. Davis said. She discussed how she was trying to get students boxed lunches since they qualified, how she wanted every site to have a web page, how she wanted teachers and students to communicate through email, and how she would be hiring a job coordinator to assist students with finding the employment they were promised for entering the program.

These changes would be initiated in the third trimester, because by then, every site would have fewer students since a bunch would have fulfilled their graduation requirements. The students were also, apparently, "obligated" to fulfill ten hours of community service. It was all a "testing ground" for what we were going to do with Twilight next year. While she spoke, some teachers dozed off. A few were reading magazines.

We were again broken into groups by site. The objective was to develop a project for the students to complete during the eleven weeks or fifty-five hours allotted for the Interblock.

For starters, I questioned how shortening academic periods for the nebulous Interblock could be successful. If students wanted to improve their English skills, they needed to be reading and writing. Reducing class time for a "work in progress" project just didn't make sense. Students needed to be working on more essential skills in a structured environment. The student project concept was too unclear. Supposedly, the Interblock would also be used for clubs, but there were no guarantees. Then again, if Mrs. Davis was going to be held accountable, maybe these ideas could yield positive results.

Our group had ideas for a trip to a senior citizen home and another to a youth center. Other suggestions included making dinner or presenting a puppet show or having a talent show with singers and poetry.

"I could bring in my video camera," Nicotina said. "The students could tape this and then edit it together and conduct interviews and take photographs and then we would have a presentation at the end of the year." She was being grossly optimistic.

Someone asked, "Are we going to have money for this?"

Nicotina suggested that the staff donate some. I almost laughed. In another conversation, Rhonda explained how Faith went to the hospital but was being forced to wait because of some doctor strike.

I offered little to the brainstorming session. Some of our students were gang members and criminals. What senior citizen home or youth center was going to let them through its doors? I understood the value of human experiences, but our students weren't up for these kinds of challenges. It barely sounded real.

Reducing class time would make teaching even more difficult. Already too much time was wasted settling everyone down and getting them to work. Cutting more class time would eliminate real instruction. I would try if that was what Twilight wanted, I guessed. And the mere suggestion of being asked to contribute money for any venture was completely unacceptable.

We all finally returned to the conference room to discuss our ideas. One group was going to make a giant mural of civil rights leaders. I didn't understand how the students drawing and painting were going to prepare them for the future.

The younger woman from the educational institution intermittently chimed in and called the presentation "awesome" and "kinda cool." Me hoped I speaked more better than that.

-10-

ANOTHER WEEK HAD GONE BY and my transfer still wasn't finalized. When I entered the Twilight office yesterday, Nicotina asked me if I wanted to contribute money toward a pool of tickets for tonight's lottery drawing for $125 million. I happily obliged, because I couldn't think of a scenario more appropriate than us Twilight teachers winning the jackpot, and one really had to play to win anyway. Nicotina conjured up an image of us all standing behind and holding a huge cardboard check. I found it entirely reasonable to think we were going to win.

During the Twilight day, students were already spending my winnings.

"Can I have $500?" one student asked.

"You're the best teacher ever," another said. The student had never even been in my class. Another told me numerous reasons why I should give him $3,000.

"I haven't won anything yet," I told them all, "but if I do win, I'll be spending money on a bodyguard to protect me from everyone asking me for money."

Before I could leave for the night, Jack pulled me aside to inform me that the paperwork for my transfer was in but was still not officially finalized. It was yet another communication about my pending departure that would be happening any day now. That night we didn't hit the lottery.

Today, the Day School students were dismissed early for report card distribution to parents and guardians. Because of their Open House, all Twilight staff started the day an hour earlier at the Board of Education. Our school day also ended an hour earlier. When I arrived at the meeting at 1:00 p.m., the only seat available was next to Faith.

All four Twilight staffs were broken into two groups, and each group had to present a seminar modeled by the educational institution. KetchupBoots was our moderator. We discussed a speech given by Dr. Martin Luther King. The seminar ran flawlessly since it was a group of teachers, not students. I felt the educational institution was in denial about how disruptive a student seminar could be. We were dismissed at 1:25 p.m.

While on the computer back at the Twilight office, Faith and Shirley discussed how Dinesh, Jack, and I should bring something on Friday to celebrate Valentine's Day. Mariella was working at the table. The conversation was thankfully broken up by the appearance of Miss D's cousin, who wanted to order Chinese food and have it delivered. Lately, students were getting lunch delivered to the office.

The school was supposed to provide lunch, but cafeteria service ended way before Twilight. The vending machines that were supposed to be providing sustenance were empty, unplugged, and turned to face the wall. It surely diminished the odds of their glass fronts getting smashed.

I hated the Chinese food system because of the lingering smell that pervaded my classroom. Students who came late missed their designated time to eat, so when they arrived, their delivery was waiting for them in the classrooms. The soiled containers and utensils in the garbage emanated the pungent remains of a Chinese lunch. Thankfully, Hero the janitor emptied my garbage can numerous times each evening. I didn't like teaching in this makeshift cafeteria.

Only four students showed for the first block. I gave them their assignments. Minutes later, Iverson arrived to announce that he "bust a nigga's ass." Sometimes I couldn't distinguish if his announcements were for everyone, someone specific, no one at all or just for me.

"Another offense?" I asked. "Sounds like a new addition to your criminal record." This softened his swagger. He gave me his scowl and looked at my pants.

"Cords, huh?" he said. "I used to have those when I was two and shit. Wearin em to church and shit." I congratulated him.

"You wanna go down to the basement and play basketball with me and Marvin?" he asked.

"I would like to, but I happen to be in the middle of the English class I'm paid to teach," I said. I didn't have flexible options allowing me to just leave my class and do whatever I wanted to do. He had those options.

"How many threes I hit last time?" he asked.

"You hit a bunch," I said.

One day weeks ago, on a day with many absent students, I agreed to take a group to the gym so we could play basketball. I should have known then, and undeniably know now, that I have no business ever playing basketball with anyone, especially a group of inner-city men who play all the time. Despite my humiliating performance, I think they appreciated my effort.

"Look, you gotta bounce it out for now," I told Iverson. He could hang around and talk all night if I let him.

"Bounce it out!" one girl yelled. It was one of the catch phrases I said over and over again all day every day, since students just walked into my class all the time, and I wanted them to leave.

Marvin started physically bouncing. As Iverson was bouncing, he began singing something like: "Like dick or what cuz it's all I'm givin up."

My small class returned to silence, and all were working intently. I answered some questions. I left to take a quick look in the other classrooms, because maybe that was where all my missing students were.

I got to the first class, the science room, and saw four of them talking and laughing with some other students who were supposed to be there. Just the other day, the science teacher, who was from another Day School, was fired. He had been permanently subbing for our science teacher, who had yet to return from a death in his family. From what I've heard, there was a stipulation in the Day School teacher contract preventing him from teaching at Twilight because the time for the two positions overlapped, so now we just had another substitute. I didn't think we would ever get a science teacher. I wondered if the students were going to get science credits for nothing.

The Day School science teacher was also black, and it was important for the school to have a man of his stature in Twilight. He was teaching the students, they were learning and they liked him. I thought the students were resentful of the fact that none of their teachers were black. Only the administrative staff was.

I walked into the science room, extended my arms and offered the countenance of utter disbelief.

"I'm not sure who is supposed to be in here," the new

substitute said. "They all said this was their class." My students were avidly contributing to the loudness and the disarray.

"What are you doing here?" I asked. I made eye contact with each of my students. "I just don't understand why you bother coming to school. If you're not coming to class, what is the point?" I was going to black out, so I turned around and returned to my class.

One at a time, each student returned, and each time a new one came in, the class was again distracted by the newest intrusion. I exchanged words with each new arrival.

"I don't care if I'm failin," one girl said.

"It doesn't matter, you're leaving," another kid said.

I was getting upset. I wondered if they would ever have any regard for school. Their demeanor and the overall lack of accountability sickened me. It gave me headaches and made me nauseous. My frustration continued building. I disturbed the class to remind them of exactly why they were here and what they had to gain from it.

"Let's just put this in monetary terms," I said. "If you make this much now, you'll make this much more with a high school degree. With a high school degree, you can get into college. Men and women with college degrees get better jobs with better pay."

"There are easier ways to make a few g's," Foolio said. He wouldn't elaborate. Obviously it was illegal. He laughed when I asked him to be more specific.

"It's easier to sell drugs to white people like you," one student said.

"Your method bears great consequences since dealers get killed and incarcerated all the time," I said.

"You just gotta do your time," one kid said. "And when you get out, you just start all over again."

The block ended as the conversation trailed off. I felt ill and hated how I failed to get my point across. It all seemed so clear to me. Nothing could have made me feel better that day.

A block later, Tanisha told me how psyched she was that she was going to finish reading *Great Expectations*.

"I never thought I could finish it since it was so long," she said. I hated leaving my students hanging despite all the problems this year.

During the next block, I finally got my class settled, accounted for, and working. I heard someone rapping, and it was getting louder and louder. It disturbed everyone and continued unabated. When I went to my doorway to investigate, I saw a kid I didn't recognize. I motioned for him to go elsewhere, but he kept rapping.

"Can you please be quiet?" I asked. "You're disturbing my class." When he continued, I repeated myself in a louder voice. Jack must have heard my voice, since he came from the office to get the student.

As the students were dismissed for the day, someone slammed the door. I was surprised the glass didn't shatter. I saw the girl who did it laughing and running down the hallway. I saw her through my window, which allowed me to see across the courtyard.

Hero came in to clean up while I was packing up.

"I'm being transferred," I told him. He looked shocked.

"Why would they do that?" he asked.

"I blame (Miss D) and the administration's decision to separate us," I said.

"It's always the teachers' fault and never the students'," Hero said. His inflections denoted how ridiculous he considered the decision.

"These kids always find an excuse for their problems

and are always blaming others," he said. He ran off a laundry list of excuses: "You're white, you have money, you're Spanish."

"It's a truly terrible cycle of life emanating from these schools," I said. "These kids are going to end up poor, dead, or incarcerated."

"Many of them will probably die young and probably expect to anyway," Hero said. "This lazy culture must remain in this area because it's the kind of mentality that must never spread to other areas of our society."

As I walked out the front door, Jack and Faith were smoking cigarettes on the school's front steps. After I said goodbye, Faith reminded me about Valentine's Day on Friday.

-11-

ALTHOUGH I WAS GETTING TRANSFERRED, I was still getting observed by the English supervisor of the high schools. After signing in, I went to the library to prepare for the observation, which would be occurring in the first block.

Considering that the majority of class time involved using worksheets, and despite the fact that it was yielding results, it wasn't the kind of demonstration that the head of the English department wanted to see. She wanted to see how I interacted with the class, how I conducted myself, and what they were learning. I needed to provide a demonstration of how I would teach if I didn't have the kind of problems Twilight provided.

First block was English 1, and we were reading *Great Expectations,* so the lesson revolved around that. I took a seat at a table in the library and began going over my lesson book, which contained all my worksheets. I had to utilize the fifty-five minutes in the block effectively and have the students illustrate various skills. Sitting at a desk with a lethargic demeanor was a terrible quality to show any supervisor.

My plan was to write, "What was the last good deed

you did for someone?" on the board. As the students arrived, I would distribute paper and pens and have them write a response. Once the writing waned, I would ask volunteers to read their responses aloud. Having students write and participate in a discussion were the kinds of activities the observer wanted to see. I estimated that it would take fifteen minutes.

Once those responses waned, I would move onto *Great Expectations*. Since I had worksheets for every chapter, compiling a list of the most pertinent questions in the first thirty chapters was easy. The students should all have read to chapter forty, but most were at least through thirty. I wrote a list of questions in chronological order and made an effort to word my questions so that they were not answered with one word, like a name, and were never answered with a yes or a no. I estimated it would take ten minutes. I would be flexible if one of these activities was running particularly well.

Once the questions got to the first appearance of Miss Havisham, I would ask the class to list characteristics of her so they could better understand what kind of person she was and what her intentions might be. I would write her name in the middle of the board, circle it, and draw lines to other circles with adjectives of her characteristics. Observers liked when the chalkboard showed student responses and webs. The class would flow into more questions about Miss Havisham. It would take maybe five minutes.

Then I would move to the questions and, hopefully, a positive conversation would ensue. Maybe it would evolve on a relevant tangent. I wanted to keep the students contributing, and I didn't want to be lecturing. I needed to make sure to have activities in case no conversation occurred at all. On a positive note, the discussion would fill in the gaps for any confused readers.

In theory, I would have liked to have activities like this once a week, but the absentee problem prevented the students from reading together as a class. I hated the idea of students solely filling out worksheets from what they heard in discussion rather than reading and understanding the questions and answers like the more conscientious students were. It was always the students trying to find the short cuts that needed the most help and needed to make up work. Then again, did my holding back for these students hamper the progress of those doing the work? I could only hope my one-on-one instruction helped to bridge the gap.

For the final fifteen minutes, I wanted the students to write a response to more questions on the board: "Where do you see yourself in one year, five years, in twenty years? What can you do to make your dreams come true?" After giving the students ample time to write their responses, and once I saw that they completed their assignments, we would have another discussion until the period ended. The students would be held accountable for today's lesson, because I would collect their papers at the end of the period to evaluate what they wrote.

I was confident that it was going to get a positive response from the English supervisor. The lesson gave students an opportunity to write and to discuss the book we were reading. It also helped to tie in some of the novel's themes with everyday life. Being over-prepared would ensure the class was active and alive. Observers hated seeing empty blocks of time, and rightfully so.

At around 4:00 p.m., I went into Nicotina's room and showed her my lesson. She looked it over and said she felt it was great since the students were asked to do numerous activities, and it also gave them a break from the worksheets. I mentioned my desire to have weekly lessons like this, and then I briefly explained my reasoning for not having them and my abhorrence at the students' attendance.

At 4:20 p.m., no one arrived for class, and I already saw a bunch of my students in the hallways. The English supervisor had not yet arrived.

At 4:25 p.m., I went into the bathroom, retrieved a few of them, and sent them to class, but I knew there were still others around somewhere. I walked down the hall and looked into the other classrooms. Three of my female students were in Nicotina's room. They thought by avoiding eye contact with me that my eyes wouldn't see them. I stood in the doorway aggravated because I didn't understand why Nicotina allowed these students to stay in her class. The students seemed somewhat shocked by me making my rounds, although they knew I did it all the time.

"Why are you in here?" I asked. They tried evading the question. One girl put her jacket over her head.

"There's no point comin since you leavin," another said. The entire charade got me so upset that I just returned to my class and proceeded with the worksheets.

Our new boss, Mrs. Davis, was in the building, and midway through the block she entered my class and asked to make a few announcements.

"I will be running Twilight," Mrs. Davis said. "There are going to be big changes. We are going to distribute Twilight newsletters."

"I never got one," Tanisha said. Mrs. Davis reiterated her desire to get them distributed. The way she phrased her statements seemed like a jab at Miss Carter, who made many empty promises.

"I am preparing a new newsletter and taking pictures," she said. "Can I ask you all to respond to a question? Why is Black History Month important?"

She told the class to give written responses to me or to Jack. She thanked them and left. I tried to get my class back on track, but no one was listening. It seemed like everyone was asking me questions from the worksheet rather than making any effort to read from their books. They were frustrated that they couldn't find answers by just skimming.

At the end of the block, Rhonda's nephew handed me his response to the question. I looked it over. He wrote about how February was the month that the slaves were freed and how he was personally a slave to the white man. He elaborated by explaining that when you're eighteen, you have to vote and go to the army. He wondered why he couldn't control his own fate and then explained that he didn't mind February after all because he was a slave. His response made me ill.

In the next block, G-Black entered and asked for work. He no longer stayed in my class; he took his work elsewhere and did it at his leisure. He reeked of marijuana, and his eyes were bloodshot. I reminded him of this fact.

"You're wrong," he said. "You won't be around longer anyway."

"Where'd you hear that?" I asked.

"They already got rid of the science teacher."

All day Faith was in and out of my classroom removing students at different intervals, and I was never sure why. She bothered the class every time she did this, and every time she pulled someone out of class, the rest wanted to know why. And Faith always asked whether she could disturb the class as she was doing it. It was a never-ending cycle. I wished she understood the effects of her behavior and how these students needed to be in school and not bothered with frivolous social activities. These students were still talking about a prom that was months away.

Maintaining order was difficult. I asked one girl to do some work, and she blacked out and told me she hated me and hated school and didn't understand why she even had to come to school. She recently had a child, and the baby's father was also here. I really hoped they both got their diplomas, so they could get jobs to support their baby.

By third block, I was physically exhausted and ill from this grind. I had to go searching for the students again. There were some in the science room, and others were in the vacant art room. There was music playing. A bunch of kids were on their cell phones. Even Miss D.

"Get out!" one voice yelled.

"Go fuck yaself," another voice yelled. Hero was also in there cleaning.

"These students are pretty lucky," I said. "My high school never gave my friends and me all this time to be social." It was all so totally draining.

I returned to class and tried to get everyone working, but it was difficult. Kia just wouldn't be quiet. I told her at least twenty-five times at varying volumes to be quiet. Iverson walked into class, and I led him back out.

"You know where to get sucked," Miss D yelled at him as he left.

When I objected to her remark, she replied, "You is dumb."

I corrected her and said, "You are dumb." I felt so sick.

"You so red," Kia yelled. There were students in

the hallway; I counted eleven. Pandemonium was everywhere.

I went into the Twilight office to get Jack since they weren't listening to me. He cleared the hallway.

I returned to my class and everyone was giggling. I blacked out about why they weren't working and returned to my seat. As I put my legs under the desk, I nearly kicked Shenequa, who was hiding there. Everyone laughed, and she exited the room. She yelled something before leaving, and she didn't even close the door behind her. No one ever did when exiting.

In fourth block, I gave Ken the written assignment for the lesson I never presented, since no one ever came to observe me. I didn't bother giving him any worksheets because he was definitely going to fail. But, since he came today, he could at least write about his intention of being a fashion designer and keep busy. His absences were plentiful, and his reading and writing skills were atrocious; yet he made no effort to better himself. I was surprised he didn't verbally express his hatred for me today. He was often in school and just wouldn't attend my class.

At some point, Tanisha entered the classroom to retrieve a jacket she had left earlier.

"Please remember to bring your stuff with you since I can't be responsible for it," I said.

"But you are responsible," she said. Suddenly, she realized that she was missing a glove and began yelling at me. Obviously, it was my fault.

"I am an English teacher and not the coat check," I said. She started blacking out on me but left on her own.

Moments later, Shirley came in and asked the class

who took the glove. Imagine if someone actually admitted to taking the glove?

As the block ended, I collected the assignments. I overheard Ken and Joe speaking, and then they were high fiving each other about how they were almost eligible for welfare. I was sickened even more. No one was getting justice. I felt totally broken.

The students were dismissed and the janitors were cleaning the floors. It reeked of chemicals. Tanisha was yelling and accusing everyone of taking her glove. She was our A student, who completed all her work well but had no idea how to act in society. I recalled reading an SAT passage in class on Jane Austen earlier in the year and how Tanisha called her a "bitch."

I saw one girl walking in the hallway and asked her where she was today since she was absent.

"I forgot," she said.

With the students gone, I read Ken's assignment about his intentions for the future. He wrote about being a fashion designer and how he needed to stay focused to accomplish his dream, but he failed to actually complete the sentence. I read Joe's paper about how he wanted to be a "modle."

Before I left, Jack told me that Friday, which was Valentine's Day, would be my final day here.

-12-

"What lies behind us and what lies before us are tiny matters compared to what lies within us."   -Ralph Waldo Emerson

IT WAS THE QUOTE ON the front of the card I received from the students and teachers on my last day of Twilight at this high school. It was Valentine's Day. It was cold, and I sat a few minutes warming up my car to go home.

The card was filled with signatures and messages from whatever students and teachers were in school. Since it was Friday and a half-day, more than half the students were absent. No Foolio. No Marvin. No Tanisha. No Shenequa. No Iverson. I wished I could have said goodbye and good luck to them. Even Miss D failed to grace the school with her presence. She could be relied on to fail though.

The students wrote me a few good lucks, some hollas, some God blesses, a few best wishes, and even some thank yous inside the card.

One girl wrote, "Think you," but I knew what she meant.

G-Black wrote, "You be cool k. dog white man get jump." I needed a translator.

Two girls wrote to tell me never to come back to school and that they hoped to never see me again, but I knew they were kidding.

I waited for this day and the impending transfer for weeks, and now that the final day had passed, it was anticlimactic. Most students were shocked by my departure, although some already knew the "secret." I hated how students knew my business. Considering how security issues supposedly attributed to my transfer, my status was still compromised.

Because of the half-day, the lack of students, and the news of my departure, there was no work in my class or in the other classes for that matter. Some students asked how come I didn't tell them earlier, and I gave numerous excuses about how I didn't want it to affect their performance and that I wasn't exactly sure when it was going to happen anyway. The majority of the students were cordial, and their demeanor was not one of ubiquitous delight that I expected.

First block consisted of a flock of girls telling me how much they were going to miss me.

"It was my job to make problems and to tell you to go fuck yaself," one girl said.

"That shouldn't have really been your role," I said.

Another girl looked sad and shocked and kept repeating that she couldn't believe it.

"You want to go fuck me in the bathroom?" Kia asked.

"Please act appropriately," I said. I wanted to report her because it was clear she needed to speak with someone about her promiscuity. Considering how I've been supported though, I figured any report would morph into charges against me. I had to leave this place.

Rhonda's nephew came in laughing that I was leaving.

"I'm going to rip those cornrows out like I'm ripping ivy off a brick wall," I joked. I was still deeply troubled by his written response to Black History Month.

Earlier in the Twilight office, I was trying to clarify with him whether he truly believed all eighteen-year-olds were sent to war, and he said yes. When I asked him how old he was, he said he was nineteen.

"His answer is correct," Shirley chimed in. "You asked his opinions and opinions aren't wrong." I disagreed vehemently, since his answer was not based in reality. Open-ended questions encouraged students to think, but lines needed to be drawn when insanity took over. It was classic Twilight.

"Everyone has a right to an opinion, but that opinion has to be within reasonable parameters," I explained. "If someone asked me what my favorite baseball team was, and I said, "Mars smells like green crayons," it wasn't really an answer to the question."

Rhonda's nephew started making references to other untruths, and I got so frustrated that I left.

Quotes and lines attributed to me were repeated throughout the day. There was "fly fly fly," which was always accompanied by a wave of my backhand. It was my nice way of getting students to go away after dialogue was exhausted. I got it from Hannibal Lecter, who said it to Clarice Starling in *The Silence of the Lambs*.

Students told me to "stop being so dead up, yo," when I was annoyed and fired up. When I repeated it to another student, he told me to "breathe easy, son." Both became important in my repertoire.

Kia reprised the three-tap song that I started a few weeks ago. The rhythm of the tap was simply one-two-three, one-two-three. It meant "spesh-shul-ed, spesh-shul-ed." Sometimes it was easier to tap my finger on the table in this rhythm rather than black out in response to some poor behavior. They got the message, some people laughed, and then they got back to work. In retrospect, it was bad to refer to my class as special education students if in fact they actually were. Then again, they shouldn't be in my class if they were. And other times I had to get past their distractions in any way possible.

At the end of the day, when the students were all in one room, I took my last stroll down the hallway. I looked into the Day School teachers lounge. I remembered the time when I was using the microwave and nearly fell over a Muslim woman praying. I looked into my old classroom. I couldn't believe how long ago that was.

On my way back, I looked into Dinesh's room. I turned the lights on and startled a giggling Ken and Joe. Joe was fixing his pants. I told them to get where they belonged, but I didn't have the same energy to fight every single moment anymore.

When they were back in class, Ken sat in the back sweating and silent, while Joe was laughing and being boisterous. Ken and Joe were surely ecstatic about my departure.

Ken was wiping his forehead with the sleeve of his Sean John shirt, and I happened to know that his particular shirt cost $175 because I priced out his designer clothing out of curiosity since certain students wore this brand despite being very poor.

I couldn't understand why some person in Ken's life

was providing him with money for these clothes and not giving him the proper guidance to get an education. He wanted to be a fashion designer but could barely read or write. His mother had been brought in for conferences, but nothing changed. I hoped neither Joe nor Ken passed, because neither deserved to. I hoped they were not given sympathy because of their sexual orientation either. It was a hard cross to bear for them, but giving them passing grades without proper English skills was positive reinforcement for non-existent accomplishments.

My departure was surely consistent with how figures moved in and out of their lives, since few were members of a typical nuclear family. Going to school was an important routine that could provide them with some stability, but an ever-changing staff prevented it from occurring. They didn't even understand how their education was affected. They couldn't rely on the kind of school support they really needed. It prevented them from living better lives and achieving worthy goals.

I wished these students could have learned earlier that an education was important. They really couldn't fathom why they had to do work in school. There were so many aspects of English to address that I would always come up short as a teacher when giving myself a personal evaluation.

As teachers, we spoke about how students couldn't tell time without an electronic watch or read Roman numerals or understand the coin change they received from the store. I promised myself to go over these concepts, but it was so easy to get consumed by everything else that I never got around to them.

I believed that some students would miss me, while others would understand in the future how I was working in their best interests. There was no way of finding out

John J. Kaminski

though. Some students read novels in my classes and understood some of the themes, and that was indeed quite an accomplishment. I could think of many ways I could have and should have done better, but the conditions were so dire that I couldn't be expected to achieve better results. I wouldn't break my arm patting myself on the back though, because it wasn't enough.

Teaching was a job just like any other job, but when the education of students was your daily task, performing poorly at your job affected people and their futures. And since teachers were paid so poorly compared to other jobs, the profession couldn't possibly attract the most ideal candidates. The wheels of the system were thereby incapable of providing students with a real education of the necessary tools to succeed in our world.

Despite how awful some of my students were, I sometimes called them Mister and Miss, because I was sure no one ever called them that. I tolerated the swearing when I shouldn't have had to. I tolerated the scattered incidents of poor behavior from better students when I knew I shouldn't have. I compromised at every level when deciding what issues should be reported and what should be tolerated. It was exhausting. My time could have been better spent. No one would ever call some of them Mister or Miss again.

In the Twilight office, I was presented with the card and given hugs, kisses, handshakes, thank yous, we'll miss yous, and good lucks by the staff.

"I didn't write anything in the card because the words would not reflect how much I am going to miss you," Mariella said. I was sure that the cafeteria duties would be reshuffled, but I could only imagine her down there by herself, since the students assigned to be there were out at the deli or elsewhere. I exchanged goodbyes with Nicotina and Dinesh.

Rhonda gave me a hug and a kiss and reminded me how everyone was only a phone call away, and I thanked her. She was a deeply religious woman and brought up the power of God in numerous conversations. She worked in two Twilight Programs and at youth shelters. I just couldn't understand how she could believe she was doing her best by coddling the students and not supporting the teachers more. By drawing these lines, achieving staff unity was impossible, and the students knew where to go to complain and not be held accountable.

Faith kissed me, hugged me and wished me good luck, and I hated the phoniness of the entire affair but I played along. She made my life here so difficult. I hoped she treated the next teacher with more respect and realized that she was not a teacher or the boss. I wasn't going to feel guilty just because she was black and earning a measlier wage than I was. She never even returned my papers. I wondered how she could honestly think I wasn't doing my job or that she was doing right. When she referred to the library as the lie-berry, I wanted to make a joke about how the library was not like a strawberry or a raspberry, but that would be rude, although it would help her pronounce her words. I was sure I wouldn't think about being so rude if she treated me with even a shred of professionalism.

I naively wanted the school to fall apart without me performing the daily tasks that weren't in my job description. It was unsettling to accept how easily life here was going to simply move on next week without me. There would be a substitute teacher and then a replacement. The school would remain open. Twilight would go on. Life would go on, as would my job in another school.

My car was finally warm enough to drive away from this place forever.

IV.

A New Beginning

-1-

THE FIRST DAY AT MY NEW SCHOOL was delayed two days because of a major snowstorm that crippled the area. Including Presidents Day, teachers were blessed with a three-day break, although we would lose our official winter break.

After meandering my car through the city streets left in disarray by snow drifts, snowed-in cars, and other parked cars hanging out into the streets and disrupting traffic flow, I finally caught a glimpse of my new school a few blocks ahead. It was the largest high school in the city. I heard that it had around 3,000 students. I also heard that it used to be a fort. It sat strategically on a hill, which provided a splendid view of Manhattan. The school was three stories high. I counted thirty-nine columns of windows along the face of it.

I parked outside the gated perimeter and walked toward the doors at the end of the sidewalk. I pulled on the door handle to make my grand entrance, but it was locked. I noticed an intercom, pressed the button, and waited. It told me to go around to the front entrance of the school around the bend.

I made my grand entrance to nonexistent fanfare. I

asked the guard at the front desk where the Twilight office was, and I was directed to an open circular staircase that led to the basement. My descent led me to an open area with beige walls and wooden classroom doors. Each door had a small window and was distinguished by a labeling scheme of painted white numbers and letters. As I looked for the Twilight office, I glanced into one of the windows to see what a classroom looked like. I caught the eye of the teacher, so I moved on. I regretted disturbing her.

I finally found the door that had a little burgundy sign with white lettering that read "Twilight." Next to that was another sign with white lettering that read "Speech Therapist." Another sign stated that "Twilight students are not permitted to enter the office without permission." I wished my old school had a sign like that on the office door.

I twisted the knob of my new office. To the right was a desk, and on the desk was the sign-in book. Behind the desk was my new clerk named Patricia. At a long, wooden table sat KetchupBoots and the roving gym teacher, Mrs. J, smiling at me. I was smiling and saying hello to everyone. The guidance counselor introduced herself. Pleasantries were exchanged. I was introduced to two security guards, one of whom was also new.

"You're definitely going to have a better time here than at your last school," Mrs. J said.

"I was looking forward to this," I said.

Both KetchupBoots and Mrs. J explained that Todd was a great person to work for, and I told them that I was glad. I wouldn't dare complain to them about my last job, because gossip tears through Twilight and I didn't want to badmouth anyone. Soon the math teacher arrived, and we were introduced. Once Patricia left, KetchupBoots warned me that she couldn't be trusted. Todd arrived, shook my hand, and welcomed me to my new position.

We were to be in our classrooms by 3:45 p.m., and the students arrived before 4:00 p.m. There was no cafeteria duty because the cafeteria was located in another building and that building was located on the opposite side of the school. Absenteeism and lateness were still problems, but a new policy was just enacted that sent students home if they didn't arrive by 4:00 p.m. Although sending students away from school sounded unreasonable, it sent a message that they wouldn't pass and graduate if they continued to come in whenever they pleased. Attending class on time was important. In the real world, one was not rewarded for simply showing up.

When I got to my new classroom, it was locked, so I asked one of the guards for a key.

"You don't need a key, just a pen," he said. I was befuddled. He showed me how to unlock my door with a pen. I thanked him.

I entered and glanced around, looking for a light switch in the place where I thought there should be one. I found an open metal box with two buttons surrounded by wires. Pressing these unsteady buttons turned on the lights. Fiddling with the wires would most certainly lead to an electric shock.

Half of the left wall was covered with blue construction paper. In the middle was a white sheet of construction paper that read "Shakespeare in Love" and was decorated with markered drawings of ivy and a heart. There was a quote from *Hamlet* as well. Personally, I wouldn't have selected a line from *Hamlet* for a display centered on love.

On smaller sheets of white paper were other quotes from other plays and sonnets. Also on the blue paper were painted white stars and a crescent moon, as well as other hearts conveying Valentine's Day wishes. My favorite was one to the Day School teacher, which referred to her as "the best zero giver ever." Also on the wall was a corkboard adorned with papers that illustrated the three steps of writing a paper: planning, editing, and revising using a web, a rough draft, and a final draft. A long wooden table was pushed toward the left side of the room. It had two computers on it; one worked and had internet access while the other functioned better as a paperweight. I was unsure whether the printer worked. The computers were both old and dirty. There was a clock and a security phone nearby.

Along the right wall were two old and worn chalkboards. An American flag hung from the top frame of the right one. The left board was so worn that it had cracks revealing cardboard underneath. Since the right one was mostly filled, I erased some of its contents so I could make room to write Langston Hughes' "Sliver." Although I wanted to introduce myself and talk to my new students, I also wanted to prepare an assignment and be overprepared in case the conversation ended quickly. After writing it out, I realized that a small chalked note in the upper right hand corner of the board read "Do Not Erase." Oops.

On the far wall was a metal desk with the Day School teacher's files, books, and a photograph of her family. Four rows of desk-chairs led the way. Behind the desk were two bookshelves. On the side of one of the bookshelves were more photographs of her family and friends as well as an obituary card from her grandmother's funeral. On the back wall were two windows that looked out on the Manhattan skyline. I would have been able to see the Twin Towers.

On the back of my door was a sign listing the student dress code. It was tagged numerous times with graffiti. The highlights of the sign, which I always considered to be givens, were "Girls are not permitted to wear transparent blouses," "Pants should not hang as low as to expose underwear," and "Clothing that would cause damage to any student or school property is not to be worn." I was glad to not be the person who had to enforce the listed and unlisted rules that were so painfully obvious. I could only imagine the amount of time wasted on teacher/student conversations about issues like transparent clothes before the signs were finally printed. Maybe school uniforms would eliminate the mess.

By 4:00 p.m., I had two students in my class. In the hallway, the janitors and the security guards were laughing and joking loudly.

"They're always loud," the students said. I wouldn't quiet them today.

I introduced myself to each arriving student and talked a bit. It was still settling in that I was in a new job because I didn't last at my old one.

"I'm going to be here for the remainder of the school year," I said.

"That's what the last teacher said," one girl said.

Throughout the day, I had about twelve students, one of whom I would have twice a day. We talked about a range of topics. This Twilight had half the students my last school had, and the snow kept many of them away. I told them where I used to work, and we talked about what the last teacher and the substitutes were doing in English. They told me that their old teacher gave them books and asked them to read in class and answer questions about the passages. They all said they enjoyed the worksheets. These students needed small, reachable tasks every day.

I met their old English teacher at the Black Issues Convention. She had liked the worksheets, since they held everyone accountable, but I knew I needed to engage in more diversified instruction. I would love to have kids who came to class every day. I would love to have classroom discussions and more interaction. With three weeks left in the second trimester, I decided to read *The Catcher in the Rye* for the first two blocks and *The Great Gatsby* for the last two.

Throughout the day, my classes discussed how the school was much more diverse than my last one, which was predominantly black. There were also Hispanic students and white students. Some spoke Spanish in class, but I urged them to stick to English. One kid was from Latvia. There were also Indians and Pakistanis in the hallways of Day School.

I tried making a joke about the dress code rule about clothes that hurt people and damaged property, and they said that some students used to wear spikes to school and that the pain and damage the clothing caused was indeed a reality.

Someone asked me for a rubber band, so I looked in the desk and couldn't find any. I did see a Valentine's Day card for the Day School teacher, though. I opened it up and saw that all her *Romeo* had to say was "Love You."

I asked the students about the other Twilight teachers' names, but they all seemed to refer to them as Mista and Miss. One student referred to the math teacher as Mutumbo because he resembled the professional basketball player. He was very soft-spoken, so the students couldn't hear him pronounce his name well. I needed to learn his real name since I hated getting names wrong and needed to get better at it.

I explained to my new students how I didn't accept

being called Mister and that my one class rule was not to call me Mister. Later, when students called me "Mista," I reminded them about my rule, and they actually apologized. I told them not to worry. When one girl swore while speaking, she apologized. These students were so much nicer.

We talked about how my old school was in the worst section of the city and how it had terrible problems with drugs and violence. Everyone was chiming in.

"High school kids deal drugs cuz they need protection and want to belong."

"They need to make money for their families, who may also be doing drugs."

"Drug dealers try to get younger kids to deal for them since the dealers won't have to bail them out when they get busted, like they do for the older dealers."

"Low-paying jobs send people down the wrong path."

"The cops there are racist."

"All cops are racist."

"A cop was shot outside the school over a parking ticket."

A small brown mouse appeared and ran around the corner of the room before darting away.

At some point, Todd came in and distributed Twilight newsletters, which explained the new hours for the third trimester. There were photos of the different sites and some quotes about Black History Month. I never handed in Rhonda's nephew's response.

The newsletter also had a picture of my old site. In the photo was our crock of a student council. Faith and Shirley were also in it. In another photo was the art teacher who came once a week. It said a lot to not have any of the other teachers in the photo. It felt like such a complete lack of recognition and respect.

At the end of the day, I returned to the Twilight office.

"You must have done pretty well since the night ran smoothly," Todd said.

"I tried checking up on you, but your door was closed all night," KetchupBoots said. She was also short, so I was sure she was unable to get the best view from the little window in my door.

"I had a great day and am glad to finally have my first day behind me," I said.

We all exchanged farewells and began walking through the school to a door that opened to the parking lot. As I walked, KetchupBoots called out to me to wait up, and when she caught up, we started recounting the day. Todd, however, called her back to the office.

The rest of the staff and I ascended a staircase and waited for security to give us the clearance to leave the building. It took a few moments, and someone expressed fidgetiness. The door opened and the teachers scattered throughout the parking lot. It had begun.

-2-

I WALKED INTO THE TWILIGHT OFFICE, waved greetings to the room, and hung my jacket on the right door of a tall, black cabinet filled with office supplies. The room was like an old storage room. There was also a refrigerator, a microwave oven, and an ancient porcelain sink.

Eight people occupied one table, and there was no room for me to work. One of the two tables was covered with books. Adella, the science teacher; Juan, the Spanish teacher; and Mutumbo were sitting around it working from their laps. I sought out the library.

KetchupBoots handed me a paper with two websites of lesson plans. She had been offering her help since I arrived, and I appreciated it. I was thinking about teaching *Black Boy* since we had a set of them.

It was Friday, which was Pizza Day. Todd bought lunch for the staff.

"Don't tell Jack I do this," Todd said.

"The secret is safe with me," I said. I thanked him.

Our staff didn't have access to a copy machine, but we had a man working in the bookroom who made copies. They had to be dropped off a week in advance, though. Last night, I retrieved my worksheets for *The Great Gatsby* and *The Catcher in the Rye* so I could get copies made. It would be a quick way to evaluate the students and get started.

I asked KetchupBoots where the bookroom was, and when she started giving me instructions I lost interest. She tended to be longwinded. She agreed to walk me there after eating her pizza. It was right upstairs.

Niles worked with KetchupBoots last year and told me all about her. She had a serious crush on him too. She asked him once if something was going on between them, and he said no.

We entered the bookroom, and the copy guy was on the phone. He saw us but made no gesture for us to hold on; he just continued his conversation. It gave me a chance to check out the bookroom, which was in complete disarray.

After a few more minutes, he finally got off the phone and granted us the pleasure of his assistance. I introduced myself and returned the books signed out by the last teacher. KetchupBoots returned downstairs.

"Could I have some copies for Monday?" I asked him.

"Maybe," he said. I needed ten copies of two pages.

"I wish we had a copier to use," I said. He didn't convey any sympathy.

"Maybe it'll be done by Monday," he said.

"Could I look around the bookroom to see what's here?" I asked.

"You need to bring a supervisor up here to take out books," he said.

"I just want to check out what you have first," I said. He directed me to the English books in the half of the bookroom to his left.

The area was a mess, with piles of books everywhere.

There was no method to the madness but only a classic case of utter dishevelment. I missed the organized Polish woman who ran the bookroom at my other school. It also had fewer books than the last bookroom. It did, however, have numerous copies of *Great Expectations,* so I planned on doing that next trimester since I had the first forty chapters outlined.

I wanted to have weekly discussions, show movie excerpts, and do some other activities that were more interactive and diverse so I could make my class more interesting. Hopefully, the attendance problem wouldn't hamper continuity too much.

Before I left, I asked the copy guy where the library was, and he gave me the simple directions. I found it and entered, walking between three rows of tables to get to the main desk. It was long and narrow, and I was in the middle. To the left were about ten computers behind a wall, and to the right were more bookshelves and a few administrative offices.

"Hello," I said to the black librarian, but she didn't respond. I walked over to the computers, sat down, and began accessing the internet.

"Excuse me," someone said. It was the librarian. Apparently, I could use the other computers but not this one, so I moved over to another vacant one.

I sat next to a middle-aged woman who was doing her lesson plans on the computer. She was working right onto a template, and having these resources would make my lesson planning much easier, so I struck up a conversation.

"I just transferred here," I said. "I work in Twilight." We talked about how awful my old school was and what patience I must have. She looked over my lesson plans.

"You need to work harder on these," she said. "They're

comparable to what a substitute would have." She showed me exactly how to fill them out, because I didn't even know what some of the acronyms stood for. I couldn't thank her enough. I knew the paperwork for a formal observation was on the way.

"No one ever showed me how to fill these out before," I said. I really tried to convey my appreciation.

"We have a great atmosphere here," she said. "We're bringing in a lot of new teachers because so many are retiring." She told me where the Day School English office was and mentioned the names of other teachers who might be able to help me. She took the time to retrieve for me a disk with the lesson plan template.

She then introduced me to a younger teacher who sat down next to her and had a small class using the computers. She was an Hispanic woman who ran her class with an iron fist, and I admired that. I was sure she connected with her students, since it was probably easier to do the work than deal with her wrath.

On only my second day, people here were so nice and helpful. It was such a better overall feeling to be with co-workers like this.

Their day ended, and before they departed for the weekend, I thanked them both again for being so helpful. They offered me additional help in the future.

Another older, white librarian came over to me and introduced herself, and we began chatting. Once I mentioned I was a Twilight teacher and where I used to teach, I was lauded as some saint because the perception (and the grim reality) of my old school was just horrible. She offered me assistance, and I thanked her for being so nice.

"We have bad students, but we also have a lot of great

teachers and students," she said. I was so thankful to be in a better environment.

Around 3:40 p.m., I went down to my room and got ready for the day. Todd came in, sat at a desk-chair, and asked me to sign a paper authorizing an observation by the Twilight boss Mrs. Davis. I signed it. She could now observe me anytime within the next twenty school days. I had to get my lesson plans in top form and make sure my rosters and grading system were intact because she would evaluate me on all these areas.

"Mrs. Davis is going to be here today, so we're going to run through the new schedule that we're beginning next trimester," Todd said. The blocks were going to be forty minutes long, and the day would begin with a fifty-minute Literacy Lab beginning at 3:50 p.m. There would also be a seventy-five minute Interblock between blocks three and four.

"What should I do?"

"Just participate when you want to," he told me.

The Literacy Lab finally began around 4:10 p.m. by the time everything was completely organized. Todd sent home about eight students for showing up after 4:00 p.m. I sympathized with them since they were here, but sending them home was exactly what needed to be done to get these students to really understand school rules.

The Literacy Lab would be a class conducted by each teacher with a focus on practicing reading and writing skills. I told Todd that I wanted my Literacy Lab used for students who had fallen behind on their reading since their absences were so frequent, and he agreed. I also wanted to take in any other students from the other Literacy Labs who needed to catch up. It would not only relieve all the other teachers, but actually help the students complete their tasks. I didn't mind taking a large group of students, because it was clear that when you sat them in a room and made them read and demanded accountability through the worksheets, they had to perform or they would fail. Nothing could be fairer.

Todd began Literacy Lab by explaining how the new schedule was going to work next trimester. He continued by talking about the plans for a student council and a future election.

"I'm votin for me and I ain't runnin," one student yelled.

Todd discussed the horrendous attendance problem. He got agitated when students entered the meeting late, and he had to leave the room with them to send them home. Miss Jackson, the black social worker who worked two Twilight sites, took over the meeting. Her serious demeanor was apparent by the first words from her mouth.

"Ninety-eight percent of you are in attendance violation," she explained. "You're only allowed six absences per trimester and some of you have twenty-two. The Day School controls the attendance and the superintendent wants students to be held more accountable."

"Last year, the superintendent signed off on a few students graduating, but he's probably not going to be as sympathetic this year," Todd chimed in. "Graduation is an important moment of accomplishment for your family to see you graduate from high school at the ceremony." He had everyone's attention.

"If you're running late and have a legitimate excuse," Miss Jackson said, "you can always call in, but you can't do this every day." (Later, the staff laughed about how one student called in to say that he couldn't make it to school since he was at his sister's wedding. When Patricia called the sister, she said she was already married. He was busted.)

Miss Jackson's hard-line yet honest approach was commendable, and I was happy she was on the staff. All in all, the first Literacy Lab helped develop a school community, since all students didn't leave at the same time of the day together. There were also no dominating negative distractions during her speech despite the efforts of one fool.

In first block, two girls showed up. One was a Filipino girl named Angela and another was a Hispanic girl named Anna. They were very polite. We talked briefly and then they got involved with reading *The Catcher in the Rye*. They completed their worksheets in half the time allotted for the assignment, so I kept feeding them more, and they kept reading. Angela called me "Mista," and before I could say anything, she apologized because she remembered my one rule. I was making every effort to be nice to them because they were just nice high school girls, and I was growing all too accustomed to being rigorously defensive. It was obvious that the attitudes were completely different here, and if I did black out, I'd better have a really good reason to, because I would lose any credibility I had thus far. I was happy to have both of these students again in the fourth block.

In second block, Carlos entered, introduced himself, and shook my hand. I heard his name mentioned yesterday as one of Twilight's more boisterous students. We talked briefly, and I explained my Mister policy and how his performance would be evaluated through the worksheets. I got him settled, and he got to work.

KetchupBoots' class was next door behind the wall with the Shakespeare display. There was a space for the pipes near the ceiling so when she raised her voice, which she did numerous times, everyone heard it clearly.

"Shut up!" Carlos yelled.

"Take it easy, please." I said. I hoped she didn't hear him.

One black girl, Yolanda, kept burping loudly, over and over again.

"Please excuse yourself," I said. She burped again.

"I am going to teach you some manners," I said.

"You have to let me burp, since I always have a lot of gas," she explained.

"I'm going to try to get you to stop doing that," I said, but she said she couldn't.

"Maybe I can at least get you to do it without being so disruptive and loud."

"You're all lucky I ain't fartin," she said. I couldn't help but laugh. Maybe she was right.

One girl asked to go to the bathroom, and I let her. Carlos asked next, and I let him go too.

"I'm so lazy that I'm gonna wait until I can't wait to go and then I'm gonna go," he explained. I laughed at his intended plan.

Two girls whispered briefly when they should have been reading, but at least they were whispering and got back to work without being cajoled, so I didn't say anything. Carlos finally went to the bathroom.

The block ended when someone banged on the door. I was still not used to the schedule, and with the different time on the different clocks in the different classrooms, it was not an exact science either.

After Block Two, we had the inaugural Interblock while Mrs. Davis observed the new Twilight brainchild. KetchupBoots ran a seminar on Martin Luther King, the same seminar she ran at the Board. She began by establishing the rules and explained that it was not going to be like Jerry Springer. The rules were to not speak when others were speaking, to address others by name, and to not make disparaging comments about anyone.

KetchupBoots passed out the speech, and everyone read it. Soon we began a round-robin conversation about what the most important aspect of the piece was. When Mutumbo spoke, his accent was so deep that even I was unable to really understand what he was saying. Someone actually yelled, "What?" but we moved on. Juan, the Spanish teacher, also had a very deep accent when he spoke.

As the conversation progressed, KetchupBoots was documenting what was said by whom so she knew who was participating. It was exactly how the educational institution taught her to do it, but I thought she should be more involved in the conversation as a participant and less as a secretary. This was best illustrated when someone asked her what she thought about the question, and she said she hadn't thought about it since she was listening and writing. There were a few sighs. I felt she lost credibility in the eyes of the students. It made her disconnected.

We moved on to what Dr. King thought about how character and intelligence made an educated man. No one was participating, so I mentioned that the science in nuclear, chemical, and biological weapons was being used to destroy life rather than sustain it and how dangerous that was and how that illustrated a danger of education. The students started chiming in since these issues were at the forefront of current events, and we needed a forum for the students to understand the issues at hand. Yolanda made a few contributions, but KetchupBoots, unfortunately, moved on to another question from her list, and the conversation died. Again, I thought there needed to be more flexibility in the discussion.

When I later mentioned this point to Niles outside of school, he said that KetchupBoots was doing exactly what she was taught to do and that she needed to keep the students focused like that. I still felt that everyone needed to participate and be flexible even though the students should be talking and not the teachers. I thought conversations and discussions needed to have guides that were more alert.

At the end of the seminar, KetchupBoots mouthed, "Thank you," to me because I was helping move the conversation along. I was more than happy to. Dead air was awful, and anyway, we teachers were all going to be conducting seminars for the rest of the year, so we should always be supporting each other.

A dilemma developed as KetchupBoots passed out paper for the post-seminar activity, which was a response to the speech. Some students wanted to know exactly if and how they were being graded, and I understood their point.

"Why should we do this if we ain't gettin graded?" one student asked.

"It's going to be graded by one of your teachers," KetchupBoots said. She was scrambling for an answer and mentioned how the grading policies would be established later.

"Spelling doesn't count either," she added. "I'm not a good speller." I didn't think she should be revealing her weaknesses or undermining herself. Spelling was important. She needed to be better at dealing with questions off the cuff. They would take advantage of her if they thought she was weak.

In the next two blocks, my biggest issue was one girl

complaining about how Todd asked her to wear different clothing from now on because she was exposing too much cleavage. She was definitely exposing too much.

At the end of the day, Todd handed me a packet about Women's History Month and said that he wanted some of my students to enter the city essay contest. He told me that Mrs. Davis was involved and wanted Twilight to be too. The deadline was in a few days, but I told him we would have something.

Before we left for the night, someone expressed their thanks that Yolanda didn't fart during the seminar or we would have been forced to evacuate the premises. Everyone laughed. I laughed too.

3

YESTERDAY, I RECEIVED an official observation from my English supervisor during Block One. I thought that the window for my observation expired, but maybe it was one of the final official days; either way it was fine with me because I wanted to start getting these mandatory observations out of the way. Maybe I could have complained to the union if I wanted to make something out of nothing.

Only Anna showed up, and she was typing up a paper for the Women's History Month essay contest, so that was my observation. During my evaluation, I spoke with the English supervisor, Dr. Larson, about my transfer and about my lesson plans. I discussed what I was going to do if the rest of my students were here, and we spoke about the attendance problem. She told me that she ordered a number of books for the Twilight English staff, and I shared in her enthusiasm. I told her about the *Great Expectations* lesson I prepared for her when she was supposed to show up to my last school, and she apologized for missing the appointment.

"What are you going to do next year?" she asked.

"I need to get certified," I said.

"You should get transferred to the Day School," she said, and I agreed wholeheartedly. She told me she would work on it for me.

When I initially arrived at the Twilight office, KetchupBoots wanted to know if I wanted the old English files stored in two crates because people in the office wanted the crates. I told her I would get to them by the end of the day, and she thanked me. In between, I heard someone say that Mutumbo's car got stolen in front of his house and how he saw the thief drive it away.

I went up to the bookroom to find out if the copies that I had ordered were made. They weren't. I asked the guy in the bookroom if I could have the originals back since I needed them for today, and he told me to come back later.

I went to the library and greeted the less than enthusiastic librarian before heading for the computers. I was going to keep smashing her with my sledgehammer of kindness until she relented. Her demeanor lacked any inkling of hospitability or politeness. I again saw the teacher who helped me with my lesson plans, and she asked for my help since she wanted to do some research on a computer and had no idea how to use a search engine. It took only a few seconds and she was thankful, and I was glad to help. The nice librarian came up to us and we all talked before the Day School day ended.

I returned to the Twilight office, and everyone wanted to know why I didn't have a coat since it was chilly outside. I left it at a friend's house and I didn't really want to get into it, and there was nothing really to get into anyway. And then someone wanted to know what "friend" and all of the ladies were laughing, so I just made something up because the situation was completely uninteresting.

"Do I have to remind you to sign the attendance

book like the students?" Patricia asked jokingly. I kept forgetting to sign-in until the end of the day. "Are you just like the students who need to always be reminded, John?"

"Yes, absolutely," I said. "I'm worse than them since I'm supposed to be responsible and actually have things expected of me." She laughed.

I picked up both crates of English stuff, brought them to my classroom, and put them on one of the desk-chairs next to the computers. I went to flip on the light switch and found that there were only wires hanging from the light switch box, and I wasn't going to feel around and investigate. I recalled that someone mentioned worker's comp the other day. Playing with these wires would surely bring us together.

As I was leaving, I noticed something on the floor in front of Adella's door. Upon closer inspection, the numerous circles and the small, red puddle sure looked like blood. I went to the office to find Todd, but he wasn't there. I quickly went upstairs and found all my copies made, so I thanked the copy guy. I returned to my dark classroom and emptied the files from one of the crates. It was student work from about three years ago and no one wanted it, and I sure didn't. There were no lesson plans I wanted, so I threw everything in the garbage can minus the hanging file folders that KetchupBoots said were salvageable.

Todd arrived and I showed him the puddle.

"Looks like blood to me," he said. He told me he would call the custodians and then unlocked a new classroom for me.

"You need to take extra special care of this room though," he told me. "In the beginning of the year, Twilight students tore it apart by writing all over the walls and the desks. They actually kicked holes in the walls." I couldn't imagine my present students doing any of that, but maybe he was being sincere when he said there had been improvement in student behavior. Todd then demonstrated how some students wrote on walls with pens behind their backs. I told him I would do my best to keep the room in order and that I didn't anticipate any sort of problem.

I returned to my old classroom for my possessions and the crate that I was supposed to empty. I stopped first at the Twilight office to drop off the other empty crate.

"I was just kidding about your jacket before," the nurse said. "It was a joke." She was wondering whether I could take jokes.

"Don't worry about it," I said. "I can take a joke, but when my verbal wrath comes out, you're gonna be running for cover." She laughed, and I left.

I placed the crate on a table next to a crate that belonged to the Day School teacher whose room it was. It was then that the stars aligned signaling disaster, but I didn't recognize the signs. In Block One, Angela was my only student and had reading to do, so I emptied the contents of both crates, but not before jokingly pleading with her to not vandalize the class.

With Angela reading, I brought the two empty crates to the Twilight office, and as I put them down, I saw what I thought was the same crate I just emptied. Could I have just made the mistake of throwing out another teacher's files?

"Are you going to be able to get a coat?" the guidance counselor asked. "I have an extra one I can bring you tomorrow." I assured her that I had one. I was hoping the unfunny commentary on my wardrobe would come to an end as well.

I considered whether I really could have made the mistake of throwing out some other teacher's stuff, and I must have looked pale white. Jenny, the Twilight librarian, asked me what was wrong, and I told her that I thought I might have just thrown some of the wrong files in the garbage. She wanted to know if I needed her help sorting it out, because that would be no problem, and I thanked her very much for her support but was hoping to figure it out myself.

As I walked back to the classroom, I thought about Jenny because I wasn't used to such basic courtesies. I was used to squabbling with my old staff. I feared I was being apprehensive about conversing with her, but so far she was nothing but nice to me.

I guessed I found myself thinking that Jenny was a librarian like Faith and she was black and that they might speak about how I was some white oppressive force beating down on the minority students I taught. I was very disappointed with myself, and I hoped not to get trapped into thinking certain ways simply because some people put a bad taste in my mouth.

I returned to the classroom and began frantically searching through the files in the garbage so I could determine whether I threw everything out or not, but I couldn't tell. They were all mixed up, and if I was to guess, it would be that they were all old. Many papers were dated, but none of them were dated after the fall of 2002.

A few minutes into the third block, Carlos arrived and asked why I switched classrooms. I told him about the light switch. He told me that he turned it on and that it wasn't an electrical hazard at all. He was right. The day ended, and I forgot all about the files.

The next day, I entered the Twilight office and Todd greeted me.

"I'm going to kill you for throwing away the folders," he said.

-4-

IPULLED INTO THE SCHOOL PARKING LOT, and the guard was sleeping at his post. I rolled my car by so I could look for a space in a lot that greatly exceeded its maximum capacity. Some cars completely blocked in other cars. There were never ever any spots at 1:25 p.m. or before, so I drove around in circles until I was lucky to find an early departing staff member. You needed patience. Finding a spot on the street was a whole other animal.

In the evening, community college occupied numerous classrooms within the school as well. Sometimes when I was teaching at night, announcements were made asking individuals to move their cars from fire zones. The speaker was always very polite.

Because of the parking scheme, I found myself arriving later and later to the Twilight office because I could never find a place to park until after I was supposed to actually sign in for the day. I was able to rationalize and legitimize my lateness. Since we didn't really have actual responsibilities until 3:45 p.m., I didn't believe my pattern bothered anyone, although my initial entrance into the Twilight office made me a little uncomfortable.

Upon my late entrance I stated twice how I was

campaigning for worst employee ever, and twice I was told not to worry and to just sign in at 1:25 p.m. It's not like I was taking the attendance of my co-workers, and they weren't sitting in the office waiting for me either.

As I entered about fifteen minutes late, I learned that it was KetchupBoots' birthday and there was a cake.

"You're just in time for some," KetchupBoots said. Later, one of the guards entered and she told him that he was just in time for some too.

Patricia explained that Ms. Garcia was trying to reach me, but since she wasn't working at the other site today, she would be calling back around 3:00 p.m.

The entire 'throwing the student folders in the garbage' incident was weighing heavily on my mind as an unbelievably asinine albatross of a situation that I desperately needed to rectify. I asked Todd exactly what the Day School teacher's name was and decided to simply wait until the end of the school day to speak with her. Her room was just down the hall from the office.

Today, though, I was speaking with Ms. Garcia when the bell rang, and my good intentions were again left unfulfilled. Ms. Garcia told me that certain people were trying to change Miss D's grade and that she wouldn't be signing off on anything. I agreed with her decision and reiterated the reality of the grade and the fantasy of me signing anything.

Right before the students arrived, the guidance counselor reminded me that Carlos' father was coming in to speak with his teachers. Seconds later, Carlos came into class to ask me to please tell his father that he was doing well and was never absent.

"There's no way I can tell him that," I said. Carlos had been absent.

"Please!" he begged.

"Sorry, but there is no way," I said. I did tell Carlos that I would tell his father that I was new here and that I have had no problem with his work or his behavior.

"I appreciate you saying that," Carlos said. And I told his father just that.

In Literacy Lab, we had a class meeting, and the new schedules for third trimester were distributed. Seventeen of twenty-six students were present. An immediate hoopla erupted because there were ubiquitous scheduling dilemmas.

"Guidance counselor stuck up," someone yelled. It was quelled when a signup sheet was placed on the office door for students needing assistance.

Todd began the meeting by explaining that there were some issues with Twilight that needed to be addressed and immediately fixed since he had a meeting with the Day School principal, who was not at all pleased with our program. Yesterday, the principal needed to use our bathroom, and it was a boys room that was supposed to be monitored by a security guard who allowed girls to use it as well. The principal went in and found two boys and one girl inside. They weren't engaging in any kind of inappropriate behavior other than the fact that there was a girl in the boys room. The principal was appropriately not a proponent of coed bathrooms.

Todd reiterated to the students, as he did to the teachers earlier, the new rules for the hallways.

"No one is allowed to just leave class unless it is a life-threatening situation," he explained. "If a student wants to use the bathroom, the teacher has to make eye contact with the monitoring security guard to prevent further snafus from occurring." The principal also said he was going to fire the guard that was supposed to be on duty.

Todd went on to discuss a new no-tolerance policy

that was going to be instituted tomorrow. Walkmans, headphones, and cell phones weren't permitted in school, but the students required constant nagging to put them away. When I asked them to remove them, they either indicated that they weren't listening to any music or they named another teacher who allowed them to wear the headphones. Numerous students told me that they were able to study and read and talk with the music. I reminded them about the concept of impossibility each time. Hats were the same kind of problem. The second that the nagging ended, they were back on. It irritated the principal. And me.

"From now on, teachers are going to be written up for allowing this behavior," Todd said. "So if students refuse to listen to their teachers, they are going to be written up." Hearing the same point restated a million ways was so boring.

"Metal detectors are also going to be installed," Todd continued. "You're going to have to walk through them every time you enter the building." He reminded the students about the sensitivity of the machines and how having tin foil in a pants pocket would trigger the alarm.

"So consider this a warning," he said. "If the alarm goes off, an officer is required to search you."

"Is the cop fat or not?" Jason, a student, asked.

"I don't know," Todd said. He couldn't really follow the question.

"Well, I hope the cop is fat so I could run away when I set off the alarm." Everyone laughed. I did too, but to myself.

Conversation shifted to the topic of student government elections; we teachers were installing a puppet regime of students who would actually do the work required for these positions. Latoya was going to be the president; Anna the vice president; Julia the secretary; and Tiana the treasurer.

When the day was finally over, I heard someone mention that Mutumbo's car was returned to him in one piece.

A few days later, I was able to apologize to the teacher whose files I disposed of. She kindly forgave me for being an idiot.

B ETWEEN FIRST AND SECOND BLOCK, Todd came to tell me that the Interblock was going to begin earlier because he wanted to have a meeting with the staff. During our meeting, one of the security guards would oversee our students watching a video from *Frontline* that delved into the roots of Saddam Hussein.

After dropping off my Journalism class, I went to the Twilight office where everyone was talking about how Yolanda was transferred to my old school. Apparently, she assaulted a Day School student before stealing his wallet. She was identified by the victim and had his wallet. In her defense, Yolanda said that she found it on the ground. The Day School didn't even want her in Twilight since she had shown many times that she was a menace by engaging in other similar antics. Todd transferred her to my old school in the hope that she could graduate in June.

Todd finally entered the Twilight office after setting up the video. He discussed the possibility of a red-level terror alert, which indicated that a terror attack was imminent. President Bush's ultimatum to Saddam was expiring around 10:00 p.m., which meant a war with Iraq could begin at any time. When darkness fell on the Middle East tomorrow, we would be in school. Considering that the terror alert for New York was elevated to orange and that we were right across the river, our school, which was the designated emergency shelter for the area, needed to be prepared for a catastrophic event. We all needed to be briefed on our roles if the area was brought under Marshall Law. If the terror alert was raised to red, our school would be closed indefinitely until Marshall Law was lifted.

"We all need to make sure we have clothes for a few days and medicine if we need it," Todd explained. "If we go into red alert, we would be under lockdown, and if we leave anything in our cars, we won't be able to get it." He also mentioned the reality of a military presence maintaining order on the streets.

"The auto shop (in the school) received a delivery today for a four-day supply of water for teachers, students, and staff. That would account for over 3,400 people," he said. He mentioned that he was given keys today to all of the locks in the school including the cafeteria freezer so that in case we were stuck in school, we had food to eat. I heard something about also receiving a supply of granola. It was all so surreal.

Todd went on about our would-be duties, roles, and responsibilities. He wanted to know if any of us had any kind of medical training or counseling experience; some members of the staff did, and I definitely didn't. Some of us would be serving as sweepers if we needed to move people to different parts of the school, which would be serving as a crisis-center hub for a large portion of the city. We would have to walk our students to another school that would serve as a center for all students so their parents could reach them.

"You need to all make arrangements with your families because of the job obligations that will keep you all here," Todd said. "Along with clothes and medicine, you should also keep some extra toiletries in the office."

"I'm going to take a sick day tomorrow," the art teacher said.

"Me too," said KetchupBoots.

I was glad we had an emergency plan in place; it was a bit reassuring, but it was also plain frightening. Todd apologized in case anyone thought it was frightening.

I returned to the room with the students, but no one was watching the movie. It was a bit rowdy and although the guard was watching them, it was apparently not his responsibility to make sure they were quiet. Nevertheless, the guards always seemed enthusiastic to help. Sometimes you needed someone to watch over your class if you needed to use the bathroom. Niles told me his guards were too incompetent and rude to do anything like that. I walked to the back of the room and waited for the rest of the staff to return. The class quieted down little by little.

Some students were trying to hide that they were throwing sunflower seeds despite the fact that I watched them do it, saw the hit, saw the ensuing reaction, and watched them stare at me to see my reaction. My combination of stares and hand gestures finally quelled any further developments with everyone other than Ivan, who still thought I was blind to his mayhem.

In the video was Iraq's invasion of Kuwait. Most students were talking.

"Can you be quiet so we can actually watch the program?" KetchupBoots said to the class.

As Iraqi troops pulled their military into the country, they were physically abusing Kuwaitis along the way. A bunch of students were laughing, and Jason seemed to be leading the charge. The images moved on to assassinations and hangings, and the entire classroom got silent.

Todd came in and turned the video off so he could talk about the "red alert." He went through the same motions. It seemed somewhat sugar-coated compared to our meeting, but there wasn't any real sugar-coating; rather, my mind was far from thinking clearly since I was so disturbed. You could tell by the looks of the students that it was no laughing matter, and although the questions after the initial announcement and dissemination of the superintendent's newsletter contextualized it all for students and parents, having it verbalized to everyone as a group was distressing.

"Where we gonna sleep?" one kid asked. "There's mice here."

"Hopefully we won't have to worry about that," Todd said.

"Are we going to sleep on the floor?" another student asked.

"If we have to, we will probably sleep on the exercise mats from the gym," he said. It was all much to the chagrin of the students.

"I hope we have a red alert till the summer so we won't have to come to school," Jason said.

"If we had Marshall Law, no one would be able to leave home," Todd said.

One of the Twins, who were nicknamed the Good One and the Evil One, and could only be distinguished by a facial birthmark, asked, "Are jets going to come from Iraq and bomb New York?" She was serious.

"There is absolutely no way any planes are going to be dropping anything ever since we have a homeland defense that will protect us," I said.

"Then how come no one stopped the planes crashing

into the World Trade Center?" someone asked. I had opened up the ole can of worms and Pandora's Box. Nothing seemed easy to explain.

I left the classroom despondent and craving the beginning of the next block. I wondered whether my facial expressions reflected my feelings. The security guard told me to remember that they were just a bunch of kids and that they just didn't get it. I said something about how they weren't that young. I wished they would get it.

-6-

IN THE TWILIGHT OFFICE, Patricia joked that all the red alert talk scared KetchupBoots into taking a sick day. KetchupBoots, however, insisted that she was sick, but I knew she wasn't coming to school since she told me. I also noticed for the first time that KetchupBoots had clear braces.

I went to the library to use a computer and once again said, "Hello," to the mean librarian. She sort of just looked through me, but I continued smiling as I walked past.

The other day, I heard her voice behind me growing louder and louder as she said, "Hey," "Hey," "Hey." I knew she was heying me, but she had seen me here for two months and never even made the slightest inclination to introduce herself or make any effort of any kind to remember my name, which I have said to her numerous times as I repeatedly introduced myself. Beating her with the sledgehammer of kindness had not been successful.

Thankfully, it wasn't personal, since she was equally mean to the students. The other day after school, one kid came in and asked to use a computer, but the server was down. The mean librarian mumbled to the enthusiastic kid as he barreled toward the computers. Once the kid realized that the server was down, he asked the mean librarian what was wrong, and she started talking about how she "woulda told ya if ya listened to me." When the kid said he would try back tomorrow, she waved her arm and said, "Whateva."

Her voice was capable of selecting the proper intonation of a word that would make that particular word sound extremely rude. I admired her for her consistency at being a complete jerk.

Upon returning to the Twilight office, I was introduced to Mutumbo's mentor. I really needed to get a mentor myself. I had not done anything for my certification, and it was going to come up eventually.

Todd met me in my room, and we talked about next year's Twilight.

"You got a good thing going here," he said. I agreed. The work environment was great; I liked the staff and the students. Jenny just the other day took me aside and told me to please come to the office if there were ever any problems, and I thanked her. My face must speak for itself sometimes. but these little bits of support here and there were encouraging, since I really didn't ever want to involve anyone with any problems I had. Nevertheless, the feelings from my last job were still lingering, and I still had feelings of apprehension for staying in Twilight. Maybe I should move to the Day School if given the chance.

Since my working conditions were that much better, I strived to be a better teacher. Dr. Larson gave me ten copies of *Lord of the Flies,* and we were about halfway through it already. We still read the chapters in class and the students still answered questions from a worksheet, but I was able to add other activities related to the novel.

In one recent class, I broke everyone up into groups

and they had to come up with a list of rules they would compose if they were stranded on an island. Then we compiled one main list while discussing all the different rules and the problems with them. I played the role of devil's advocate to keep the conversation moving and the students thinking about potential problems and various perspectives. Then the next day they went back into the reading, having had a discussion about rules. It made it easier for them to understand the breakdown of the children's society as the plot progressed.

I also tried to have 'Quote of the Day' at the beginning of every block. It gave students a chance to write a response to a statement, and then take part in a class discussion. I selected the quotes from a website that had an unlimited supply of *famous* ones. In the last week, we had quotes from Thomas Jefferson, George S. Patton, Indira Gandhi, Pablo Picasso, and Yoda. Some discussions went on longer than others, but it brought the class together at the start of class and was a worthwhile activity. Niles had great success with it at his school.

My first block always benefitted from the additional forty minutes of Literacy Lab. Therefore, we were able to do the 'Quote of the Day' every day, and no students were behind in their reading.

Third and fourth blocks were always only forty minutes and sometimes even got shortened because of an extended Interblock. Everyone was on different parts of the book because of this, and I already lost two books to students who brought them home to catch up. I wished we could have consistent 'Quote of the Day' sessions, but the students needed more reading time.

By this point, I understood the majority of the slang. Whenever I used their words, I made them uncool, so they stopped saying them. A bunch of kids also spoke

Spanish, and I didn't speak a word of it and didn't pretend that I could. I was sure that they tested whether I understood it, but I only hablo español muy un poco y no bueno. Sometimes they spoke Spanish and laughed hysterically. I was probably better off not understanding them.

Like Abbott and Costello's "Who's on First," I noticed the same phrases going back and forth repeatedly. They were "Word is bond" (pronounced bawn), "Wha Happen," "True," "Word," and "Yeah, Ah-ite." I could easily overhear a conversation of a "True," then "Word," then "Yeah, Ah-ite," and then someone new would enter the conversation and say "Wha Happen," and then the cycle of nonsense would begin again. As foolish as I may have thought of it, I actually understood where they were coming from.

They also ruined words in my vocabulary. When I would tell students to leave, I used to say, "Bounce." But now when I said that, too many students would bounce in place. So, they took back that word. Now, I rarely used it, unless I chose to say it to certain students who broke into dance, which made everyone laugh.

I was still adamant about no cursing in class and no racism whatsoever, even though it was often the way many spoke. Carlos would respond to a regular "no racism" from me by calling me "white boy," but it was just because he was a wiseass. He sometimes called me Mr. KKK when I reminded people about no racial comments. I never imagined such a backfire. My other favorite lines were, "Just because you could talk, doesn't mean you should speak," and, "Just because you are a jackass, doesn't mean you have to act like one." In the former, I sometimes interchanged talk, speak, or anything about having a mouth, and my point was clear. For the latter, I generally followed that by asking that particular student to please surprise me today by not being one.

I was still talking to Todd about working here next year, but I needed to get started on my state certification.

"Even (Mutumbo) has a mentor already and is getting his certification in order," I said.

"I'll mentor you then," Todd said.

Before I could answer, Mrs. Davis greeted us both and asked for my signature, which gave her the right to observe me in the next twenty days. We all began talking, and she explained that she would be spending the first two blocks at our school and would be conducting a seminar during Interblock.

In the hallway, I saw Carlos with his arm around the Evil Twin as they walked by, and Todd just looked at me dumbfounded. The relationship between the Twins, the Good and Evil identical ones, and Carlos was quite puzzling. One day he seemed to be with the Good One, and on another day he seemed to be with the Evil One. Once, when we were watching a clip from the black-and-white version of *Lord of the Flies*, Carlos asked if we could turn the lights off since he was sitting next to the Good One. I said, "Yeah, Ah-ite," hitting every necessary sarcastic intonation.

Right before Mrs. Davis' seminar, two of the candidates for student council offices would be giving their speeches. The election was already fixed, but the speeches maintained the illusion of reality. Latoya and Tiana were absent today, so only Anna and Julia would be speaking.

As I was proofreading Anna's speech for vice president in first block, one girl came up to my desk and started looking at a picture of the woman teacher standing with her family that sat on the desk I used.

"This family's fuckin ugly, Mista," she said, while laughing a funny laugh.

"Please be nice," I said.

"You can't say they're not fuckin ugly, Mista," she said.

She demanded that I look at the picture, but I feared that if I did, in combination with her cackle, I would start laughing. I needed to maintain a professionalism that didn't include mocking other staff members with students.

At the beginning of Interblock, Anna gave her speech to the class and it sounded very positive and made clear her goals and her conscientious attitude. Julia, the candidate for secretary, went next. I didn't read her speech before she gave it. Julia talked about the same types of goals and how she'll work hard as an officer. The tone changed quickly, however, when she darted into her other goals.

"We need better teachers at Twilight because some of them are absolutely terrible," Julia said.

Todd put on the same dumbfounded face that he had on earlier and one that I would see again and again. Surely my jaw dropped to the desk while Mrs. Davis was sitting next to me. Julia later told me that she wasn't talking about me though, but it was still tough to hear that kind of criticism about the other staff members.

The awkwardness ebbed when Mrs. Davis began her seminar. Basically, it was an activity to give each student and teacher an opportunity to learn about each other. People needed to learn one quality about every person in the room, and you couldn't tell two people the same thing about yourself. The next twenty minutes or so, everyone was asking everyone questions about themselves.

Once everyone completed the assignment, each student went to the front of the class, and in an organized manner, everyone around the room stated a quality about that person. It was funny to hear how certain guys were referred to as playas and pimps. Other students were called drinkers, while others were called cigarette smokers and marijuana smokers. Although these were negative traits, at least it was an honest forum, and everyone enjoyed learning new things about each other.

I was troubled and surprised to hear how many students actually had children. I already knew that Latoya, the class president, had a baby. Carlos had two babies and one on the way, all from different mothers. Other kids had babies. The students had more than the staff.

Twilight served an important purpose if these students could get their high school diplomas. I couldn't imagine any of them raising children. The teenage pregnancy epidemic was relentless.

Julia recently told me that she was pregnant, and Tiana also told me that she was pregnant. It wasn't a secret.

"What are you going to do about it?" I asked Tiana.

"I'm keeping it," she said. "I already had an abortion once."

I remembered hearing at my other school how some female students wanted children so someone would always love them. And they all questioned me persistently and never understood why I didn't have any yet.

-7-

EVERY THURSDAY, WE USED the Interblock from 6:00 p.m. to 6:55 p.m. as a gym period for all Twilight students. The gymnasium was split in half for two different games: basketball and volleyball. Mrs. J also taught gym during the individual blocks, but it wasn't done consistently, and frankly, having students pulled from my class to go to gym was pretty pointless. Gym was simply not as important as English class under any circumstance.

Teachers weren't forced to play, but it was fun to get involved rather than sit on the sidelines and watch or sit in the Twilight office. Since I knew quite well the grim reality of my basketball-playing ability, I played volleyball. The basketball game was pretty intense, so all the girls were pretty much eliminated from that game by the boys, who never passed the ball or let them shoot anyway.

Mutumbo and I had been playing volleyball from the beginning while Todd switched sports. Maybe it had something to do with making even teams in basketball but I wasn't sure. Either way, Todd and I would sweat during Interblock. I began bringing gym clothes.

We played with a volleyball that was a bit softer than

the standard one. Mrs. J kept insisting we use a standard one, but the girls complained that it hurt their hands. Led by the Twins, a bunch outright refused to play. I didn't understand why Mrs. J was making such a big deal about it. Mrs. J was also the worst volleyball player ever.

When I played, I did my best to get everyone involved and to get my team to rotate positions so that everyone had an opportunity to serve. I wanted to get them to understand how those in the back row could feed the ball to the front row, so people in the front could try to spike it. Unfortunately, everyone chased after the ball so they could hit it and most never did. Without sporadic reminders, a team could easily just be one big line in the middle of the court chasing after the ball and never returning it over the net. Thankfully, my team began to understand the strategy and took advantage of a team that was playing like that.

When I served, I always served to a student, and I always told him or her where I was going to serve it. I tried to make it more fun by being sarcastic and falsely competitive. I tried to hit it to whoever was least involved or whose mind wasn't in the game, so everyone got involved and stayed involved. I started taking my serve too seriously, and when a few students started making fun of me, I toned it down. If Mrs. J happened to be the one to receive my serve, it was never returned.

I always played on the team against Todd when he played, and everyone enjoyed him missing a shot or getting spiked on. Obviously everyone enjoyed watching me miss shots and fall on the ground. Carlos enjoyed calling me "white boy" when I missed, and I had no problem hitting him in the back with the ball when he mocked me. Mutumbo always hit the ball with his head at some point, and everyone laughed.

The teachers and the school never forced students to take part, so some sat on the side and watched or played cards. Juan, the Spanish teacher, never played, and KetchupBoots never played. Jenny was sometimes in the gym talking with some students, as was Catherine, the guidance counselor. Just recently, Adella started playing volleyball, and she succeeded at being even worse than Mrs. J. Carlos got a kick out of showing her how to play and demonstrating to her how to hit the ball. During a break, I saw him coaching her as she hit the ball against the wall to get used to the return.

During the last Interblock gym, Tiana was demanding to know what the score was since she wasn't keeping score and no one else was keeping score and I didn't care to keep score. She needed to know what it was so she could talk about how her team was winning and was better. In the midst of this, a pigeon flew down from the rafters and landed on an empty section of the gym floor. Everything in the gymnasium ceased. There were no more bouncing balls or squeaks of sneakers. Everyone was locked in on this pigeon that was cooing and walking around. Soon the volleyball was flung at the pigeon and the pigeon jumped. Everyone was chasing it so they could get it to fling at the pigeon. No other teachers were around as I joined the game of chasing after the ball to prevent it from being grabbed and flung at the pigeon. A basketball was soon in the mix. Thankfully, Todd returned to stop the madness.

Realizing it was under constant fire, the pigeon flew up to the rafters and still captivated everyone in the gym. Some students yelled for others to throw something. We got the volleyball back.

The Cancer returned from getting a drink and threw

himself into the fray. He was about to whip a basketball before Todd stopped him.

The Cancer got his name because he used to be at Niles' school, and Niles, who was rarely critical of people, referred to him as "the worst human being I ever met." For numerous reasons, the Cancer was expelled from Niles' school and transferred here for another chance to get his high school diploma. His father was apparently one of the biggest drug dealers in the city. The Cancer still sold drugs outside Niles' school.

"I have to make a living," he told Niles. The Cancer also told Niles that I had to "step off." I mentioned to the Cancer that I knew Niles from high school. He also told Niles that I demanded that he get his assignments done.

On his first day, the Cancer was trying to make his mark by having a smart mouth in my class. It was not the best method of getting my attention.

"What school are you going to get transferred to next?" I asked him. "What is going to be the next excuse? Are the teachers not fair here either?"

Later when I told them about my responses, Niles and his colleagues appreciated my honest approach with him. Their school was better without him. Even the Cancer's old friends who followed his every move told Niles and his colleagues that they were glad he was gone.

The Cancer appreciated my brand of honesty, and I thought I was growing on him. He wasn't really that bad either; I would take him over most of the awful students from my old school. He tried to ruffle my feathers by calling me Mr. Gay, but my persistent sarcasm slowed him down. He made his remarks under his breath, so only I heard him. He didn't strive for attention from others.

Because of his attempts to mock me, he got a new

nickname. If Jennifer Lopez can be JLo, then the Cancer could be KLo. I called him KLo and referred to him as KLo to the other teachers. No one else called him KLo, though. KLo forgot to write his name on his paper a few days so I wrote his name on it for him: KLo.

The other day, I went to the bathroom in between blocks and saw KLo and Carlos talking, and obviously KLo was holding a cigarette behind his back since the bathroom reeked of a fresh cigarette burning.

"I'm not stupid, just smoke your cigarette," I told him. He was doing all his work, and I didn't have the energy to tell him to put it out. I would be thrilled if he didn't wear his hat or his headphones in class. After using the proper urinal, I heard numerous threats about how they were going to "get me" now that I was in the bathroom.

"You're far too intelligent to make a mistake like that," I said.

When I was washing my hands, KLo told me how he once smashed a male teacher's face against the wall while the teacher was urinating.

"Stop playin me," I said. He said he wasn't.

"Word is bawn?" I asked.

"True," KLo replied.

After KLo's story about assaulting a teacher, Carlos countered with his own teacher assault contribution. KLo, who could never be outdone, told another story about how once a teacher put him in a headlock, and he unloaded on him and he didn't even get in trouble because the teacher touched him first and he was just defending himself.

"You best not get tangled up with these fists," I said, sarcastically, as I showed them both my clenched hands. "These are lethal weapons." They both laughed.

"Seriously though, please stop assaulting teachers,"

I said. "Even though it sounds like they deserved it, violence can't always be the solution."

I let them finish their cigarettes and held the door for their exit.

"I'm not gonna call you Mr. Gay anymore," KLo said.

"Don't worry," I said. "There's no way I'm going to stop calling you KLo."

-8-

"**S**O WHO CAN TELL ME the four bodily fluids that are infected with the AIDS virus?" began the young lady from the AIDS awareness center. It was her third appearance as a guest speaker for Wednesday's Interblock. She was very informative and frank, and the students needed to be informed about the dangers of sex.

I heard a horrendous statistic about Niles' Day School. After a student was shot, students were asked to donate blood, and forty of them did. Twenty-four were HIV-positive. Apparently, numerous students in the area were infected with AIDS at birth and their guardians kept it from them. From what I could gather, students hardly ever used protection. The numbers could be overstated or entirely false, but such a seemingly realistic and horrific health epidemic failed to make me breathe any easier. If the number of students' children was any indication of their sexual habits, it could very well be true. I told my students the statistic numerous times because they really needed to think about it and be afraid. Just the other day, both Twins were absent because the Evil One had to get an abortion.

"OK, so we have blood, we have breast milk, we have male cum…"

It was very difficult to look at the smirks of the students and watch them whispering and laughing. When I was in school these kinds of health seminars were a hoot. I remembered watching a film about childbirth and someone yelling, "I wonder how that smells." I remembered hearing a twenty-three-year-old blonde alcoholic tell of her problems and how once she found herself hundreds of miles from her house sleeping in her car, which was filled with beer cans from her driving bender. The first question asked to her by a student observer: "How quickly can you chug a beer?"

I always had a tendency to laugh at people laughing, so since I was by the door, I went to the bathroom and tried to find the more composed and mature self I knew was inside me somewhere. And I almost did.

When I returned to class, Pablo threw a card on my desk, and a bunch of students were looking at me and laughing. He said, "I ain't readin this shit." The card read: "Sexually abstaining but has had sexual intercourse."

Quickly another card was thrown on my desk that read, "Giving Oral Sex with a Condom."

A couple of students were laughing, and it was apparently my turn. I was unclear what the cards were about, so I threw them on Pablo's desk and the AIDS lady moved on. I learned that I was supposed to recognize my situations as high risk, low risk, or no risk.

Todd was in the office but finally returned and sat down. The 'Giving Oral Sex with a Condom' card was thrown his way, and all the students laughed. I was unsure if they even knew he was gay.

"I've been framed," he said. The students laughed for one reason, and the staff laughed for another. I wondered if the kids would give him the same respect if they knew of his homosexuality. His business was his business anyway, and he didn't have to tell anyone. I was amused when KLo got "Mutual Masturbation."

The conversation turned to people putting on condoms incorrectly.

"They fit everyone's dick," someone yelled.

Carlos said, "Mista K could tell you that they fit the smallest ones." I grit my teeth and slightly smiled. If I dished it out, I had to take it. I knew how to get laughed at.

As the conversation continued, one girl kept asking, "Isn't it true when you drunk you want to fuck?" The chatter got louder and starting getting out of hand.

"Mista K's like a woman who likes gettin beaten up and smacked around," Pablo said. Although the banter was losing focus, most students were too inattentive to notice.

The Q&A moved on to dildos. The students asked questions, and for me, the talk of dildos was difficult to sit and listen to.

"Can you get AIDS from a dildo?" someone asked.

"Wash the dildo first," someone replied.

"Get your own dildo," another suggested. "Quit usin someone else's."

Some of the other teachers chuckled, and I tried hard not to laugh as well. Some students were making funny comments, and being an adult that was supposed to keep them on track and scold them was difficult and fruitless.

A bunch of students thought the AIDS lady and I were a good match. One of the girls said, "You need to start hittin that since she needs a man and you're both white."

A month ago, a woman spoke twice about abstinence.

At the second presentation, she said that condoms were scientifically ineffective, and she had medical quotes backing her up.

"My two daughters are saving their virginities until they're married," she said to a roomful of teenage parents and sexually active teens.

She checkered her speech with ghetto-type lingo like, "Even though I'm fifty-five, I still like gettin some." Equally ridiculous were the role-playing scenarios where the kids were supposed to say no to sex and to better understand the realities of pregnancies.

The abstinence platform for the inner-city students disturbed the lady from the educational institute who was observing that day, and I couldn't agree with her more. She wrote some harsh comments when the abstinence lady passed out comment sheets for the staff. The southerner felt that it was irresponsible and ridiculous, and she was right. These students already had sex, and the abstinence woman failed to properly address reality.

I was glad the Texan from the education institution was speaking up. At the four school Twilight staff meeting, she used such speaking gems as "Duh" and "That's awesome." She made the latter reference to how my old Twilight site had given the students an Easter Egg Hunt, since many students had never been to one. To me, it was a waste of time. They were adults clamoring for a high school degree. An education was more important than the experience of an Easter Egg Hunt.

Also at this Twilight meeting, I learned from Niles that Mariella's husband/boyfriend supposedly cheated on her with an assortment of strippers that he routinely slept with. He bragged to Niles about it. I felt bad for Mariella. My situation was so much better now that I rarely thought about my old school.

At the meeting, I even got a chance to meet my replacement; he was an older, white man with a gray buzz cut. He sought me out to ask me how I got "them" to have a discussion and not leave the class and how I was able to get any work done.

"I'm glad I got transferred," I said. I told him to hang in there and to try different teaching methods because the students were awful. They seemed even worse. The new teacher brought up Miss D. I also was sorry to hear that Mrs. Davis' husband had colon cancer.

Between the abstinence lady and the AIDS lady, a naval spokesman came to visit. This was when I thought about Nicotina. As the Iraq War was becoming more of a reality, Nicotina went into a tirade about how wars were for poor people and minorities to fight and die in and how unfair that was. I understood her point, but she always put this slant on it about how I would never have to go into the service because of my background and my ethnicity. Nicotina had a way of making me feel guilty about who I was, and I thought that was unfair; it was difficult to not get into it with her. The reality was that the navy had wonderful opportunities for some students, and they could and should take advantage. I was sorry that any soldiers died.

At another Interblock, a representative from the Newark Bears independent baseball team came in to talk about careers in sports. He provided us with promotional materials about the team but not any free tickets. Most students couldn't even get summer jobs. They couldn't afford to go to Newark to see the Bears.

Hudson County Community College gave a presentation too. Any student who got a Twilight diploma got a scholarship to HCCC. I never stopped emphasizing this to students. I hoped some would take advantage.

-9-

IT WAS THE FIRST DAY back from spring break, which was extended from a half-day on Holy Thursday to Monday. I entered the Twilight office, and after the usual greetings and corresponding chitchat, Todd proclaimed that there were only forty more days until summer break. He suggested having a numbers board that would be reduced on a daily basis. Everyone laughed.

When asked about my break, I explained how I went to Schroon Lake, NY with Niles. Todd made a joke about how I was in Screw Lake, and that joke went on and on. There was something ironic about a homosexual making a comment about two male friends and a screwing fantasy. I always tried to not divulge too much of my life. Work was for work.

"Midterms are next week so please give me copies of them," Todd told us.

My classes only had two chapters remaining of *Lord of the Flies,* but a handful of students needed to catch up because of absences or just not completing their work. I tried helping them get through it. Unfortunately, of the ten extra books I had, I was down to five, so I needed to get more from the library. I also wanted to show them the newer version of the movie on Wednesday and Thursday between reviewing the themes of the text. The visual would be helpful for students to fill in the gaps, although they would overwhelmingly prefer to watch the movie without ever having to read the book.

As the day was about to begin, I enthusiastically but sardonically greeted the students back from break. No one wanted to be back. I got my class together, and we went straight into the 'Quote of the Day,' which was one by James Baldwin. It flowed smoothly into today's reading of chapter eleven. The class was exactly where I wanted them since they benefited from having the Literacy Lab, which gave them extra time for the quote and to read. Even the new student was on chapter eight.

Jason was suspended for cutting school for falsely signing in two weeks ago. Ivan would also be enjoying an additional week of break for the same offense.

As the extended second block got underway, I divided the class between Journalism students who only took Journalism and Journalism students who also took English class. I wanted to make sure everyone was going to finish their book before the midterm. The Journalism students had to read sections of the Sunday paper, copies of which I was able to get from the payroll office, and write up summaries using the format from our meeting on Holy Thursday. If the English students completed chapter eleven, I would move them onto the Journalism assignment.

Getting the students to understand and complete their assignments, unfortunately, was a frustrating exercise. It was hard distributing the different assignments with no access to additional copies because of the preposterous copying system in the school. I passed out the originals, so they could copy the questions. Such busywork was a monumental waste of time.

Nothing was easy, and today KLo was one of the central culprits. He was so high with his eyes so red and barely open. After my incessant nagging, he eventually took off his hat. Trying to get him to sit still and do work, though, and not talk and not rap, was an exercise in futility. He started calling me Kay Gay under his breath, which only served to irritate me. He kept touching Tiana next to him, who called him one of her papis in the last block, while staring at the Good Twin, who was playing right into his flirtation. I was unsure whether KLo was the father of Tiana's unborn baby.

Pablo, meanwhile, couldn't be upstaged. He elected to keep his hat on despite me asking him to remove it. I had to stand next to him and remove it or he would put it back on his head the moment I moved a few paces away from him. He kept it off after succumbing to my persistence.

Pablo was way behind in the book, but he insisted he would pass the class and the test.

"I beg to differ," I said. "I have to sign off on your grades."

"I don't care," he said. Obviously, it was better if he got a high school diploma rather than not get one, but he had to learn something about responsibility and accountability. Todd already told me that he would pass, but I was going to make sure he did something for that meager grade. He was making no effort to complete any work, and I had him again in the fourth block. I just wanted him out.

My relaxed self from break had disappeared. Between KLo and Pablo, there was just too much noise, and if some people were talking, others were compelled to talk.

No one could or would complete any assignments. I was flustered.

"Look you two," I said, "my life will be easier with one of you outta here. You should just shoot it out to see who gets chucked." This backfired. They started shooting it out with their hands as guns from one side of the room and into the middle, as they tapped their feet to the rhythm of their arms.

"Get out!" I said to Pablo. "Go to the office." Before he could refuse, I went to the office to tell Todd I needed him out. I returned and handed Pablo his work. KLo settled down. His eyes were open much wider. He finally got busy.

As the block progressed, Pablo was able to leave the office, look in through the window of my door and stare at me, with his hat on, of course. I went to the door to speak to him.

"Why are you even in the hallway?" I asked him.

"The office threw me out," he said. "I gotta pee." I began my discourse on irrationality and impossibility.

"You just a dictionary," he told me. "You ain't from the street."

Despite the fact that KLo and Pablo annoyed me terribly and frustrated me immensely, their behavior was more from the wiseass vein than from some of the threatening kind I experienced at my last school. In the midst of our verbal sparring, I laughed at times because they were funny and not being violently malicious.

Pablo told me how he was going to smack me or give me a "one-hitta quitta," which would be one punch by him that would knock me out. He was filled with bullshit.

"If you did hit me," I said, "we wouldn't have any more issues." I implied that he would be gone.

"If I hit you and got put away, I'd get jacked in jail

and then beat you again when I got out." I removed his hat for him.

The second block madness ended and the third one began, but not before KLo and Pablo returned to socialize with the class. They felt compelled to visit me at all times because they loved the attention. I had to physically escort them out of my room.

The Twins were getting a lot of attention, and it seemed everyone wanted to speak with the Evil One. Finally, I got everyone settled and reading. The class was only forty minutes long, and by the time they were all working, we already lost ten minutes. We could rarely do 'Quote of the Day' in blocks three and four.

The room was quiet and I tried getting on the internet, but the server was still down. It's too bad they were unable to fix these computer problems during the ten days the students and staff were away.

Carlos finally arrived and stated how he was completely caught up by handing in all his work. I was sure he just got the answers during his first two blocks, but at least he did it. His understanding of the novel would be in the results of his midterm exam anyway.

When he finally got started on chapter eleven, Todd came to tell me about the rapid dismissal. He knew I was having a bad day.

"Would you rather be at Screw Lake?" he asked. I begged him for a few more days off.

In the previous block, no one showed up for the first ten minutes, and I was tired of looking for them and dragging them to class. My job was to teach English, but there were so many responsibilities and decisions that were never mentioned at Twilight meetings.

Finally, Pablo, Dino, and the Twins arrived. The Evil One didn't actually have class, but she sometimes waited for the other one. I didn't mind her waiting in my class since her only real problem was having every male member of the class vie for her attention. She helped Carlos with some of his work, and he needed any help he could get.

The Twins always completed their assignments. They needed to get their diplomas and go to a real school. I was glad to hear that they were taking advantage of the free community college scholarship offered to them after graduation.

Dino and Pablo, on the other hand, were really behind and didn't want to do anything. They gave me numerous reasons why they should be allowed to take the book home.

"I don't have enough books," I said. "Schoolwork is supposed to be done in school anyway."

I once again played the hat game with Pablo and asked Dino to remove his do-rag, but he apparently needed it for his hair, and I lacked the energy to argue about it. Pablo felt compelled to then put his hat back on, but I removed it.

I asked the Twins to go to the bathroom for awhile so these guys could get to work. These guys wouldn't stop flirting with them. The girls loved the attention so they wanted to stay, but they reluctantly left. Dino and Pablo continued talking while doing nothing. I tried to get through to them that they wouldn't pass, but Pablo insisted that he would. He enjoyed interspersing his argument with the phrase "balls in your mouth," which obviously was unacceptable and frustrated me.

"I don't want to know what you did all break," I replied. Dino and Pablo laughed.

I decided to go after Dino. I reminded him that he should have failed last trimester, but he ended up passing with a 70. It got him working. Even Pablo began working, but then the Twins returned.

At some point, the Twins became silent and Pablo and Dino got working, but then Todd knocked on the door to announce the rapid dismissal fire drill, and that was that.

We went through the procedure and brought the students outside. They made their ways away.

"Spring break was extended," I said. "You don't have to return for the rest of the week." Patricia, some students, and a few other teachers within earshot laughed.

As I tried to leave the parking lot, Dino and Pablo walked passed my car, and the smoke from their marijuana poured into my car, temporarily making it reek.

"I found the roach I lost in your classroom," Pablo said. It explained why he kept coming into my classroom at every opportunity between and during my classes.

I couldn't believe summer break was only thirty-nine days away.

-10-

IN THE TWILIGHT OFFICE, KETCHUPBOOTS was in somewhat of a foul mood. As she left to make another cell phone call, Patricia, Catherine, Miss Jackson, and Jenny started talking about KetchupBoots' boyfriend. Apparently, he had two different names. I couldn't help but laugh. I was told that KetchupBoots stayed up late playing pool at a pool hall and didn't get any sleep. The entire notion was odd. I didn't know any pool halls open at 6 a.m. when KetchupBoots was done playing. She had been bringing her briefcased pool stick to work. I guessed she didn't want someone stealing it from her car.

"How come you didn't hear anything about this?" Patricia asked me.

"I have no idea what's going on," I said. She laughed.

I often used a computer in the corner of the room near Patricia's desk and people talked all around me. Sometimes I'd hear snippets of conversations and laugh and Patricia would accuse me of listening in. I told her I was focused on my job and not constant gossip. Then, Miss Jackson blindsided me.

"So was it you who wrote that story about Faith and

Shirley?" she asked. Jenny started laughing. I tried not to get nervous and didn't think I did.

"I did write a story," I said, "but someone stole it from my desk so I don't even know what the names were in the story, since it was never returned to me."

"I remember you walking into one of the first Twilight meetings in August with a pair of sandals on," Miss Jackson said. I laughed but didn't remember if I was wearing sandals.

I looked different than when I first began working here, since now I weighed twenty-five pounds less and made much more of an effort to maintain a better professional appearance. At my last school, there were numerous people whose lives were simply pages and pages of excuses, and when you are in a situation like that, you'd best look in the mirror and begin fixing your own problems or your life will become one of making excuses. I hoped I would never forget that.

The Twilight experience was coming to an end, though. Mrs. Davis, after returning a satisfactory evaluation form, told me that I would be recommended for the Day School so I could take my certification classes and get certified at the end of my first or beginning of my second year in Day School. I tried to get a guarantee of where I would be, but I couldn't. I did, however, fill out a paper concerning my employment next year, and according to the contract, they were required to notify me if I wasn't being retained and that time had passed. I later heard rumors that some teachers would not be back, but I didn't know who.

Mrs. Davis understood the kind of progress I made because in one Twilight meeting she said, "Without naming names, one teacher actually has students reading in his class."

Niles, who was always vocal in these meetings, looked over at me, but I shrugged him off. Despite this, I still wished I could be more interactive with my classes and less of a manager of work.

They were reading, but the classroom discussion element was gone. They came in when they wanted and completed assignments when they wanted to. They wanted their diplomas. I could only hope these activities were making them more literate. These kids could get a diploma by completing their English requirements in less than two years, which didn't include the amount of class time they wasted before entering Twilight and didn't take into account their performance in other subject areas. I hoped they appreciated the accomplishment of reading an entire book.

I found the students benefited from regimentation. When Pablo and KLo were caught up in World Literature, it was an accomplishment. They understood the themes in *Things Fall Apart*. When I tried to mix in any other teaching methods, they were so distracted by anything new that I had to work back to the standard regimentation. 'Quote of the Day' was difficult to do with them and ended up being a nuisance. Giving them work once they walked through the door was much easier, which allowed for the small amount of time we had together to be used more effectively.

I was back in my room sitting at my desk and filling out my lesson plans when the students began walking in, and every day was generally the same. Each morning, they walked in and I greeted them enthusiastically in the hallway, welcoming them to another day in school. Generally, none of them reciprocated the greeting. They went into the office, signed in, and returned to my class to eat lunch, which in theory they weren't supposed to be doing in school.

Once they were inside my class, I mildly teased them as they ate: "So what did you bring for me today?" or "Hmmm, that smells delicious. What are *you* going to eat?" Each day might be different and there was no particular line that was a constant, but the spirit was there.

Most students had absolutely no concept of manners. Even my nicest students never said thank you. When I asked them how they were, they just said "OK" and never asked me how I felt. Nevertheless, many offered me food whenever I got into my routine. It was nice because they absolutely never had to offer me anything.

"MY SON!" I yelled operatically in the hallway. The student known as My Son entered school with a smile.

"How are you?" I asked My Son.

"Nunya," he said.

"What's that mean?" I asked him.

"Nunya business, muthafucka," but the motherfucker waned out and wasn't as completely disrespectful as it seemed. I sure didn't take it as such and he didn't give it that way.

Whenever I yelled, "MY SON," someone yelled, "MY DAUGHTER!" Apparently, I was the daughter in the exchange.

When I saw who said it, I put on a face to convey that I was incredibly insulted, but they knew I was holding back laugher.

"MY SON!" I yelled again as he entered the room. The last English teacher also had a nickname for him and some of the teachers still called him that, but everyone else knew it was My Son now.

"MY DAUGHTER!" another student said in an operatic voice.

"You want a vacation!" I said. It was my sweet way of threatening a suspension for disrespect I wasn't actually disrespected by.

"Well, you got one, Mister. Say it again?" I was copying *The Breakfast Club* scene where the moron kept punishing Judd Nelson over and over again with detentions. They hadn't seen the movie, but I was amused. I offered *vacations* to everyone in the class.

At 4:00 p.m., I insisted that the do-rags and the hats and the headphones be put away, but who was I kidding? It would be the same exact battle over every object as it was day in and day out. It was difficult to have authority while also joking around.

My Son offered me a small roll from the Filipino bakery around the corner, and I graciously accepted it because those rolls were delicious. The bakery sold a bag of them for a dollar, and a bunch of students bought them and gave them out at school.

Latoya came into my room and took orders for the school store, which had become my newest vexation and the newest student distraction. The funds were to be donated to the graduating class.

The school store was Todd buying cookies and chips, and students selling them at a small markup. All these kids were buying junk food at the local stores, so it was good business to undercut the crap out of them. Latoya and Anna were the chief salespeople.

Initially, I had a disagreement with Latoya, our best student, because she wanted to sell food rather than do her work. Anna used to enter my class and apologize for disturbing it before taking snack orders.

"Just because you are telling me you are disturbing my

class doesn't mean you have a right to disturb it," I said. I threw her out a few times. Thankfully, they stopped doing this.

It was almost 4:00 p.m., and I decided to bring my students outside to enjoy the spring day. We would go down to the Vietnam Memorial and sit in a circle and read *Of Mice and Men,* although we would probably end up just talking. The outdoors was a positive change. I could only do it in the first block, since those kids were pretty well-behaved. The sun was always brightest then too.

The last time I was outside with them, someone saw a caterpillar and no one knew what it was, so we talked about caterpillars. Tiana eventually killed the caterpillar, but it cheered her up after she alluded to numerous sexual situations she had been in. She may have done some stripping or worse, but I wasn't sure. Another time we talked about how none of them had been successful at getting jobs. I explained how even people with degrees were unemployed, but they had a better chance than people without educations.

Soon, the calm before the storm was upon us with gusts of wind and swishing, milky clouds.

"We gotta go inside," Latoya demanded. "It's gonna rain."

"Just enjoy the weirdness of it," I said.

A few minutes later, she demanded we return inside.

"It's only fifty yards to the door," I said. "We could run back inside if it starts raining." I didn't want her just running away.

Latoya turned her head again toward Manhattan. It quickly got darker and the gusts burst with varying speeds and temperatures. She started crying.

"Please let's go in. I'm scared of lightning," she begged.

There wasn't any lightning, but we all got up together and started walking back. An hour later, it started raining.

In second block, we were halfway through *Things Fall Apart* in World Literature. Maria was fidgeting about needing a pen and wanted to go to the office to get one. My supply of pens and pencils was again depleted.

In the interim, KLo arrived and sat in Maria's seat, which was in the back of the room near Tiana. Once Maria returned, she screamed at KLo to get out of her chair. The reaction gave KLo more of a reason to stay seated.

"Can you both please realize what a ridiculous situation this is?" I asked. "Can someone please just move?"

"But it's my seat," Maria said.

It was her seat, but the swearing and the screaming exacerbated the situation. Maria's tone was always confrontational. She was small in stature, and had a filthy mouth that threatened many guys in the school. She couldn't have been justified every time. At one of the sex seminars about penis size, she said, "If guys are big, they retarded."

Todd was in KetchupBoots' class listening to the incident. He heard the sides and wanted me to assign seats for class from now on; we all decided that it was Maria's seat today and KLo had to move, which he did reluctantly. Later in the day, I thanked KLo for moving his seat and told him she could have been nicer.

Miraculously, Pablo was silent during the entire incident and continued his work. He was in a better mood since he got his arm cast removed. He broke it while skateboarding a few weeks ago. He was trying to hold onto a bumper of a car and things went awry.

Pablo was almost expelled a few weeks ago with less

than two months to go. He had a nasty, disrespectful mouth and was still arguing about wearing his hat and his headphones. Todd had to call his father about it. Pablo's attitude changed; rather he toned it down a little. Since I knew he could be the worst, I tried to keep him busy and I stayed consistent. I had to keep telling him: "No hat." "No headphones." "No swearing."

I had to be a robot, and although I hated being one, I had to be relentless about the rules. Lots of teachers were giving breaks and not enforcing them. Every break showed how weak school rules were. If I wasn't consistent, then why should they listen to anything? I stood firm, but it was a waste of energy that had nothing to do with instruction.

Lately, Pablo was getting me upset because his behavior was too unreasonable to tolerate. He never threatened me; he was just so annoying in every class. Whenever someone tried to discipline him, he stated with confidence how he was going to graduate "no matta what."

Despite having absences and suspensions, he completed his work in every class. I tried getting him expelled, but when asked by Todd whether I honestly wanted him out of the program, which would prevent him from getting a high school diploma, I couldn't agree to it. I hated having to concede, but it was better that he have a high school diploma than not have one. There were enough people in the city who didn't have one, and I was sure the few jobs available wanted employees with diplomas. I hated how he failed to understand how much his behavior was affecting everyone and how terrible he was being.

One day, he got me so mad.

"You're a complete fuckin asshole," I said to Pablo.

"I can't believe you said that, Mista," Carlos said. Everyone was shocked. Pablo smirked. He broke me.

The next day, I tried to forget the entire incident, although many students wanted me to tell the story and elaborate for other students. I tried hard not to hold a grudge against Pablo. He was just a stupid teenager, much like the rest of the students. I was a stupid teenager once too.

V.

The Last Hurrah

IT WAS THE FIRST TUESDAY after the Memorial Day washout, and I heard before we left for our three day break that we only had four more Fridays until summer.

I recently realized that someone was tampering with the McDonalds billboard located a one block from school. Across the street from the billboard was one focused on the problems with gang violence and the appropriate numbers to call so one could report it.

At the top of the McDonalds billboard, the copy read, "East. West. North. Mouth." Front and center were numerous menu items like burgers, fries, and salads. At the bottom, underneath the food, someone attached a banner saying, "Watch Your Diet Go South!" Another sticker read, "SUPERSIZE YOUR THIGHS!" Both new attachments blended in nicely with the color scheme of the billboard.

I wondered who was trying to coax the community into thinking about its eating habits. All my students ate tons of fast food, and the daily school sales of chips and cookies certainly didn't help matters. A few kids insisted how they ate fast food every day and never gained weight.

"One day your metabolism is going to slow down," I said.

When I mentioned the billboard down the block and how someone was trying to make a point about how fast food was bad, Anna insisted that Burger King was better than McDonalds.

In first block, I held up the class while waiting for Latoya to do a food inventory in the Twilight office. I just finished *Of Mice and Men* last Friday, and I told them we would watch the movie the next two days before Friday's exam. Since the first block had an extended period with me because of Literacy Lab, I wasn't as crunched for time. Plus, I wanted Latoya to see the movie.

The idea of waiting a few extra moments for the movie to begin was evidently too much for Tiana to handle, and she insisted that we begin immediately. She was outright disgusted at the prospect of waiting for anyone, even if it was only for another minute. Latoya arrived, and we began the movie.

Ten minutes into it, Tiana began reading a Victoria's Secret catalog.

"Can you watch the movie please?" I asked.

"I wish it started earlier," she told me.

"Can you please put that catalog away?" I asked.

"Wait a second," she said.

Thirty minutes later, she left for a thirty minute bathroom break and then returned with her prom pictures. She offered them to me, and I looked at them. No one was really watching the movie.

No one showed up when second block began, even though the ten students in the class owed me quite a bit of work. Even though kids like KLo were distractions for the most part, they were completing their academic obligations.

The students trickled in one by one. It was the same affair each time a student entered. The arriving student distracted everyone already in the room. Everyone needed to check out who was coming in and what his or her story was.

Pablo and KLo arrived, and soon Carlos was pushing into the classroom because he wanted to use the Instant Messenger on the computer. I let him use it once during third block, and now he came in to use it every block of every day. He had a series of reasons as to why he was allowed to use the computer. I made him return to his real class.

Enforcing the rules about wearing hats and headphones made me feel like Bill Murray in *Groundhog Day*. I wondered how many hours of my life I'd already spent repeating these rules. I had to remain steadfast.

In class, KLo and Pablo both refused to remove their hats. It was like one was trying to outdo the other at my expense.

I kept nagging KLo to remove it, and he responded by telling me to "go fuck yaself."

"I can wear my hat," he explained. There was a threat after that.

Pablo said something about "balls in your mouth," while keeping his hat on. It was followed by numerous comments about my mother. Pablo told me how there was no way he was going to fail the class or get expelled.

"Will you guys never learn about accountability and consequences?" I asked. My *Groundhog Day* was a lot less charming.

"I will never remove it," Pablo said. "And I'm passin."

KLo started bothering one of the girls and then

started rapping when he didn't get any attention. Even the students were bored by the charade.

"You puppy dogs have to stop begging for attention from the big dog," I said. I returned to my desk, and without any attention, their hats remained off as they read.

"If you want to pass, you're going to finish reading *Things Fall Apart* and pass the exam," I reminded everyone. Everyone worked in silence.

At about 5:55 p.m., Adella came to my room.

"I am giving the seminar today," she said. I was hoping we had extended blocks, so my students could finish their reading.

At 6:00 p.m., getting the students to Juan's room was easier said than done. All the students hated Interblock and exclaimed how boring it was. And, as I got one student to leave my room, another got on the computer. We used to have three computers, but only the brand new one was working. I often found the students downloading music, and I suspected that was slowing it down. When I asked them to not download music, it was an argument.

I had to ask the computer technician what the password was for the new computer because I thought the Day School teacher was locking me out. It was no surprise that the students wanted to know the password. If you want to log in, just type in B10BSE. The first four digits of the code was the basement room number, and the second two letters stood for special education.

At 6:06 p.m., I got everyone from my room and the hallway into Interblock. In the Twilight office, Tiana and Maria were talking with Jenny.

"We need you guys in the Interblock," I said. "Can you come with me and not let your classmates down?" I asked.

"I'm comin," Maria said. She didn't come to second block, since she was finishing some art project. Because she was always absent, late, in the office, or working on some other project, she was probably not going to pass World Literature.

Todd walked out of Adella's room as I exited the office.

"Are any students in there?" Todd asked.

"Yes!" I said.

"We need to get started," he said.

When I reached Juan's class, the Twins and Anna exited the room.

"Where are you going?" I asked.

"To the office," one of them said.

I started talking with some students here and there. Some of the nicer students like Angela said hello. KLo and Pablo had their hats on. Carlos was being obnoxious, and Ivan was following someone new at every moment.

There was screaming in the hallway, and I saw the Twins and Maria getting separated by Todd and some other staff members. The entire class poured into the hallway for a look.

The Good Twin was screaming at Maria about how she was going to go to a certain street to get her tonight. Todd quelled the disturbance.

I addressed the crowd of onlookers: "Get back to Interblock, ladies." A security guard arrived to investigate the disturbance. Todd brought all the students from the office so we could begin. During the ruckus, someone took Adella's videotape from the VCR. I looked at KetchupBoots, and she rolled her eyes.

My futile attempts to bring order were met with verbal jabs from the class. According to Pablo, my grandmother had "camel toe." According to Carlos, my grandmother flashed her breasts on *Girls Gone Wild*. Their gang was all laughing.

"I beg you both to please get an understanding about cleverness and wit," I said. "Please be funny when you are mocking me."

Pablo repeated that my grandmother was on *Girls Gone Wild*, and the same group began laughing again. I left the student desk area to talk to KetchupBoots near the front of the room.

"I hate Interblock," she said to me. I agreed.

"You're getting her number so you can fuck her later," Pablo screamed from the back of class. He said something about me "scammin."

I pretended not to hear him and ended the conversation. I went back to my seat near that group. KLo had his hat on.

Twenty minutes later, the seminar began with Adella having no control. Her accent made it very hard for anyone to understand her.

"No one can understand a fuckin word she's sayin," KLo said. Everyone was talking. No one was even trying to listen.

During her Interblock, she passed out cards, showed a video clip, and used an overhead. I wasn't entirely sure of its focus. I also stopped myself from constantly disciplining the students, since Adella needed to learn how to be more assertive. It was difficult to watch.

"They don't know what she's sayin," Latoya later said to me. "And she don't even know what *they're* sayin."

When Mutumbo had a seminar, I tried to let him find his way but ended up doing most of the reading. Some teachers needed to do a better job of pulling their own weight. There were more than whispers about Juan,

Adella, and Mutumbo being unable to pull their own weight.

The seminar concluded with Todd explaining to the class that Adella was trying, and that since she was there for them, it showed she cared, so they should respect her. The students desperately needed more assertive and tougher teachers.

"The drugs probably haven't worn off from the weekend," KetchupBoots said to me. I didn't think that they were all on drugs, since they had no money to buy them. Sex was free to have, on the other hand.

Todd's attempt to put a positive spin on Interblock did little to change my mood or opinion. During third block, Carlos talked non-stop. I was so glad when it finally ended.

Carlos wanted to remain in my room to use the computer, but I physically tossed him out. KLo was soon visiting and refused to leave.

"You have to stop lookin for love in here," I said to him. After our standard back and forth, he left. Again, I was fine with this sarcastic banter. These students weren't being mean; they were just being wiseasses. I hoped they understood that at least I was being consistent and honest, as opposed to the other teachers that they treated like doormats.

Pablo soon began acting up. He couldn't stop talking about how his friend let him drive a car around. It was the same friend who hit him when he was on his skateboard and caused his broken arm. His "balls in your mouth" routine soon progressed into some commentary about how I was the "pink ranger." It went on and on.

I tried not to laugh at the image of me in a white and pink leather cowboy suit riding a white stallion. I had to send him to the office.

"I'm gonna pass," he reminded me before leaving. He had one up on me ever since I swore at him.

When I returned to the Twilight office at the end of the day, Jenny asked me if "Johnny" had a bad day.

"Johnny did," I said. Soon everyone was laughing.

Miss Jackson blurted out how I was the "pink ranger." I couldn't help but laugh with everyone.

-2-

I ALWAYS HAD A BRIGHT SMILE to greet the students arriving for school.

"Welcome back, JDs!" I began. JD stood for juvenile delinquent.

As they walked passed me, some made sarcastic and profane comments. Others just laughed or tried unsuccessfully to ignore my rambling banter. I called everyone by name as they came in. Mostly, the students signed in and then congregated in my room. I always provided them with words of encouragement.

"Keep your drinking and your drugs and your unprotected sex off school grounds, people."

My Son had been absent for the last few days.

"My Son!" I bellowed, "Don't you know by now that your classroom participation is essential to creating an environment conducive to learning?" I asked. "Where have you been?"

"Nunya," he replied.

"Nunya?"

"Nunya business, muthafucka." Just like it always was. Like clockwork. I had to laugh. Nuyna was funny. My Son was a good kid. He had a B in both classes with me. Adella told me that My Son used to come to school drunk in the beginning of the school year, and he was evidently a mean drunk. He was graduating in two weeks. I was glad he didn't come to school drunk anymore.

Right before 4:00 p.m., KLo arrived with his lunch, his hat on, and eyes that were barely open. He stunk of pot and completed his assignments. I couldn't help but question the level of difficulty of my classes when KLo had an A.

"You're not supposed to even be here," I said. "Your hat is on. Just go to art class." He sat still.

"Your eyes are red and you reek," I said.

"KHo," Tiana called out. He finally left. No one ever laughed or got into the conversations between me and KLo because he was a criminal "on the street."

Around 4:30 p.m. I saw Ivan in the hallway and addressed his lateness again.

"Almost on time, Ivan," I said. "Almost."

Ivan walked past me without saying a word, and silence was not his forte. He went into the office and didn't come out as quickly as signing in should take, so I returned to class. Sometime later, Jason was pulled from my classroom by Todd, so I went into the hallway to investigate.

"You nosy," one of my students said. I couldn't argue with that.

KetchupBoots was standing in the hallway waiting for Ivan. Ivan was her only history student in the first and fourth block, so when he was absent, which was more than once a week, she had two free blocks. Because of her small classes, it was difficult for me to ever sympathize with her plights.

"I hate the rain," she said. "And it's so humid down

here." I had a class, but I wanted to know what happened to Ivan.

"He got mugged on the way to school," she told me. "Someone put a knife to his throat and took his Iverson jersey." Just the other day, students were mocking Ivan since his jersey was counterfeit and cost only forty dollars rather than the authentic jerseys that other students bought for over a hundred dollars.

Right before Interblock, I changed into my gym clothes, which were red exercise pants and an undershirt because I forgot my gym T-shirt. Even though it wasn't the scheduled day, I was ready to kick some ass in volleyball.

My newly-improved gym-attired self entered the office, and Jenny, Miss Jackson, and Patricia laughed at my getup. Two students in the office also laughed. I pretended to look appalled by their insults.

"What baby you rob that shirt from?" Miss Jackson asked.

"You need a T-shirt bigger that hangs down to your knees," a student said.

In silence, I continued looking upset, aghast, and shocked at their suggestions as I looked around at everyone smiling and laughing. I departed for the gym to impress everyone with my stellar volleyball abilities and workout ensemble.

Once in the hallway, I saw Pablo slowly meandering his way to the gym, and there was an infinite number of comments I could have made to him since he was failing my class, was often absent, and didn't even attend my class during Block Two.

"Where've you been?" I asked. He was arrogant as usual.

"I don't have to come here or finish my work and I'm gonna graduate," he said. He smirked.

I needed to get serious. He needed to get it through his head that I was going to hold him responsible for not completing his work and that it wouldn't be me preventing him from graduating but his grades. He didn't really want to discuss it, but I was feeling loquacious.

We walked into the gym, and as we entered, a bunch of students laughed at my red pants. I walked Pablo back to the side so I could talk to him. He was supposed to graduate but really didn't deserve to. His inability to recognize the direness of the situation disgusted me. I really wanted him to fail because he needed to understand accountability. Considering the way he acted toward everyone on a daily basis, along with the fact that he was not completing the bare minimum expected of him, simply graduating wasn't going to do him any justice. What would he learn by graduating this way? What would happen once he could no longer get his high school diploma in Twilight? Was it better for society for me to give him his diploma and hope he had a better chance to get a job and turn his life around? I still couldn't sign off on his expulsion.

I tried speaking to him, but his smirk was too much for me to handle. I walked away.

I felt a stream of water strike me in the middle of my back and drip down my spine. I turned around to see Pablo laughing at me. Another student stood still looking.

"Did you just spit on me?" I asked.

"Yep," Pablo said, with his smirk. I was in a state of shock. I couldn't believe he really spit water on me.

There was a basketball game being played on the other side of the gym, and Todd was playing. I went over to the game and stopped it. Pablo needed to be dealt with. I was trying not to get angry, but I couldn't have students spitting on me.

"He just spit water all over me," I said to Todd while pointing at Pablo.

I went to the office. Todd was seconds behind me.

"I just sent him home," Todd said. "He can't return to school unless his father comes with him."

I recounted the incident for the office. Miss Jackson and Catherine called for Pablo's immediate expulsion. There was absolute justification for expelling him not only because of this, but for poor grades and attendance. He was failing Adella's science class and his art class, and there weren't many days left. What would a suspension in June achieve?

"You could bring up charges," Todd told me. But I obviously wasn't going to.

"If you weren't new here and had been here for a few years, you'd think differently," he said.

I returned to my classroom and was angry and shocked. I didn't know how many minutes elapsed before I went to the bathroom to change. I forgot to bring my work pants, so I went back to class in my button-down shirt and red pants. Todd came in behind me and told me that Pablo and his father were here, so I was to come to the office for a meeting.

Todd, Catherine, Jenny, Miss Jackson, Patricia, Pablo's father, and Pablo were in the office. Everyone except Patricia and Pablo were standing. Todd recounted the incident and the problems we had with Pablo. I shook hands with his father. His were heavily calloused.

"I'm sorry," he said. "I'm embarrassed I have to come down here again." The routine was new for me but not for everyone else.

"He doesn't deserve to graduate," Pablo's father said. "He's gonna get thrown outta the house."

Pablo sat there smiling. There was not a shred of remorse to grab onto.

Later, Pablo said, "I never spit water on him. He just said that."

"You already admitted to doing it," I said. "You're already guilty. And there's lots of other problems, too."

Pablo and his father were asked to wait outside, and the discussion about his expulsion began.

"You gotta stop savin the world," Miss Jackson said to Todd. "He don't deserve to be here."

"I can't help the situation," Todd said. "He's gone too far." We discussed how we would all have to sign off on the expulsion.

When asked to make such decisions, there are a lot of things to think about: Will an expulsion teach Pablo a real lesson? Will not getting a high school diploma be the best way to get through to him? Is society better off if he just got the diploma? Would he ever take the time to get back into a high school program to get his diploma so he could move onto something else? Is this the appropriate revenge for someone who treats you poorly, disrespects you, and spits water on you? I couldn't do it.

"But he has to get suspended," I said.

We suspended him for the rest of the week and gave him an in-school suspension the following week so he could complete all his work. He also had to apologize if he wanted to graduate. Pablo and his father came back into the office. Todd gave them our decision, and they left.

Miss Jackson started telling me that I should fail Pablo.

"I can't bring myself to do it," I said. "Without a diploma, he has an even greater chance to fail in life."

"You gotta stop savin the world like him," she said, and nodded toward Todd.

I wished Pablo understood all this. Maybe my red pants could help me save something.

3

IARRIVED TO WORK ABOUT thirty minutes late. Upon entering the office, I was informed that a librarian was looking for me because I had not yet returned a VHS copy of *To Kill a Mockingbird,* and the library was trying to straighten out its records before summer.

I signed it out one day a few months ago when attendance was low. The students weren't really into it, but My Son was. Mutumbo's mentor asked to borrow it, and I let her. Then I forgot all about it. The librarian wanted me to return it as soon as possible.

I looked through my shelves of books for the video, but I knew I didn't have it. Jenny looked through the file cabinets and found it. She handed it to me, and I departed for the library.

The white librarian and the black librarian were sitting behind the main desk. I handed it over to the black librarian, and the white librarian thanked me. Suddenly, the black librarian began ranting.

"You returned the wrong tape," she said. "This isn't the right label."

"I think that's the one I borrowed," I said. She continued on about the label.

"Keep an eye out for another copy," the white librarian chimed in.

"I definitely will," I said.

I returned to the office to discover that someone robbed our student store overnight of its cookies and chips. Thankfully, Todd took the store's bank home with him, so the money remained intact.

Discussion moved to the present lottery jackpot, which topped $100 million. Thirteen employees had been throwing in two dollars each for every one of these big jackpots. I really thought we had a chance of winning. What a great way for everyone's school year to end! What a perfect ending for me!

Soon, it was Juan, Patricia and me, and Patricia and I were talking about the lottery.

"You should go buy more," she urged me. Maybe she was right.

Before I left, Juan asked if I would buy him a few tickets, and I did. His English was very poor. I heard from Niles that he might not be rehired next year, but KetchupBoots was unable to confirm it.

I took a nice stroll in the spring sunshine to the store that sold the lottery tickets. On my way back, the sidewalks filled with students who were just dismissed from the Day School. As I walked by the Filipino bakery, which smelled absolutely delicious, I saw a young black kid pushing a Middle Eastern kid into the wall and demanding money from him. I moved along past them with the crowd but stopped before getting too far.

I looked again at the robbery, and an even younger black kid was looking at me.

"Move along," he said to me. He lifted up his shirt to show his empty waistband. I smiled at him and walked over.

"Yo he's coming," the younger cohort said.

I got right next to the Middle Eastern kid and the black kid.

"Come on, boys," I said. "I hope there's not any trouble here." The Middle Eastern kid ran away and everyone dissolved back into the crowd.

I headed back to school and felt like those two black kids were following me, but when I turned around before crossing the street, they were gone.

Before first block began, I was talking to Angela.

"I'm disappointed that no one's going to give me a birthday present," she said. She told me again about how her boyfriend was in jail.

"He didn't do it," I deadpanned. She said he never did anything. Maybe he never did.

Angela told me that she wanted me to buy her a book called *B More Careful*. I told her I would have it for her on the last day of school.

Carlos arrived and asked, "Do you like my silver bag?" Before I had a chance to give my opinion, he told me that he robbed some kid for it.

"No, you didn't," I said.

"Yeah, I did," Carlos said. "I just put a knife up to this kid's throat." He once showed me a small knife he carried around. He showed me his paintball gun once too.

"You can't tell me these things because I'm going to have to report you," I said. I doubted he was telling the truth. He lied a lot. The other day he told me that he had only one kid. I thought he had three. Then after speaking to him about his kids the next time, it seemed as though he had two.

"Everyone in Twilight is corrupt," Carlos said. He said I wasn't though.

"Once the cops came here lookin for me, and (Todd)

let me out the back door," he said. I didn't know why he wanted me to know these things.

During second block, one girl was filling out an application and asked for help. The application called for her ethnicity, and she was unclear what circle she should fill in. There was a laundry list of racial options, and I had no idea what she should fill in since she was an Arab American.

"Just leave it blank," I suggested. Many of the other students had parents of different ethnicities, and I wouldn't know what to tell them either.

As I was about to go to Interblock for another session with the students and the woman from the AIDS awareness center that the students called the Sex Lady, Catherine came to class to tell me that Mrs. Davis would be observing me during third block.

"Thanks," I said. I told her I wouldn't be attending Interblock so I could make sure I was prepared, and she told me it wouldn't be a problem.

Every teacher had to be observed three times a year, and although I was observed three times, there were only two official observations on paper. Miss Carter observed me, never filled out the proper paperwork, and left Twilight, so my initial observation didn't count. I signed a paper a few weeks ago allowing Mrs. Davis to observe me within the next twenty days, and I was glad to get it out of the way and have it completed before school was over.

My lesson plans were updated, as were my attendance records. Most of my grades were done, since I gave my *Of Mice and Men* final two weeks ago. I needed the Interblock time to grade some *Things Fall Apart* assignments. Mrs. Davis would be here around 6:55 p.m.

At 7:10 p.m., my class assembled. The Sex Lady's

presentation ran longer than expected. Mrs. Davis followed soon after. I began the class with the 'Quote of the Day' for eight minutes. The students then began reading selections from *Things Fall Apart*. Two students arrived late, asked for their work, and got reading. After the class, Mrs. Davis stayed briefly to speak with me about the lesson.

"I liked how all the students knew what was expected of them," she said. We spoke about the different aspects of Twilight.

"Interblock cuts into too much class time for the third and fourth blocks," I said. "First block gets more time with Literacy Lab and the second block benefits from the two days we don't have Interblock." She understood my point.

Then we started discussing my prospects for next year. Since I had to take certification classes, I was getting transferred to Day School, so we talked about the transition.

"Classes will be bigger and eighty minutes each," Mrs. Davis reminded me. "The students in Day School don't do homework either." She endorsed how I had students reading in class, and I was glad. She departed.

During fourth block, I had only one student since the Good Twin was talking to the Sex Lady, as was Ivan. When they returned, the Good Twin began telling me how I "had to date" the Sex Lady. I tried moving on. KetchupBoots asked me to momentarily watch Ivan, so he was soon in on the conversation.

"How come you don't talk about your sex life?" Ivan asked.

"I don't think I should be talking about that with the high school kids I teach," I said.

"Mutumbo talks about his life," Ivan continued. "He has a bad marriage and gets hookers."

"I don't know what Mutumbo does, and I'm not interested," I said.

Before the students were dismissed, a bunch of guys were waiting in the hallway. One ran into a wall with a slam and another followed suit. Another then slammed into the lockers and was followed by another kid. Soon, they were all slamming their heads into lockers.

"We're copying *Jackass*," one of them said.

"You should join in," Ivan said to me. I declined.

The next day was our Twilight end-of-the-year party. We invited another Twilight site to join us, since they had only twelve students. Pablo wasn't allowed to attend. Each staff member donated twelve dollars and brought in a food item. I brought potato salad.

I forgot my radio in the car, so I went to get it. Outside were Carlos and Ivan.

"Are you going to put me in my place?" I said to them. They both surrounded me. I started laughing. Ivan sort of pushed me and Carlos nearly tossed him to the ground.

Back at the party, I had problems mingling. It was boring, and I didn't want to goof on the students in my usual way since it was their event. I was having trouble making anything other than the most banal of conversations.

Carlos came up to me and asked to use my computer and since I wanted to grade papers, we spent the beginning of the party in my classroom. A few times staff members asked us to join the party, and eventually we did.

I got a chance to speak with Yolanda, who used to go here but got transferred to my old school. She attended the end-of-the-year party there, so I asked her about the students and the staff.

"Wait," she said. "You're the Mista K who used to be there?" I nodded my head.

"Everyone thinks you're a bitch," she said.

"Every single student thinks that?" I asked.

"Yeah," she replied after burping. I wished it wasn't so unanimous.

At the party, the gym was divided so some students could play basketball while others could congregate on the chairs strewn against the walls. One student brought in his DJ equipment, and some students danced. A few administrators like Todd and Mrs. Davis made some formal comments. And we all ate.

At the end of the day, the students were dismissed and our guests left. We all sat in the office surrounded by leftover food.

"What happened to the chocolate cake?" KetchupBoots kept asking. She really wanted to eat some and when she went looking for it, it was gone. Todd asked me if I could drive Jenny home.

On the ride, Jenny and I had a few laughs about KetchupBoots' desire for the chocolate cake.

"She should've kept a closer eye on the desserts so she wouldn't miss out on them," Jenny said.

When I dropped her off, she asked me where the chocolate cake was.

"I have no idea," I said.

She said it was in the bag she was carrying. We both laughed.

4

IT WAS THE LAST DAY of work. I remembered thinking about how this story was going to end, but that was before I got transferred. I thought it ended with me and Dinesh basking under the hot summer sun in the parking lot, shaking hands, and me thinking about who was going to be here next year and making an epic comment like, "Some I may see tomorrow. Some I may never see again." But it didn't end that way.

I began the day by going on an interview at a Day School downtown. Dr. Larson left me a message a few days ago about how it was impossible to park there.

With a copy of the school address I got from the internet, I was able to find a spot, and soon was walking to my destination. I found the door to the address and it was locked. It sure didn't look like a school.

I asked a few people if they knew the location of the school, but they couldn't help me. I found it just around the corner. The address I had was wrong.

It was a dismal brick building. Directly next door to the school was a vacant lot, and in its center sat what looked like an oil rig. The idea of locals going mad and blindly drilling for oil in the middle of the city entered my mind.

I made my way to the principal's office. A lady outside the office asked me if I needed help, so I mentioned my appointment. She stuck her head into the principal's office and said my name. I was directed into the office, where two men were standing. They motioned me in.

The bald man shook my hand and then I shook the other man's hand. The other man looked exactly like my friend Niles if he was thirty years older with a beard. It was absolutely uncanny. I took a seat. It was also the school where Niles' girlfriend worked. She later became his wife. Maybe I would meet my wife here too.

I ended up not taking the job, and instead accepted a job at Twilight for next year. They were going to help me get my state certification. Next year, I would be able to leave school every Wednesday to take evening classes. It meant that I only had to teach Monday, Tuesday, Thursday and Friday. They were also going to find me a mentor.

When I finally got back to the office, it was empty. Everyone was running errands or just left early. It was sad.

I looked over at the table and remembered the night the art teacher left paper mache eggs on it before departing for a long weekend. When we came back, rats had eaten them and left feces all over the office.

The school's solution was to put rat poison in the office. The rats came out at night, ate the poison, and went back into the walls, where they died. The stench of the rotting rats was unholy. Patricia actually worked in a surgical mask. Eventually, the smell dissipated, but a few weeks later, the stench returned. Apparently, a new wave of rats consumed the poisoned rats and they were then subsequently killed by the poison.

I started thinking about KLo and how on his final exam, he wrote about the theme of *Things Fall Apart* and concluded that "with great power comes great responsibility." Just like in the *Spider Man* movie.

I also remembered how he was talking about his gang The Dark Side.

I said, "Ooooh, are you going to come with Darth Vader and the stormtroopers?"

Nonchalantly, he replied, "No, we gonna kidnap you and your mom and you're gonna watch us rape her." I had to get everyone back into *The Great Gatsby*.

I thought about how Pablo seriously explained to me how he was going to sue me if I failed him and how if he brought a tape recorder then he'd get sued. I couldn't make any sense of it. I wondered what he would do with his high school diploma.

I thought about how the students complained about the SAT and how boring it was and the problem I encountered when we were discussing analogies. The analogy was lubricate: smoothly.

I thought about KetchupBoots and how she used a plastic bag and an easel as a marker board in her class. She didn't have a real chalkboard.

I thought about taking the students outside to read Emily Dickinson and having to come back inside because some of them were afraid of bugs.

I thought again about how disappointed Angela was the other day because I didn't really buy her the book I said I would. Right then, Jenny said, "You don't have a halo over your head anymore." Angela also told me that she was so embarrassed by the red pants I wore in gym that she couldn't even take a picture of me.

I thought again about how it would all end, but it already did.

THE END

Breinigsville, PA USA
22 December 2010
251999BV00001B/3/P